Worker and Family Assistance: Guyana Tragedy Points to a Need for Better Care and Protection of Guardianship Children: HRD-81-7

U.S. Government Accountability Office (GAO)

The BiblioGov Project is an effort to expand awareness of the public documents and records of the U.S. Government via print publications. In broadening the public understanding of government and its work, an enlightened democracy can grow and prosper. Ranging from historic Congressional Bills to the most recent Budget of the United States Government, the BiblioGov Project spans a wealth of government information. These works are now made available through an environmentally friendly, print-on-demand basis, using only what is necessary to meet the required demands of an interested public. We invite you to learn of the records of the U.S. Government, heightening the knowledge and debate that can lead from such publications.

Included are the following Collections:

Budget of The United States Government
Presidential Documents
United States Code
Education Reports from ERIC
GAO Reports
History of Bills
House Rules and Manual
Public and Private Laws

Code of Federal Regulations
Congressional Documents
Economic Indicators
Federal Register
Government Manuals
House Journal
Privacy act Issuances
Statutes at Large

Report To The Congress
OF THE UNITED STATES

Guyana Tragedy Points To A Need For Better Care And Protection Of Guardianship Children

About one-third of the 913 individuals who died in the 1978 Peoples Temple tragedy in Guyana were children, few of whom were wards of adult members of the Peoples Temple. The tragedy raised many questions about the adequacy of protection afforded children under the guardianship of adults not related to them.

The Peoples Temple tragedy points to a need for the Department of State to establish specific procedures for reviewing passport applications for guardianship children. Furthermore, the Department of Health and Human Services should increase the protection afforded California guardianship children and make sure that they are not placed in homes with more children than can be adequately cared for. The Department should also recover Federal overpayments to States for guardianship children not eligible for foster care maintenance assistance.

114028

HRD-81-7
DECEMBER 30, 1980

COMPTROLLER GENERAL OF THE UNITED STATES
WASHINGTON, D.C. 20548

B-201398

To the President of the Senate and the
Speaker of the House of Representatives

This report describes how the Departments of State and
Health and Human Services can help improve the care and
protection of guardianship children. This report also discusses (1) the placement of foster and guardianship children
with Peoples Temple members and (2) excessive Federal payments to California on behalf of guardianship children.

Our review was made at the request of the Chairman,
Subcommittee on Child and Human Development, Senate Committee
on Labor and Human Resources.

We are sending copies of this report to the Director,
Office of Management and Budget, and the Secretaries of State
and Health and Human Services.

Comptroller General
of the United States

GUYANA TRAGEDY POINTS TO A NEED
FOR BETTER CARE AND PROTECTION
OF GUARDIANSHIP CHILDREN

D I G E S T

The Chairman, Subcommittee on Child and Human Development, Senate Committee on Labor and Human Resources, requested GAO to review the placement of foster children with members of the Peoples Temple. After finding that some of the children had guardians, GAO expanded its review to examine guardianship children in California.

GAO found that:

--No children, while in foster care, died in Guyana. However, a few of the victims of the tragedy were wards of Peoples Temple members and were taken to Guyana without court approval.

--California guardianship children frequently did not receive all the protection intended for them by State law.

--California received Federal foster care maintenance payments for guardianship children who did not meet Federal eligibility criteria.

--The health and safety of some children may have been jeopardized by placing them in small foster family homes which housed children in excess of capacity.

CHILDREN WITH THE PEOPLES TEMPLE

Of the 294 children who died in Guyana in November 1978, GAO found that:

Tear Sheet. Upon removal, the report
cover date should be noted hereon.

i

HRD-81-7

--None was in foster care when they died. Seventeen had been in foster care, but were terminated from such care (returned to parent or guardian, or adopted) before the tragedy. (See p. 8.)

--Twenty-one were wards of Peoples Temple members. Nineteen of them had apparently been relocated to Guyana without the court approval required for changing the residence of guardianship children outside California. (See p. 13.)

--Peoples Temple adult members and their children usually did not travel to Guyana together. However, no fraudulent activities relative to taking children to Guyana were identified by U.S. Passport Services' investigations. (See pp. 14 and 15.)

To exercise better control over the travel of children, the U.S. Passport Services should verify before issuing passports that, where required, guardians have obtained court approval to take their wards outside the country. (See p. 16.)

SERVICES TO CALIFORNIA
GUARDIANSHIP CHILDREN

To determine the type of protective services provided to California guardianship children, GAO reviewed such activities in three counties. In two of the counties, required suitability reports on petitioners for guardianship of nonrelative children, usually were not prepared, and other protective services were not available to all the children. (See p. 21.)

Those suitability reports that were prepared included good assessments of whether the petitioner could meet the child's psychological and social needs, but these reports could have more comprehensively addressed the child's physical well-being. (See p. 23.)

State regulations covering assessment and reassessment of guardianships were inadvertently terminated in January 1980. Even when in effect, the State regulations had not been fully implemented. (See p. 25.)

In fulfilling the Federal role as an advocate for the welfare of the Nation's children, the Secretary of Health and Human Services (HHS) should direct the Office of Human Development Services to encourage California to

--reiterate to State court judges the importance of county social workers' preparing suitability reports on petitioners for nonrelative guardianship children,

--help the counties expand suitability report criteria to more fully address the physical well-being of guardianship children, and

--reissue regulations specifically covering guardianships and require compliance by county social service agencies. (See p. 27.)

FEDERAL OVERPAYMENTS FOR
GUARDIANSHIP CHILDREN

Guardianship children do not meet the Federal eligibility criteria for foster care maintenance payments if their care and placement is not the responsibility of the California Department of Social Services, the State agency designated to carry out the federally funded foster care program.

Federal overpayments occurred in the three California counties reviewed because the counties obtained Federal reimbursement for guardianship children whose care and placement were not the responsibility of the Department of Social Services. These overpayments totaled $320,000 for 104 children.

The overpayment period per child ranged from 1 month to 6 years. (See p. 29.)

The Secretary of HHS should direct the Office of Human Development Services to:

--Issue instructions to all the States notifying them that guardianship children are not eligible for Federal reimbursement for foster care maintenance payments when responsibility for such children is removed from the responsible State agency.

--Obtain retroactive adjustments for Federal overpayments that were made for California guardianship children.

--Determine if other States are receiving Federal overpayments for ineligible guardianship children, and act to identify and recover these overpayments. (See p. 33.)

PLACEMENTS IN EXCESS OF CAPACITY

Children have been placed in 16 State-licensed small family homes that housed more children than they were licensed for. This situation occurred because guardianship children were not being considered or included in the maximum number of children that the homes were licensed for. (See p. 38.)

The Office of Human Development Services should work with California to assure that federally eligible children are placed only in licensed facilities that fully meet State health and safety requirements. (See p. 41.)

HHS, DEPARTMENT OF STATE, AND STATE OF CALIFORNIA COMMENTS

HHS and the Department of State agreed to take actions that, for the most part, were in line with what GAO had recommended.

The State of California has taken or planned to take actions in areas where GAO pointed out that there was a need for action.

However, while the State did not agree with GAO's conclusion that guardianship children should be counted in determining whether a licensed home had children in excess of capacity, it planned to take a number of actions relating to the licensing procedures for foster family homes. GAO believes that the State's procedures will enable foster home operators to continue to obtain increased capacity by seeking guardianship of their foster children without providing the protections of large family or group home licensing requirements.

Contents

CHAPTER

APPENDIX

ABBREVIATIONS

AFDC   Aid to Families with Dependent Children

GAO   General Accounting Office

HHS   Department of Health and Human Services

CHAPTER 1

INTRODUCTION

This report discusses the circumstances of the placement of foster and guardianship children with the Peoples Temple members who died in Jonestown, Guyana; problems associated with the care and protection provided for guardianship children in three California counties under State law and regulations; and excessive Federal payments made to California for the care of guardianship children.

On February 28, 1979, the Chairman, Subcommittee on Child and Human Development, Senate Committee on Labor and Human Resources, requested us to review the placement of foster children with Peoples Temple members. (See app. I.) In accordance with the Chairman's request, our initial objectives were to determine:

--The extent and circumstances of such placements.

--The amount of Federal funds used to place and/or support these children.

--The circumstances under which foster children were removed from the United States to Guyana.

--Whether any foster children died in Jonestown.

--Whether any Federal funds were diverted from their statutory purpose.

On May 31, 1979, we testified before the Subcommittee in Los Angeles on the results of the initial phases of our review. At the time of our testimony, we agreed to expand our review to determine the:

--Legal requirements and restrictions placed on nonrelative guardians by California statutes.

--Extent and adequacy of reviews of potential nonrelative guardians by social services agencies.

--Extent and adequacy of continuing social services agency evaluations of nonrelative guardianship children in unlicensed homes.

1

--Extent of foster care payments to nonrelative
     guardians and the Federal portion thereof.

     The following sections provide background on the Peoples
Temple, foster care, guardianships, and freedom of citizens
to leave the country.

BEGINNING, GROWTH, AND DEMISE
OF THE PEOPLES TEMPLE

     Since the mass murders/suicides in Jonestown, much has
been written about the Peoples Temple and its leader, Rev.
James Jones, Sr. Rev. Jones started his own church in
Indiana in the 1950s. By the early 1960s, the church, now
referred to as the Peoples Temple, was listed as affiliated
with the Christian Church (Disciples of Christ). In the
mid-1960s, an envisioned nuclear holocaust prompted Rev.
Jones to settle with more than 100 followers in northern
California. A temple was built in Redwood Valley, a small
community in Mendocino County near Ukiah. Within a few
years, Rev. Jones opened facilities in San Francisco and
Los Angeles--later, the headquarters of the Peoples Temple
was moved to San Francisco. Peoples Temple members included
attorneys who assisted Rev. Jones and other members on legal
questions ranging from obtaining guardianships of children
to operating nonprofit corporations that were primarily
engaged in acquiring property for the Peoples Temple.

     Rev. Jones became involved in political activities and
was publicly identified with many political figures. In
late 1976, he was appointed Chairman of the San Francisco
Housing Authority Commission by the city's mayor. In August
1977 a national magazine article criticized life in the
Peoples Temple. By this time, the Peoples Temple membership
of about 1,000 had begun to migrate to the agricultural
development community that Rev. Jones had established in
Guyana in late 1973. Nearly half of the Peoples Temple
members migrated to Guyana in July and August 1977. In
late 1977 Rev. Jones resigned from the San Francisco Housing
Authority Commission while he was in Guyana.

     Small numbers of Peoples Temple members were still
arriving monthly at the agricultural development community
when the tragedy at Jonestown occurred on November 18, 1978,
and 913 Peoples Temple members died.

HOW CHILDREN ENTER AND EXIT FOSTER CARE

Children who reside outside the home of a parent or, in some cases, the home of a specified relative are referred to as foster children. States provide financial assistance to foster parents when the foster child is placed by a court and/or through a State-approved placement agency.

Children normally enter foster care by (1) a court directing placement because of the child's behavior and/or home situation or (2) the parents voluntarily allowing an agency, such as a welfare department, to place the child outside the home. Also, a child can enter the foster care system in California when a nonrelative legal guardian applies for foster care maintenance payments.

Children exit from foster care by (1) returning home, (2) being adopted, (3) becoming the ward of a guardian, (4) reaching majority, or (5) other ways, such as marrying or joining the military services. After children exit foster care, the State social services agencies do not have any further responsibilities to them unless services are requested in the children's behalf or a complaint is filed with the social services agencies concerning the children's well-being.

FEDERAL FUNDING OF FOSTER CARE PROGRAM

Title IV-A of the Social Security Act (42 U.S.C. 608) makes Federal matching funds available to the States under the Aid to Families with Dependent Children (AFDC) program for foster home care of dependent children. In fiscal year 1979, Federal funding for title IV-A foster care was $241 million.

The Federal Government also contributes to the support of foster children through titles IV-B (42 U.S.C. 620) and XX (42 U.S.C. 1397) of the Social Security Act. These programs provide Federal matching funds to support child welfare services and social services to adults and children. In fiscal year 1979, Federal funding was $56.5 million for the title IV-B child welfare services program and $2.9 billion for the title XX social services program. The total State and Federal titles IV-A, IV-B, and XX funds allocated for foster care was almost $1.2 billion nationwide for fiscal year 1977, the latest year for which this information is available.

3

As indicated earlier, there are several ways for a child to enter foster care. Only court-directed placements, however, are eligible for Federal financial participation in the AFDC foster care maintenance payment program. Also, for a case to be eligible for Federal funding, there must be a plan containing information on the foster child's needs and a redetermination of Federal eligibility every 6 months. No Federal regulations require visits by social services caseworkers to check on the well-being of foster children.

While there is no Federal program specifically dedicated to aiding children living with guardians, Federal title IV-B funds can be used for maintenance payments to guardians, and title XX funds can be used to provide services to guardianship children. In chapter 4, we explain why guardianship children are not eligible for title IV-A Federal foster care maintenance payments. The Federal programs for aiding children are administered by the Department of Health and Human Services' (HHS') 1/ Office of Human Development Services and Social Security Administration.

CALIFORNIA'S FOSTER CARE PROGRAM

The California Department of Social Services has overall responsibility for administering the State's foster care program for children. However, under State delegation, the counties operate their own foster care programs. The State gives the counties administrative guidance, program oversight, and fiscal support in operating their programs.

In fiscal year 1979, California spent about $50 million of Federal funds authorized under titles IV-A and XX and about $170 million of State and county funds for its foster care program involving about 28,000 children. The State did not spend any of its title IV-B funds for foster care.

1/Effective May 4, 1980, a separate Department of Education commenced operating. Before that date, the activities discussed in this report were the responsibility of the Department of Health, Education, and Welfare.

4

CALIFORNIA GUARDIANSHIP OF CHILDREN

Guardianships in California are based on authority
provided in the State probate code. For purposes of this
report, a guardian is defined as an adult appointed by a
court to take care of the person or estate, or person and
estate of a minor. Any person may petition the court for
guardianship of a minor. Our review concentrated on nonrelative guardianships of persons or persons and estates.
Sections 1440 and 1443 of the California Probate Code include requirements for preguardianship suitability investigations by the county agency responsible for public social
services. Section 1500 of the code requires court permission for the guardian to establish a minor's residence
outside the State. No statewide figures are available on
the actual number of relative or nonrelative guardianships
in California. Records on guardianships are on file only at
the county probate courts.

RIGHT OF CITIZENS TO LEAVE COUNTRY

Before leaving the country, citizens ordinarily come
into contact with only one Government organization--the
Passport Services of the Department of State. The Passport
Services' primary responsibility is to issue passports to
U.S. citizens. A concurrent responsibility is to prevent
issuance of a passport to an applicant who is not the person
the applicant claims to be or in any other case where fraud
is suspected.

Anyone 13 years of age or older may execute a passport
application in his or her own behalf. A parent, a legal
guardian, or a person in loco parentis (in the place of a
parent) must personally appear and execute an application
for a child under 13.

OBJECTIVES, SCOPE, AND METHODOLOGY

Our review of Peoples Temple children in Guyana was made
at the Department of State headquarters, HHS headquarters,
the HHS San Francisco Regional Office, the San Francisco
Passport Services, the California Department of Social Services, and 13 California counties. We coordinated our work
with the review efforts of the HHS Inspector General and the
California attorney general.

5

From two Department of State lists of verified and un-
verified Peoples Temple members who died in Guyana and from
a list compiled by a Peoples Temple attorney of persons who
migrated to Jonestown, we identified 294 names of children
under 18 years old who died in Guyana. We used this list to
identify and analyze foster care and/or guardianship children.

All of the names of the Peoples Temple members who migrated to Guyana were checked against the State's Medi-Cal
files. (Medi-Cal is the State Medicaid program funded under
title XIX of the Social Security Act.) In addition, we sub-
poenaed and examined county welfare records of the children
that were identified in the Medi-Cal files. With the assistance of State and county officials, we identified the children who had a welfare history and reviewed the available
case files for these children. Available court records on
Peoples Temple guardianship children who migrated to Guyana
were also obtained.

Our review of guardianship activity in California was
made from August through November 1979 at the State Department of Social Services and in three counties--Alameda, Los
Angeles, and San Diego--and included an analysis of:

--Probate court records of over 200 guardianship children to determine extent of preguardianship protection provided.

--Social services files of 385 of the over 600 children
   in nonrelative guardianship status as of November
   1979 to determine extent of Federal participation in
   maintenance payments.

--Several foster family homes or other facilities to
   determine if guardianships were being used to circumvent foster care licensing requirements.

In San Diego County, our review included files of all
72 nonrelative children available. However, because of the
large number of nonrelative guardianship children in Alameda
and Los Angeles Counties, we limited our review to files of
136 of the 233 children in Alameda County and files of 177 of
about 300 children in Los Angeles County. The files of the
nonrelative guardianship children in Alameda County were not
readily available for our review. Consequently, we reviewed
all of the files of children (136) that were given to us by
the county during our review at the county offices. In

6

Los Angeles, we selected for review 9 of the 20 suboffices that had the largest number of nonrelative guardianship children and reviewed the files of all of the 177 children at those suboffices.

The objectives of our review are discussed on pages 1 and 2.

- - - -

HHS, the Department of State, the State of California, and officials of the California Judiciary were given an opportunity to comment on our draft report. Written comments were received from HHS on October 22, 1980; from the Department of State on October 27, 1980; and from the State of California on October 24, 1980. These comments, which are set forth in appendixes II, III, and IV, respectively, have been considered by us in preparing this report. Specific comments concerning our recommendations are summarized at the end of each chapter. A California Judiciary official informed us orally on October 21, 1980, that the officials had no comments to offer on the draft report.

CHAPTER 2

CIRCUMSTANCES OF THE TRAGIC DEATHS

OF PEOPLES TEMPLE CHILDREN

The exact number and names of all the children who died in Guyana will never be known. More than 200 of the young victims of the tragedy were not individually identified before burial in California. We identified 294 names of persons under the age of 18 years who reportedly died with the Peoples Temple group in Guyana in November 1978.

Most of the children had some history of welfare aid in California before migrating to Guyana. Seventeen had previously been in foster care, but had been terminated from foster care (returned to parent or guardian, or adopted) before the Guyana tragedy. Of the 21 children who died in Guyana who were wards of nonrelative Peoples Temple members, 19 were there without the court approval required to change their residence to Guyana. Information regarding Peoples Temple children is discussed in the following sections of this chapter.

MANY OF THE PEOPLES TEMPLE CHILDREN HAD RECEIVED WELFARE ASSISTANCE

Of the 294 children identified as probable victims in Guyana, more than three-fourths (228) had a welfare history in California--206 were previously recipients of both cash grant and noncash aid programs, and 22 were previously recipients of such noncash aid programs as food stamps and Medi-Cal. Of the 206 children in cash grant programs, 189 were previously in the AFDC family group/unemployed parent program, and 17 were previously in foster care.

Demographics and other data on the 17 former foster children who died in Guyana

None of the 17 former foster children who died in Guyana were under the care and custody of the California

8

Department of Social Services while in Guyana. 1/ Since
they had been terminated from the foster care program before
migrating to Guyana, no foster care maintenance payments
were made on their behalf while they were in Guyana. 2/

Sex, ethnic background,
and age

Of the 17 Peoples Temple children who had been in foster
care, 10 were female and 7 were male. Fourteen of the children were black, and three were white. At the time of death,
two children were from 5 to 7 years old, three were from 8 to
10 years old, six were from 11 to 13 years old, and six were
from 14 to 16 years old.

First contact with
Peoples Temple

Four of the 17 children came into contact with the
Peoples Temple by placement actions of county agencies.
However, all four exited from foster care through adoption
or other court action. Three children were adopted by
their Peoples Temple foster parents. The fourth child was
a juvenile delinquent placed into a facility operated by
Peoples Temple members. The probate court later made this
child the ward of a Peoples Temple member and gave approval
for the guardian to take the child to Guyana. (See p. 11
for detailed discussion of this case.)

The other 13 children were first exposed to the Peoples
Temple by members of their own family, usually the mother.

1/On page 14, we discuss a California attorney general report
   which addresses a broader Department of Social Services
   responsibility for Peoples Temple children in Guyana.

2/One child was in foster care while in Guyana, but she
   survived because she was in Georgetown, Guyana, when the
   tragedy occurred. In this case foster care maintenance
   overpayments for 7 months occurred (no Federal funds
   involved), and the State has taken action to recover these
   overpayments.

Time spent in foster care

The time spent in foster care by the 17 children ranged from 5 to 156 months. The average time spent in foster care was just under 2 years, excluding two children who were in foster care for 13 years each. The breakdown:

Time in foster care	Number of children
Less than 1 year	5
1 to 2 years	4
2 to 3 years	2
3 to 4 years	4
13 years	2
Total	17

Ten of the 17 children spent all of their time in foster care with Peoples Temple members--including the 2 who were in foster care for 13 years each. The other seven children's foster parents were not Peoples Temple members.

Time out of foster care
before migration to Guyana

Four of the children had left foster care less than 6 months before departure, two from 6 months to 1 year, four from 1 to 2 years, six from 4 to 5 years, and one over 6 years.

For the four children who had left foster care within 6 months before their migration to Guyana, we obtained the following information.

--A child's foster parent or guardian took the child to Guyana in July 1977. County foster care payment checks were issued in July and August 1977 and sent to the foster parent's former address in California, but were returned to the county by the Postal Service. The county terminated the child from foster care as of June 30, 1977, because the foster parent or guardian failed to maintain contact with the county. The foster parent or guardian had obtained court approval to take the child to Guyana.

--In July 1977, a U.S. district court judge placed a
  mother on 3 years' probation and released her to the
  Peoples Temple agricultural development community in
  Guyana. The Federal judge permitted the mother to
  take her 5-year-old child to Guyana. The child had
  been living with foster parents from October 1976 to
  July 1977, when foster care payments were terminated
  because the child was returned to the mother. Passport
  documents show that the child was taken to Guyana in
  August 1977 by nonrelative Peoples Temple members;
  the mother did not arrive in Guyana until January 1978.

--A child who was a ward of the juvenile court had been
  living with foster parents from June 1974 to March
  1976, when the court removed him from foster care to
  place him in a juvenile detention facility. In April
  1976, a nonrelated Peoples Temple member obtained
  guardianship and court approval to take the child to
  Guyana. In June 1976, the child, now 13 years old,
  went to Guyana apparently unaccompanied. We found no
  evidence that the guardian ever went to Guyana. A
  newspaper reported that the guardian left the Peoples
  Temple group shortly after his ward went to Guyana.

--A child was in foster care from May 1973 through March
  1977. During this period, she was under two separate
  guardianships with different nonrelated guardians who
  were Peoples Temple members. In August 1977 the child
  arrived in Guyana accompanied by nonrelative adult
  Peoples Temple members. Her guardian did not migrate
  to Guyana until March 1978.

The other two children whose foster care status was
terminated within 1 year before going to Guyana were in
foster care from July 1964 to June 1977. In July 1977, their
foster mother began procedures to adopt the two children.
State subsidized adoption payments were made to the adoptive
parent concurrent with the termination of foster care maintenance payments. The two children were taken to Guyana by
their adoptive mother in April 1978, the same month that
their adoption was finalized.

For most of the other children, foster care payments
were terminated because the children had returned to a
relative, usually their mother, before they migrated to
Guyana.

Children's family status and persons accompanying children to Guyana

At the time of departure to Guyana, 4 of the 17 children had been reunited with and were accompanied to Guyana by one or both of their parents or a relative; six of the children had been living with a relative, but were not accompanied by a relative; two children were accompanied by their adoptive mother; one child was accompanied by her legal guardian; three children had legal guardians, but did not depart with their guardians; and one child had been adopted, but did not depart with his adoptive parents.

Passport applications frequently indicated trip to Guyana was for vacation

We reviewed the passport applications that were available for 16 of the 17 foster care children to obtain information on their reported reasons for leaving the United States. The passport applications showed that 10 of the children were leaving for a "vacation" for a period of from 20 days to 6 months. Of the other six children, three were reported leaving for Peoples Temple agricultural mission work, one for Peoples Temple human services work, and two did not give a reason for leaving. Peoples Temple members migrating to Guyana commonly stated on their passport application that the purpose of the trip was for a vacation. On the passport application, the section for stating the purpose of travel is optional.

Extent of foster care maintenance payments for the former foster children

Foster care maintenance payments for 3 of the children had been claimed by the State for Federal participation, while the other 14 were funded solely by the State and counties. Payments to the foster care parents of the 17 children who spent some time in foster care totaled $66,000 for the total period of foster care. This included $42,000 paid to foster parents associated with the Peoples Temple. About $5,800 of the $66,000 was provided from title IV-A funds for the three federally funded foster care children. Included in the $5,800 was $750 of Federal funds for a child placed in foster care with a person who was not

12

a Peoples Temple member. This child was a voluntary placement and was later determined by the State to be ineligible for Federal funding.

PEOPLES TEMPLE MEMBERS WERE
LEGAL GUARDIANS FOR SOME OF
THE YOUNG VICTIMS OF GUYANA

Twenty-one of the 294 children who died in Guyana were wards of nonrelative guardians at the time of their deaths. Seven of the 21 children were included in the 17 children with some history of foster care previously discussed. In addition to these 21 guardianship cases, other children had been wards of nonrelative Peoples Temple members. Peoples Temple members had filed guardianship petitions for more than 50 children. Such children, other than the 21 who were wards at the time of their deaths, reached majority or were returned to their parents before the migration to Guyana.

Guardianships used to circumvent
foster care licensing procedures

In the early 1970s, children were being placed in foster care in unlicensed homes of Peoples Temple members in Mendocino County by placement agencies of other California counties, primarily Alameda County. To stop such placements, Mendocino County officials advised the counties that this practice was contrary to State and county regulations, which required that foster children be placed in licensed facilities. Peoples Temple attorneys and members then began filing petitions with probate courts for guardianship of children for Peoples Temple members. Children were placed in the homes of Peoples Temple members who, as guardians, were exempt from the foster care licensing requirement. Only one of the seven homes receiving foster care maintenance payments for guardianship children had a foster care license.

Guardianship children were
taken out of country without
court approval

Nineteen of the 21 children who died while under California guardianship arrangements had been taken out of the United States for relocation in Guyana without the court approval required by California statutes for change of residence. Guardians of the other two children, both former foster children, had obtained court approval to take their wards to Guyana.

13

Section 1500 of the California Probate Code requires the guardian to obtain probate court approval to change the residence and domicile of the ward outside the State. The code does not require court approval for absences from the State if residence and domicile are not changed.

Proof of court permission
to take guardianship children
out of the country not required
by Passport Services

The primary purpose of the U.S. Passport Services is to help U.S. citizens obtain passports. The principal documentation required is proof of identity and of U.S. citizenship. Passport officials attempt to verify that the person applying for the passport is the person purported to be, that the person is not a fugitive, and that the passport is not being obtained for illegal purposes. Passport Services does not have procedures that require documentation of court approval for a guardian to take his or her ward outside the United States.

The Passport Services' San Francisco agency processed Peoples Temple members' applications in accordance with existing laws and regulations. Passport officials said that the number of children and elderly persons going to the jungles of Guyana was considered unusual, so they monitored applications from Peoples Temple members for potential passport fraud and kept their national office advised of passports issued to Peoples Temple members.

A California attorney general report 1/ on the Peoples Temple discusses the contact between Department of State and California officials concerning the children taken to Guyana. The report states that there were discussions between California and State Department personnel regarding complaints against Peoples Temple activities in Guyana, including possible foster children being there. However, no fraudulent activities concerning children were established by the Passport Services.

1/"Report of Investigation of People's Temple," April 1980.

MOST OF THE PEOPLES TEMPLE
CHILDREN DID NOT TRAVEL TO
GUYANA WITH A PARENT OR GUARDIAN

In migrating to Guyana, the children and the persons who had legal responsibility for the well-being of the children--biological or adoptive parent, other adult relative, or legal guardian--usually traveled separately. An analysis of Department of State passport data and other documentation concerning travel of the 294 children to Guyana showed that:

--96 traveled with parents.

--9 traveled with other relatives.

--2 traveled with legal guardians.

--147 traveled with someone other than parents, guardians, or other adult relatives.

--40 travel arrangements were unknown.

Thus, over half of the children for whom we were able to obtain data went to Guyana without being accompanied by a parent, other adult relative, or guardian.

Peoples Temple files in the custody of the court-appointed trustee in San Francisco contained documents authorizing travel of children. Typically, there were three documents for each child that were signed by a parent or a guardian:

--Limited power of attorney.

--Release of liability.

--Consent to travel and visit.

These documents had the effect of virtually turning the children over to the control and custody of almost anyone within the Peoples Temple. Without ruling on the legality of such documents, in November 1979 a California deputy attorney general told us that the existence of such authorization could establish the voluntary intent of those persons with legal custody of the children to allow other Peoples Temple members to take their children to Guyana.

CONCLUSIONS

Peoples Temple children were commonly transported to Guyana with nonrelative Peoples Temple members. While children frequently went to Guyana without their parent or guardian, no fraudulent activities involving taking the children to Guyana were identified by Passport Services investigations.

We did not identify any children who were under the supervision and care of the California Department of Social Services when they died in Guyana. We identified 17 children, under 18 years of age when they died, who had previously been recipients of foster care maintenance payments. All of the children had been terminated from the foster care program before migrating to Guyana (returned to parent, adopted, or placed in guardianship).

Twenty-one children were wards of nonrelative Peoples Temple member guardians when they died in Guyana. Guardians of only 2 of these children had obtained court approval for their wards to settle in Guyana--the other 19 children had apparently been relocated to Guyana without the court approval required for changing the residence of guardianship children outside California. No regulations require Passport Services to verify that guardians have obtained court permission to take their wards outside the United States.

RECOMMENDATION TO THE
SECRETARY OF STATE

We recommend that the Secretary require the U.S. Passport Services to adopt policies and procedures to verify, before issuance of passports, that where required by State law, guardians have obtained court approval to take their wards outside the country for travel and/cr residence abroad.

DEPARTMENT OF STATE COMMENTS
AND OUR EVALUATION

The Department of State said that its procedures could be adapted for processing passport applications of minors in guardian situations to accomplish the purpose of our recommendation. The Department also said that, under its procedures, a person who is not a parent of the minor applicant must provide proof of the legal relation to the child before a passport is issued and that passports will not be issued

if Passport Services is notified in advance that an adult
who is a parent, guardian, or person in loco parentis and
is normally entitled to travel outside the United States
with the child, no longer has that right. The Department
added that Passport Services would be willing to inform the
States of the availability of this measure to prevent the
issuance of a passport to a minor whose guardianship order
does not allow travel outside the United States.

We believe that the State Department proposal will help
prevent children who are under court-approved guardianship
arrangements and who do not have the right to travel outside
the United States from obtaining passports to leave the
country. However, we believe that there is a need to assure
that passports are not given to guardianship children when
no advance notice is given to the Passport Services that a
child is not permitted to travel outside the country and
when State law, such as the California law, requires that
guardianship children obtain court approval to reside outside
the United States. Therefore, when the Department informs
the States of the measure that it has available, the States
should be requested to provide pertinent information on
State laws regarding the preexisting conditions that are
required for taking guardianship children out of the country.
The Passport Services should use the information obtained
from the States in developing its policies and procedures to
insure that passports are not given to guardianship children
contrary to State law.

CHAPTER 3

CALIFORNIA'S PROCEDURES FOR HANDLING

NONRELATIVE GUARDIANSHIPS ARE NOT ADEQUATE TO

ENSURE THE WELL-BEING OF CHILDREN

Since some of the children who died in Guyana were under court-approved guardianship arrangements, our review was expanded to examine the care and protection provided for nonrelative California guardianship children. We found that, although probate court and social services agency protection was potentially available to all children entering or already in nonrelated guardianships in California, neither the probate courts nor the social services agencies were adequately providing this protection.

California probate laws and Department of Social Services regulations include various procedures that can contribute to the well-being of children who are, or are about to become, wards of nonrelative guardians:

1. Suitability reports--State law requires the county public social services agency to report on the suitability of a potential nonrelative guardian's home before guardianship is granted.

2. Continuing periodic reviews--Regulations of the State Department of Social Services require the county public social services agency to perform semiannual assessments of homes after guardianship is granted if foster care maintenance payments are being made to the guardian on behalf of the child.

3. Probate court reviews--Probate court judges grant guardianships and can periodically review such placements. Biennial probate court reviews are required for guardianship children who have estates.

However, these procedures were not consistently implemented, and children frequently did not receive the protection available.

Many children have become wards of nonrelative guardians who had previously obtained community care (foster care) licenses. To obtain licenses, the homes had been investigated by State or county social services agencies. Thus, in addition to the three types of protective procedures discussed above, children entering these homes obtain a fourth type of protection.

To see how well nonrelative guardianship children were being protected, we looked at the probate court files of 208 children in three California counties. Of these, 106 were recipients of foster care maintenance payments, and 102 were not. The petitions for guardianship on all 208 children were submitted after the requirement for suitability reports became effective in 1976.

Except for court reviews of children with estates, the only protective procedure required under State law is a report on the suitability of placing a specific child in the home of a nonrelative who has petitioned the court for guardianship of the child. The other procedures, such as foster care licenses, while not required, can contribute to the well-being of guardianship children.

CALIFORNIA LAW NOT CONSISTENTLY FOLLOWED AS TO WHEN AND HOW PREGUARDIANSHIP SUITABILITY ASSESSMENTS SHOULD BE DONE

California law does not require nonrelative petitioners for guardianship to obtain foster care licenses. Instead, the law requires suitability reports to be prepared to assess the suitability of the homes of nonrelative petitioners. However, such reports generally were not prepared. Therefore, children have been placed in nonrelative guardianships without benefit of an adequate investigation that might help the court assure that the child's needs would be met.

State and county officials have made different interpretations of the State probate code section requiring suitability reports on petitioners applying for guardianship of nonrelated children. While State officials believe that the county social service agency should prepare a report in every nonrelative guardianship case, some county probate judges believe that reports should be done only when the child may also be involved in adoption proceedings or when directed by the court.

19

The probate code section governing suitability reports
states:

"Sec. 1440.1 Petition for adoption; reports

If a petition states that an adoption petition
has been filed, a report with respect to the
suitability of the petitioner for guardianship
shall be filed with the court by the agency investigating the adoption. In any other case the
local agency designated by the board of super-
visors to provide public social services shall
file a report with the court with respect to the
petitioner of the same character required to be
made with regard to an applicant for foster
family home licensure."

In a September 16, 1975, letter explaining the intent of the
originating bill submitted for the Governor's approval, its
author, California State Senator Nicholas Petris, wrote:

"This bill provides that in all cases where a
petition for guardianship over a minor is filed
by a nonrelative (who was not named in a will as
guardian) a report on the suitability of the
petitioner must be filed with the court."

Senator Petris then went on to explain who must file the
report: the agency investigating adoptions if an adoption
petition had also been filed, or the foster home licensing
agency if no adoption petition had been filed.

The State Department of Social Services has interpreted
the law in accordance with the intent expressed by Senator
Petris in his September 1975 letter. In a February 1976
policy memorandum, the department communicated this to the
California county social services agencies. This policy
memorandum also explained several of the law's other provisions, describing the flow of information necessary to implement the law, such as the (1) guardianship petitioner's
attorney must submit a copy of the petition to the State
Department of Social Services' Adoptions Operations Bureau
and (2) Adoptions Operations Bureau must, in cases where no
adoption is pending, notify the applicable county social
services agency that a petition has been filed, so that the

local ag cy can begin the suitability investigation. Meanwhile, e probate court receives the petition and sets a hearing date, which becomes the deadline for the social services agency to complete the report.

Only one of three counties
routinely makes preguardianship
suitability investigation

Of the three counties reviewed--Alameda, Los Angeles, and San Diego--only Los Angeles County routinely performed preguardianship suitability investigations. Probate judges of the other two counties did not interpret the law according to Senator Petris' stated intent that a report be provided to the court in each case. Rather, they interpreted the law to mean that they should get suitability reports from the local social services agency only when requested or when an adoption petition has been filed for the child.

As a result of the probate courts not requiring the submission of suitability reports and the failure of the county social services agencies to prepare suitability reports unless directed to do so by the probate judges, such reports were not prepared for most children, as shown in the following table.

County	Number of cases reviewed that required preparation of suitability reports	Suitability reports prepared
Alameda	101	3
Los Angeles	56	42
San Diego	51	3
Total	208	48

Thus, in Los Angeles County, 42 of 56 (75 percent) of the petitioners for nonrelative guardianship were reviewed for suitability. In contrast, only 6 of 152 (less than 4 percent) of the petitioners in the other two counties--Alameda and San Diego--were reviewed for suitability. Two factors seem to account for this difference. First, Los Angeles County probate judges actively enforced the requirement for the local social services agency to prepare and issue suitability reports. In fact, the judges went beyond the State

21

law requirements by directing the petitioners' attorneys to notify the local social services agency directly to make the suitability review, instead of, or in addition to, notifying the State Adoptions Operations Bureau. Secondly, Los Angeles County judges have demonstrated a willingness to delay the guardianship hearings to allow the social services workers time to prepare the suitability reports.

When the direct notification to the county social services agencies was not required by county probate judges (such as in Alameda and San Diego Counties), the required procedure for the State Adoptions Operations Bureau to notify the county social services agency of the guardianship petition was frequently untimely. As a result, the local agency often did not have time to make the suitability review and report before the guardianship hearing date. Thus, suitability reports were not prepared unless the judges (such as those in Los Angeles County) required them and were willing to set guardianship hearing dates to accommodate the review. Court officials stated that, without suitability reports, a judge normally grants a nonrelative guardianship of a child based on the merits of the petition and the lack of relative opposition to the petition.

ALTHOUGH NOT REQUIRED, OTHER PROTECTION IS AVAILABLE TO SOME CHILDREN

We assessed the use of other procedures that could have contributed to the well-being of the 160 guardianship children for whom suitability reports were not prepared. We found that other protective procedures existed to contribute to the well-being of 129 of the 160 children as shown below.

Protective procedure	Number of children
Continuing periodic reviews and foster home licensure investigation	65
Continuing periodic reviews, only	19
Foster home licensure investigation, only	45
	129

Thus, 31 of the children reviewed (160 minus 129) did not benefit from the required suitability report or any of the other protective procedures potentially available.

SUITABILITY REPORTS AND LICENSING
EVALUATIONS COVER DIFFERENT ISSUES--
ELEMENTS OF BOTH MAY BE NEEDED

State law requires that the suitability reports be of the same character as those made regarding an applicant for foster family home licensure. However, the suitability report criteria developed by Los Angeles and San Diego Counties were quite different from foster home licensing criteria. The licensing criteria covered primarily the physical aspects of the home. On the other hand, the suitability report requirements and actual investigations were much more comprehensive in appraising the social and psychological aspects of the home environment. They also evaluated the merits of guardianship as a placement alternative for the child and the petitioner's motives in seeking guardianship.

Primarily from the perspective of the child's physical well-being, the licensing criteria included three important items not covered by suitability report requirements: (1) evidence of a criminal record check, (2) a physician's certification of the health of the petitioner and other home residents, and (3) a fire clearance for the housing of non-ambulatory children. Suitability reports could be strengthened by incorporating these licensing criteria.

ONGOING REVIEWS OF GUARDIANSHIPS
NOT PERFORMED CONSISTENTLY

Preguardianship suitability reports and placement of children with guardians who have foster care licenses do not provide assurances of the continued well-being of children in guardianships. Two types of periodic reviews can provide this ongoing protection: probate court reviews and county social services agency reviews.

California probate courts have not routinely reviewed guardianships unless the children have estates, and social services agency involvement with guardianship children has not been consistent. These findings are discussed in the following sections.

23

Probate courts do not routinely review guardianships unless the children have estates

California State probate law does not specify whether probate courts must periodically review guardianships of children who do not have estates. Although the probate code refers to periodic reviews of guardianships, it addresses only matters of financial accounting in cases where the guardian has taken custody of the child's estate. It does not address the guardian's "accountability" for a child's physical, social, or psychological welfare. Sections 1904 and 1553 of the California Probate Code require that, at the end of 1 year from their appointments, guardians must present their accounts to the court for settlement and allowance. Thereafter accounts must be presented to the court as often as required by the court, but at least biennially.

The lack of a requirement for continuing periodic needs assessments of ongoing guardianships is of particular concern for children not receiving foster care maintenance payments and not living in licensed homes. (Examples of such children are the 31 children shown as receiving no protection on p. 22.) When financial assistance was provided or the home was licensed, the Department of Social Services regulations required periodic contact with the home. However, where no money or license was involved, both the probate court and the social services agency could lose all contact with the child. Contact would only be reestablished if a complaint was made that the child was being neglected or abused.

Social services involvement with guardianship children is not consistent among counties

Although the probate courts do not monitor ongoing guardianships of children without estates, some children--those whose nonrelative guardians were receiving foster care maintenance payments--were afforded some protection through the visits of social services staff. These visits can indicate when the child's needs are not being met and could alert the social services agency of the need to apply appropriate protective service measures, such as involuntary removal of the child for abuse or neglect.

24

State Department of Social Services regulations 1/ used by county workers in reviewing the eligibility of guardians for financial assistance stated that financial assistance could not be provided until county social workers, in accordance with the "Standards for Social Services," had determined that the home or facility met the child's physical, social, and psychological needs. One section of the standards required the local department of social services to assess a child's needs and determine whether they were being met in the foster home. Another section stated that an initial assessment must be made for each child and that reassessments should be made as frequently as needed but at least every 6 months. This last clause, which established a condition on eligibility for financial assistance, meant that homes receiving assistance for their ward(s) must be reviewed by a social worker, in addition to a (financial) "eligibility" worker, at least every 6 months or lose their funding.

While Alameda and San Diego Counties were enforcing these regulations, the Los Angeles County Department of Public Social Services operated with the understanding that it had little authority for supervising guardianships, since the probate court gave legal responsibility for the child's care to the guardian. Consistent with this understanding, Los Angeles County interpreted the State's financial eligibility regulations as follows: The Department of Public Social Services could initially deny a guardian funds if the first social assessment found the home unsuitable or if the guardian did not cooperate with the social worker. However, once the home was found suitable and funding was approved, the department would not stop payments if the guardian did not allow the social worker to reassess the home. Rather, the rate of financial support would be reduced to the base level (minimum rate paid by the county), and the case would then remain open only for providing the monthly maintenance payment.

1/Although the department did not intend to reduce protection for children in guardianship arrangements, in January 1980 its regulations covering guardian situations were revised and reference to guardians was inadvertently deleted. Current State regulations do not provide guidance for handling guardianships. A State official advised us that actions will be taken to reinstate the State regulation covering guardianships.

CONCLUSIONS

County public social services agencies did not always report to the court on the suitability of petitioners for guardianship of nonrelative children. This noncompliance with California State law was attributed to (1) judges not requiring the reports and (2) insufficient time to prepare the reports before the guardianship hearing dates. The result was that most of the children we reviewed in two of the three counties did not receive the protections provided by State law.

When prepared, suitability reports included an assessment of whether the proposed guardianship arrangement would meet the child's psychological and social needs. We believe the assessment should be expanded to address more fully other areas, such as evidence of criminal records check, physician certification of health of petitioner and other residents of the home, and a fire clearance for the home if the petition is being filed for a nonambulatory child.

While suitability reports were intended for all nonrelative guardianship children, two other types of protection exist for many children. First, some children, because their guardians receive foster care maintenance payments on their behalf, benefit from continuing periodic reviews of the guardianship home by county social workers. Second, the guardians of many of the children were previously investigated for a foster care license. Nevertheless, 15 percent of the children in our review received none of the three major types of protection offered by State laws and regulations.

Although no cases of abuse were noted, one of the counties we reviewed had a policy which would allow foster care maintenance payments to continue to guardians who did not let county social workers periodically visit the home to assess whether the child's needs were being met. This policy was contrary to State regulations and should be corrected. Recent revisions to State regulations inadvertently deleted guidance to the counties on how to handle guardianship cases. According to a State official, this oversight will be corrected.

26

RECOMMENDATIONS TO
THE SECRETARY OF HHS

HHS has acknowledged its role as an advocate for the welfare of all the Nation's children. In fulfilling this role, HHS could be instrumental in improving the protection provided to guardianship children. To accomplish this goal, we recommend that the Secretary direct the Office of Human Development Services to encourage California to:

--Reiterate to the probate court judges the importance of county social workers' preparing suitability reports on petitioners for nonrelative guardianship children.

-Help the county social services agencies expand criteria on suitability reports to cover more fully the physical well-being of children, such as criminal checks and health certificates for petitioners and fire clearances for petitioners' homes.

--Reissue regulations governing guardianship situations and require compliance by county social services agencies.

HHS AND STATE OF CALIFORNIA
COMMENTS AND OUR EVALUATION

HHS

According to HHS, we were correct in stating that California should emphasize the importance of having county social workers prepare meaningful suitability reports on the petitioners for guardianship children to further ensure the children's well-being. However, concerning our recommendation that it encourage California to reissue its regulations, HHS misinterpreted it to mean that we are recommending that HHS issue Federal regulations governing guardianships where the care and maintenance of such children is not the responsibility of the State agency's federally funded foster care program. HHS, therefore, said it lacked legal authority to issue the regulations, and it did not inform us of any actions it would take in response to our recommendation.

27

State of California

The Director, California Department of Social Services, agreed with our recommendations and stated that the following actions have been or will be taken:

--Asked the California attorney general to issue, and circulate to all probate court judges, a legal opinion on the Probate Code concerning the necessity for preparing a suitability study before awarding guardianships.

--Issued directives to county social services departments reiterating and redefining their role and responsibilities in conducting home suitability studies. These directives also address the need to cover the physical well-being of children when conducting home suitability studies. Also, the directives instruct the counties to notify the court of any delay and to seek postponement of the hearing if necessary to enable them to file the report before the granting of guardianships.

--To alleviate the problem of insufficient time allotted to counties to prepare suitability studies, the department has sponsored State legislation to increase from 15 to 60 days the time frame for completion of the studies.

--Regulations governing guardianship situations are being prepared to replace the regulation inadvertenly deleted. In addition, a State law was recently enacted which specifies requirements to be met before children living with nonrelated legal guardians are eligible for financial assistance: (1) the legal guardian must cooperate with the county welfare department in developing a needs assessment, updating the assessment every 6 months, and carrying out the service plan, and (2) the county social services department must complete the needs assessment, update it every 6 months, and carry out the service plan.

CHAPTER 4

CALIFORNIA IS RECEIVING FEDERAL

FOSTER CARE REIMBURSEMENT FOR

INELIGIBLE GUARDIANSHIP CHILDREN

Guardianship children do not meet the criteria for Federal reimbursement of foster care maintenance payments under title IV-A. The Social Security Act requires, among other things, that the care and placement responsibility for foster children reside with the State IV-A agency (in California, the Department of Social Services). We reviewed cases for 385 nonrelative guardianship children in three California counties to determine whether Federal reimbursement was being claimed. We found that the counties improperly requested and received Federal reimbursement for foster care maintenance payments for guardianship children amounting to about $320,000. Generally, the counties were not aware of the Federal requirement to terminate from Federal financial participation guardianship children no longer under the care and placement of the State IV-A agency.

The following sections discuss the requirements for AFDC Federal financial participation and our findings in the three counties reviewed.

CERTAIN CONDITIONS MUST BE MET
FOR CHILDREN TO BE ELIGIBLE FOR
FEDERAL FINANCIAL PARTICIPATION

To be eligible for AFDC Federal financial participation, a child must meet the Federal requirements in sections 406 or 408 of the Social Security Act. Federal aid under title IV-A AFDC is available to

--a dependent child (1) who has been deprived of parental support, (2) who is living with a specified relative, (3) who is under 18 (or under 21 if regularly attending school), and (4) whose family meets income eligibility requirements--this category is referred to as AFDC family group/unemployed parent program--or

29

--a dependent child removed from his or her home by judicial determination (1) whose placement and care are the responsibility of the agency specified by the title IV-A plan, (2) who was placed in a State licensed or approved foster care facility, and (3) whose family meets income eligibility requirements--this category is referred to as AFDC foster care.

Nonrelative guardianship children are not eligible for Federal financial participation under either aid program. Guardianship children are not eligible for the AFDC family group/unemployed parent program unless the guardian is a relative as specified in section 406. Similarly, guardianship children are not eligible for AFDC foster care because the probate courts remove federally eligible foster children from the care of the State agency and give the responsibility of caring for the children to the guardians. The responsibility for placement of these children is also taken from the State agency and retained by the court. To remove such a child from his or her guardian, the State agency must obtain court review and approval.

At the time of our review, HHS was not aware that California was receiving reimbursement for guardianship children under the Federal foster care program. Also, HHS had not issued any instructions to California notifying it that guardianship children were not eligible for Federal reimbursement under the program.

CALIFORNIA COUNTIES RECEIVING
FEDERAL REIMBURSEMENT FOR
INELIGIBLE GUARDIANSHIP CHILDREN

Each of the three counties we reviewed had received Federal reimbursement for foster care maintenance payments on behalf of guardianship children. These Federal overpayments occurred when the county agencies did not terminate children from Federal foster care financial participation when they became wards of guardians. Such children originally met the requirements for Federal financial participation under section 408 of the Social Security Act. After becoming wards of guardians, they remained eligible for State foster care maintenance payments, but lost their Federal eligibility.

State regulations allow payments
to nonrelative guardians under
foster care provision

California Department of Social Services regulations
allow nonrelative guardians to request and receive foster
care maintenance payments for their wards. Every 6 months
the county agencies are required to assess whether the needs
of the child are being met in the guardian's home.

Federal overpayments for
guardianship children identified
at three counties reviewed

The following sections describe our findings on nonrelative guardianship children reviewed in each county.

Alameda County

As of November 1979, 233 children were in nonrelative
guardianship status in Alameda County receiving maintenance
payments under the State's foster care provisions. Upon reviewing case files on 136 of them, we found that Federal foster care maintenance payments were made for 61 children after
guardianship was granted. In most cases, dependency was terminated within a few months after guardianship was granted,
and in some cases, Federal financial participation was also
terminated. The Federal overpayments ranged from 1 to 75
months per child and totaled $173,000.

Foster care maintenance payments for 39 of the 61 guardianship children were still being federally supported at the
time of our review. Alameda County officials said these children will continue to be classified as federally eligible,
and adjustments to reimburse the Federal Government for the
overpayments will not be made unless the county is directed
to do so by the State Department of Social Services.

Los Angeles County

As of November 1979, about 300 children were in nonrelative guardianship status in Los Angeles County receiving
maintenance payments under the State's foster care provisions. We reviewed case files on 177 of them and found that
Federal foster care maintenance payments were made for 26

31

children after guardianship was granted and dependency was terminated. Federal overpayments ranged from 1 to 79 months per child and totaled $107,000.

Foster care maintenance payments for 20 of the 26 guardianship children were still being federally supported at the time of our review. Los Angeles County officials stated that appropriate actions have begun to classify all guardianship children as non-Federal and that adjustments to reimburse the Federal Government were being made in all cases.

San Diego County

As of November 1979, 72 children were in nonrelative guardianship status in San Diego County receiving maintenance payments under the State's foster care provisions. We reviewed all the case files and found that Federal foster care maintenance payments had been made for 17 children after guardianship was granted and dependency was terminated. The Federal overpayments ranged from 1 to 57 months per child and totaled $40,000.

None of the guardianship children were being federally supported at the time of our review. San Diego County policy was revised to appropriately indicate that guardianship children are not eligible for Federal financial participation in foster care maintenance payments. The county has not received Federal reimbursement for foster care maintenance payments for guardianship children since February 1979. County officials stated that adjustments to reimburse the Federal Government for the overpayments received for guardianship children will be made only if the county is directed to do so by the State Department of Social Services.

CONCLUSIONS

The three California counties we reviewed had received Federal reimbursement for foster care maintenance payments made on behalf of guardianship children who were not eligible for Federal financial participation.

Alameda County officials indicated that they will continue to claim these children as eligible for Federal financial participation unless directed otherwise by the State Department of Social Service. The other two counties reviewed have taken action to terminate guardianship children from

Federal reimbursement, and one, Los Angeles County, has initiated actions to reimburse the Federal Government for the
overpayments involved. These overpayments occurred because
the counties were not aware of the requirement to identify
and terminate the Federal eligibility of guardianship children
who were no longer under the care and placement responsibility
of the State Department of Social Services.

Because of the problems noted in the three California
counties, we believe that Federal overpayments for guardianship children could be occurring in other California counties
and other States. HHS needs to issue clarifying instructions
to all the States explaining that guardianship children lose
their eligibility for Federal foster care maintenance payments
when the care and placement responsibilities of such children
are taken from the State title IV-A agency. Also, HHS officials need to survey the situation nationwide to assess the
overall significance of Federal overpayments for ineligible
guardianship children.

RECOMMENDATIONS TO THE
SECRETARY OF HHS

To ensure that Federal financial participation in maintenance payments to foster children is made only for those
meeting the Federal criteria, we recommend that the Secretary
direct the Office of Human Development Services to:

--Issue instructions to all the States notifying them
   that guardianship children are not eligible for Federal reimbursement for foster care maintenance payments when responsibility for such children is removed
   from the State title IV-A agency.

--Follow up on Federal overpayments for ineligible
   guardianship children and work with California to
   identify and make retroactive adjustments for the
   overpayments in the three counties reviewed and the
   counties not reviewed.

--Determine whether other States are erroneously including guardianship children as federally eligible for
   foster care. If so, act to identify and recover the
   overpayments.

HHS AND STATE OF CALIFORNIA COMMENTS AND OUR EVALUATION

HHS

Regarding our first recommendation, HHS stated that:

> "GAO is correct that Federal financial participation in maintenance payments for foster care should be made only for those children meeting Federal criteria. Existing regulations clearly define the conditions under which States can claim Federal financial participation for foster care maintenance. Pursuant to the recently-enacted Adoption Assistance and Child Welfare Act of 1980 (P.L. 96-272), regulations are being developed which will further define the requirements for FFP [Federal financial participation] for foster care maintenance. The new legislation and regulations pertaining thereto, will also require States to arrange for a periodic, independently conducted audit of this program, to occur no less frequently than once every three years. This law, and the regulations to follow, also mandate a minimum set of reporting requirements to this Department relative to the status of the program. It is expected that there will be no lack of clarity in determining for whom Federal payments may be made for foster care maintenance. In addition, program reviews conducted by this Department will reveal any lack of adherence to the requirements for Federal financial participation."

Concerning our second recommendation, HHS stated that Social Security Administration regional staff will be directed to determine whether there were ineligible guardianship children for whom the State claimed Federal financial participation under the AFDC foster care program. HHS said the review will also determine whether the guardianship status of the children terminated the placement and care responsibility of the State or local agency administering the State plan or any public agency with whom the State or local agency had an agreement which included provisions for assuming development of a plan of care. A disallowance will be made for cases that are determined to have been ineligible for AFDC foster care payments under title IV-A.

As to our third recommendation, HHS stated that the Office of Human Development Services, which assumed responsibility for the AFDC foster care program on October 1, 1980, from Social Security's Office of Family Assistance, will make efforts to ensure that only children who meet the program's eligibility requirements are included in the States' claims for Federal participation. HHS added that the Office of Family Assistance will request HHS' Audit Agency to review States' expenditures for AFDC foster care for periods before October 1, 1980, and to take appropriate action.

We believe that actions to identify the disallowance of ineligible Federal foster care payments should not be delayed because of provisions of Public Law 96-272, enacted on June 17, 1980, entitled the Adoption Assistance and Child Welfare Act of 1980, which affect future payments to States for foster care. This legislation provides that the fiscal year 1978 Federal foster care payments to States are to be used as the ceiling and basis for payments to States for fiscal year 1981 and later years. The legislation also provides that payments made to States in fiscal year 1981 and beyond will not be subject to recovery for excessive payments resulting from overstated fiscal year 1978 payments. Therefore, action should be taken to reduce the 1978 base-year payments for any overpayments as soon as possible.

State of California

The State said that Federal eligibility currently exists in certain guardianship cases where the detention order making a child the responsibility of the county social services department is not dismissed but guardianship is awarded. We agree with the State since, in these cases, the care and supervision of the guardianship child remains with the county social services department. The State agreed that Federal foster care maintenance funds are not available for other children living with nonrelated legal guardians. The State also expressed the view that HHS should implement regulations which provide for title IV-A funding for such children.

35

The State also requested that all action relative to recovery of funds be postponed until (1) HHS issues instructions to the States and (2) the State of California has reviewed each case GAO found to be ineligible for Federal funds.

As previously discussed, we believe that actions should be initiated as soon as possible to follow up on ineligible payments because of the impact of Public Law 96-272 on determining payments to States for foster care starting in fiscal year 1981.

CHAPTER 5

GUARDIANSHIPS HAVE BEEN USED TO OBTAIN

CHILDREN IN EXCESS OF THE NUMBER AUTHORIZED

BY FOSTER HOME LICENSING REGULATIONS

The operators of 16 State-licensed small family homes appeared to have more children than authorized by community care (foster care) licensing criteria. More children were in these homes because guardianship children were not counted or considered as foster care children. Transfer of licensing responsibility at the State level along with failure to address the problem allowed these placements to continue for many years. Potentially, the health and welfare of all the children are jeopardized when residing in a home with more than the number of children the house is licensed for. In early 1980, the State initiated action to review these homes.

During our review of guardianship children, we noted that certain homes contained many of these children. (See chs. 3 and 4.) Using this information, we reviewed licensing records and identified 16 homes in Los Angeles County where the number of children appeared to exceed licensed capacity. No such homes were identified in Alameda and San Diego Counties.

MANY OF THE CHILDREN IN THESE
HOMES ARE PARTIALLY SUPPORTED
BY FEDERAL FUNDING

The operators of the 16 small family homes receive moneys from the California Departments of Social Services and Developmental Services for taking care of children with developmental disabilities (including mental retardation, cerebral palsy, epilepsy, and autism). The homes receive foster care maintenance payments for the guardianship children and the non-guardian foster children placed in the home. Developmentally disabled children are difficult to place and require more attention than most foster children. Los Angeles County pays individuals that take disabled children a premium rate of up to $743 per month per child depending on how much extra attention the child requires. Payments for many of these children include Federal foster care or Supplemental Security

Income funding. In December 1979, the 16 homes had 122 children for whom they were receiving foster care maintenance payments. Federal and State payments to each of the 16 homes ranged between $30,000 and $80,000 per year, with total annual payments to all the homes of about $1 million.

CHILDREN RESIDE IN 16 FOSTER HOMES
IN EXCESS OF EVALUATED CAPACITY

Social services placement agencies have placed children in each of 16 small family homes in Los Angeles County having in excess of six children, the capacity of each of these State-licensed homes.

Community care licensing laws are meant to prevent children from being placed in residences that do not meet certain health and safety standards. The standards that apply vary with the number of children for which the home is licensed. In California no more than six children, in addition to the operator's own children, can reside in a small family home. None of the homes had more than six nonguardian foster children. However, operators of the 16 homes were able to circumvent the the licensing laws and house more than six children by obtaining guardianship on some children and still have up to six nonguardian foster children placed in their homes. This occupancy of children in excess of evaluated capacity of the homes has occurred because State and local social services personnel have not counted the guardianship children among the children placed in the homes in determining compliance with licensing capacity.

Requirements for large family
homes are more stringent
than for small family homes

Homes licensed for more than six children (large family homes) must meet more stringent requirements than homes licensed for six children or fewer (small family homes). These requirements include:

--Meeting more stringent fire regulations.

--Hiring a social worker as an ongoing consultant to the operator to plan for each child's daily activities.

38

--Hiring skilled employees.

--Keeping records on revenues and expenses.

Because of the more stringent requirements applicable to large family homes, the operators of the 16 homes have benefited by retaining their small family home classification. Simultaneously, they have operated more like a large family home without having to meet the requirements for large family home classification.

REORGANIZATIONS OF THE LICENSING AGENCIES AND VARYING INTERPRETATIONS OF REGULATIONS ALLOWED THE SITUATION TO CONTINUE

The problem of whether guardianship children should be counted for licensing purposes stems primarily from the ambiguity of regulations regarding the status of such children. This ambiguity has been perpetuated, in part, because the State agency responsible for licensing has changed twice in recent years. Before 1974, the State Department of Mental Hygiene had licensing responsibility for these homes. Under its policies, guardianship children were included in the maximum number of children that could be placed in a home. From 1974 to 1978, the State Department of Health was responsible for licensing small family homes. The regulations and policies of the Department of Mental Hygiene were no longer in effect, and the Department of Health foster care regulations did not refer to guardianship children. Therefore, some State licensing offices that had managers from the prior Department of Mental Hygiene staff continued to count guardianship children, but other licensing offices that did not have managers from the prior department did not count the guardianship children in determining compliance with the licensing capacity.

In 1978 licensing responsibility was again transferred, this time to the Department of Social Services, Community Care Licensing Division. Department of of Social Services regulations state that small family homes are licensed to provide care for not more than six foster children. These regulations, like the prior Department of Health regulations, do not instruct the licensing offices on whether or not guardianship children should be included or excluded from the maximum number of children that can be placed in a small family home.

The large number of children in these homes came to our attention in September 1979, and we visited two of the homes. At that time, we discussed the problem of placements with Los Angeles County licensing personnel. In December 1979, the State licensing office in Los Angeles requested the State Community Care Licensing Division's policy staff to resolve the problem, since placing children in homes in excess of licensing regulations results in overcrowding, inadequate services, and potential neglect of children.

In March 1980, a State Community Care Licensing Division memorandum directed the State licensing office in Los Angeles to consider guardianship children in the maximum number of children (six) that a small family home can be licensed for. Homes not in compliance with required criteria will be evaluated and will be required to obtain a large home license, if they are able, or reduce the number of children placed with them if they choose to remain a small family home.

CONCLUSIONS

The health and welfare of children are jeopardized when they are placed in a home in excess of the capacity to care for them. This may have occurred in 16 small family homes in Los Angeles County which have obtained guardianship for some children. Because of ambiguous regulations and inaction by the State licensing agency, children residing in the homes (including guardianship children) have exceeded the limitation of six for which they were evaluated and licensed.

After our review, the State Community Care Licensing Division issued instructions to assess the placement of children in foster homes when total number of children in the home may exceed its capacity for care. The instruction specified that guardianship children must be considered in establishing the number of children that each home is licensed for.

Although the 16 homes in Los Angeles County are being reviewed, the placing of children in homes in excess of licensed capacity could continue if any of the homes have the capacity to care for more than six children. We believe that foster home operators can continue to obtain increased capacity by seeking guardianship of their foster children without providing the protections of large family or group home licensing requirements.

40

RECOMMENDATION TO THE
SECRETARY OF HHS

We recommend that the Secretary direct the Office of
Human Development Services to work with California to see
that Federal funding is provided only for children placed
in licensed facilities that fully meet State health and welfare licensing requirements.

HHS AND STATE OF CALIFORNIA
COMMENTS AND OUR EVALUATION

HHS

HHS concurred with our recommendation and said that a
dialogue has been initiated between departmental staff and
the State Department of Social Services regarding the review
of licensing standards, procedures, and practices and the
need for corrective action in this area.

HHS also said it would soon be issuing regulations governing the administration of the Adoption Assistance and Child
Welfare Act of 1980 that will further define and reiterate
the requirement that a foster home must meet the standards
prescribed by the State licensing agency. Further, HHS said
it would furnish ongoing technical assistance and guidance
to the State agencies and assist them in reviewing their
programs to ensure compliance with these standards.

State of California

While California did not agree with our conclusion that
guardianship children should be counted in the six foster
children that the homes are licensed for, it planned to take
a number of actions dealing with the licensing procedures
for foster family homes.

The State said that the Department of Social Services'
Community Care Licensing Division would issue a release to
all licensing agencies to reaffirm the importance of current
State regulations for small family homes and children and
foster family homes which require an evaluation of the presence of other members of the household to determine the
extent to which these individuals impair or affect the
ability of the foster parent(s) to adequately care for the
foster children. Also, after the review, the presence of

another individual could result in a reduction of the licensed capacity based on the inability of the foster parent(s) to care for a specific number of foster children because of the needs of other household members.

In addition, the State plans to propose new regulations which will

--require notification to the licensing agency when additional members are added to the family,

--authorize the licensing agency to reduce capacity based upon these additions to the family, and

--require notification to the licensing agency if members of the household leave when those individuals were responsible for the provision of care and supervision.

We believe the State's proposed action and the plans to review each of the 16 homes to determine if their licensed capacity should be reduced because of the presence of the guardianship children should be beneficial. It does not appear, however, to address the principal issue that we believe should be considered--foster homes should not be allowed to obtain guardianships in order to house more than the number of children they are licensed for. The placing of children in homes in excess of licensed capacity could continue if the homes have the capacity to care for more than six children. We believe that foster home operators can continue to obtain increased capacity by seeking guardianship of their foster children without providing the additional protections of large family or group home licensing requirements.

We believe that HHS in its dialogue with the State should emphasize that federally funded children should not be placed in facilities that do not fully meet State health and welfare licensing requirements.

United States Senate

COMMITTEE ON HUMAN RESOURCES
WASHINGTON, D.C. 20510

February 28, 1979

Honorable Elmer B. Staats
Comptroller General
General Accounting Office
441 G Street, N. W.
Washington, D. C. 20548

Dear Elmer,

A number of reports about the alleged placement of
foster children in homes or facilities operated by
the People's Temple or by its members -- and the
deaths of an unknown number of these foster children
in Jonestown, Guyana, -- have come to my attention
in connection with hearings before the Subcommittee
on Child and Human Development on abuse of children
in out-of-home placements. The first day of these
hearings was held in San Francisco, California, on
January 4; a second day was held in Washington, D.C.,
on January 24, 1979.

I believe that it is important to learn whether there
is any foundation for these reports and the extent
to and purpose for which federal funds have been
utilized in connection with any such placements. I
am also deeply concerned about the implications of
these reports for Congressional efforts to reform
the foster care system. As you know, your report
(No. HRD-77-40) in February of 1977 on foster
children and the steps for Congress to consider
taking to improve their care stimulated a great
deal of Congressional and Administration interest
in enacting reform measures. Although we were not
successful during the last Congress in seeing these
measures enacted, legislation dealing with this
problem passed both the House and Senate during the
95th Congress (H.R. 13511 and H.R. 6693 as passed
by the Senate, and H.R. 7200 and H.R. 11711 as
passed by the House). I certainly plan a renewed
effort during the 96th Congress to enact legislation
in this area.

Hence, I am requesting that the General Accounting
Office conduct an investigation of the allegations
that foster children were placed in homes or facilities operated by the People's Temple or by its
members; the extent to which federal funds, if any,
were utilized for the placement or support (or both)
of children in homes or facilities operated by the
People's Temple or its members; the extent to which
any such federal funds were diverted from their
statutory purpose; whether any foster children died
in Jonestown; the circumstances under which any foster
children were placed in homes or facilities operated
by the People's Temple or by its members (including
what information was known to the local agency when the
placement was made); and the circumstances under which
any of those foster children were removed from the United
States to Guyana (including what information was known
to the local agency immediately prior to their removal
and during their residency there).

If there appears to be any foundation to the reports
regarding the placement of foster children in homes
or facilities operated by the People's Temple or by
its members, I would also like your opinion as to
whether the reform measures which passed the Senate
(or were proposed in S. 1928 or H.R. 7200 as passed
by the House) during the last Congress could have --
if enacted and implemented years ago -- prevented or
reduced the likelihood of this result. I would also
appreciate any suggestions for improvements in the
legislation which passed the Senate.

I would appreciate very much your immediate attention
to this matter and your response on an expedited basis.
If you have any questions, please contact Susanne
Martinez, counsel to the Subcommittee on Child and
Human Development (224-9181).

Thank you for your cooperation with the Subcommittee.

                    Sincerely,

                    Alan Cranston
                    Chairman
                    Subcommittee on Child and
                       Human Development

DEPARTMENT OF HEALTH & HUMAN SERVICES   Office of Inspector General

Washington, D.C. 20201

OCT 2 2

Mr. Gregory J. Ahart
Director, Human Resources
  Division
United States General
  Accounting Office
Washington, D.C. 20548

Dear Mr. Ahart:

The Secretary asked that I respond to your request for our
comments on your draft report entitled, "After the Peoples
Temple Tragedy--Actions Required to Improve the Care and
Protection of Guardianship Children." The enclosed comments
represent the tentative position of the Department and are
subject to reevaluation when the final version of this
report is received.

We appreciate the opportunity to comment on this draft
report before its publication.

Sincerely yours,

Richard B. Lowe III
Inspector General (Designate)

Enclosure

GAO note: Page references in this appendix have been changed
            to agree with the final report.

DEPARTMENT OF HEALTH AND HUMAN SERVICES COMMENTS ON
GAO DRAFT REPORT "AFTER THE PEOPLES TEMPLE TRAGEDY--
ACTIONS REQUIRED TO IMPROVE THE CARE
AND PROTECTION OF GUARDIANSHIP CHILDREN"

GAO Recommendations (page 27)

HHS has acknowledged its role as an advocate for the welfare of all the
Nation's children. In fulfilling this role, HHS could be instrumental
in improving the protection provided to guardianship children. To accomplish this goal we recommend that the Secretary, HHS, direct the
Office of Human Development Services to encourage the State of California
to:

> Reiterate to the probate court judges the importance
> of county social workers preparing suitability reports
> on petitioners for non-relative guardianship children.
>
> Assist county social services agencies in expanding
> criteria on suitability reports to cover, more fully,
> the physical well-being of children, such as criminal
> checks and health certificates for petitioners, and
> fire clearances for petitioners' homes.
>
> Reissue regulations governing guardianship situations
> and require compliance by county social services agencies.

Comment

GAO is correct that States (including California) should emphasize the
importance of having county social workers prepare meaningful suitability
reports on the petitioners for guardianship children to further ensure
the children's well-being. However, the Department lacks legal authority
to issue Federal regulations governing guardianship when the care and
maintenance of such children is not the responsibility of the State
agency's federally funded foster care program.

GAO Recommendation - (Page 33)

That the Secretary, HHS, direct the Office of Human Development Services
to determine whether other States are erroneously including guardianship
children as federally eligible for foster care. If so, action should be
taken to identify and recover the overpayments.

Comment

The Office of Human Development Services assumed responsibility for the AFDC-Foster Care program effective October 1, 1980. Through State Child Welfare Program Reviews, and other mechanisms, OHDS will make on-going efforts to ensure that only those children who meet this program's eligibility requirements are included in States' claims for Federal financial participation.

Regarding States who may have erroneously included guardianship children as federally eligible for foster care, prior to October 1, 1980, the Social Security Administration's Office of Family Assistance will request the Department's Audit Agency (through the Inspector General's Office) to review States' expenditures for AFDC-FC for periods prior to October 1, 1980 and to take appropriate action.

GAO Recommendation - (Page 33)

That the Secretary, HHS, direct the Office of Human Development Services to follow-up on Federal overpayments for ineligible guardianship children and work with the State of California to identify and make retroactive adjustments for the overpayments in the three counties reviewed and the counties not reviewed.

Comment

Inasmuch as this recommendation pertains to a period of time when the Social Security Administration administered the foster care maintenance program, the Social Security Administration Regional staff will be directed to determine whether there were ineligible guardianship children for whom the State claimed FFP under the AFDC-Foster Care program. The review will include a determination as to whether the guardianship status of the children terminated the placement and care responsibility of the State or local agency administering the State plan or any public agency with whom the State or local agency had an agreement which included provisions for assuming development of a plan of care. A disallowance will be made for those cases which are determined to have been ineligible for AFDC-FC payments under Title IV-A.

<u>GAO Recommendations</u> - (Page 33)

To ensure that Federal financial participation in maintenance payments
to foster children is made only for those meeting the Federal criteria,
we recommend that the Secretary, HHS, direct the Office of Human Development Services to issue instructions to all the States notifying them that
guardianship children are not eligible for Federal reimbursement for foster
care maintenance payments when responsibility for such children is removed
from the State Title IV-A agency.

<u>Comment</u>

GAO is correct that Federal financial participation in maintenance payments for foster care should be made only for those children meeting Federal
criteria. Existing regulations clearly define the conditions under which
States can claim Federal financial participation for foster care maintenance. Pursuant to the recently-enacted Adoption Assistance and Child
Welfare Act of 1980 (P.L. 96-272), regulations are being developed which
will further define the requirements for FFP for foster care maintenance.
The new legislation and regulations pertaining thereto, will also require
States to arrange for a periodic, independently conducted audit of this
program, to occur no less frequently than once every three years. This
law, and the regulations to follow, also mandate a minimum set of reporting requirements to this Department relative to the status of the program.
It is expected that there will be no lack of clarity in determining for
whom Federal payments may be made for foster care maintenance. In addition, program reviews conducted by this Department will reveal any lack
of adherence to the requirements for Federal financial participation.

GAO Recommendation - (Page 41)

That HHS direct the Office of Human Development Services to work with the State of California to see that planned corrective action is taken and that Federal funding is provided only for children placed in licensed facilities that fully meet State health and welfare licensing requirements.

Comment

The Department concurs with this recommendation. Dialogue has already begun between Departmental staff and the State Social Services Agency regarding the review of licensing standards, procedures and practices, and to plan corrective action in this area. In addition, Departmental staff, in concert with State Social Services staff, will conduct follow-up reviews of other relevant areas. These will include social assessments for placements, Social Work supervision of placements and the types of children placed, monitoring of counties' placements, use and length of stay in emergency shelter care, the recruitment of foster parents, and establishing the extent to which foster parents are a resource. On site work will be initiated in January 1981.

The Department will soon be issuing regulations governing the administration of the Adoption Assistance and Child Welfare Act of 1980 (P.L. 96-272) that will further define and reiterate the requirement that a foster home must meet the standards prescribed by the State licensign agency. We will furnish ongoing technical assistance and guidance to the State agencies and assist them in the review of their programs to ensure compliance with these standards.

DEPARTMENT OF STATE
Comptroller
Washington, D.C. 20520

October 27, 1980

Mr. J. Kenneth Fasick
Director
International Division
U. S. General Accounting Office
Washington, D. C.

Dear Mr. Fasick:

I am replying to your letter of September 18, 1980, which forwarded copies of the draft report: "After the Peoples Temple Tragedy--Actions Required to Improve the Care and Protection of Guardianship Children".

The enclosed comments on this report were prepared by the Assistant Secretary, Bureau of Consular Affairs.

We appreciate having had the opportunity to review and comment on the draft report. If I may be of further assistance, I trust you will let me know.

Sincerely,

Roger B. Feldman

Roger B. Feldman

Enclosure:
  As stated

GAO DRAFT REPORT:
"AFTER THE PEOPLES TEMPLE TRAGEDY -- ACTIONS REQUIRED
TO IMPROVE THE CARE AND PROTECTION OF GUARDIANSHIP CHILDREN"

        The GAO draft report concerning the care and protection
of guardianship children states on page 24 that "[t]here
are no regulations that require Passport Services to verify
that guardians have obtained court permission to take their
wards outside the United States". The report recommends
that Passport Services establish procedures for verifying
whether the state laws governing guardianship relations
requires specific court permission to take a ward out of
the United States, and whether such permission was granted
for each guardian applying for a passport for his or her
ward.

        While such a specific regulation as GAO recommends
is not part of Passport Services procedures, present procedure is rigorous enough to be adapted for processing passport
applications of minors in guardian situations to accomplish
the purpose contemplated in GAO's recommendation. Under
present procedure a person who is not a parent of the minor
applicant must provide proof of the legal relation to the
child before a passport is issued. Furthermore, passports
will not be issued if Passport Services is notified in advance
that an adult who is a parent, guardian or person in loco
parentis and is normally entitled to travel outside the
United States with the child no longer has that right.
Such notification frequently occurs in child custody situations,
where one of the child's parents does not have the legal
right to travel with the child or to obtain a passport for
him or her by virtue of a court order granting sole custody
to the other parent.

        Present passport regulations are fully compatible with
denying passports based upon notice and the presentation
of an order by a court establishing a guardianship relation
for a child which does not permit the child's travel outside
the United States. Such notice would be effective everywhere
within the United States, and would be specifically applicable
only to those few cases of guardianship where foreign travel
is not permitted, while not inconveniencing the majority
of guardians who have the right to travel abroad with the
ward. Furthermore, it does not incur the risk of a guardian
successfully evading the wishes of the court by misrepresenting
the terms of the guardianship relation.

Passport Services would be willing to inform the States Attorneys of the states, territories and the District of Columbia of the availability of this measure to prevent issuance of a passport to a minor whose guardianship order does not allow travel outside the United States. Passport Services further proposes to emphasize to its agents that all guardianship situations do not contemplate or permit travel outside the United States, and to change the relevant internal regulations to reflect this situation.

October 23, 1980
Date

Diego C. Asencio
Assistant Secretary
Bureau of Consular Affairs

ATE OF CALIFORNIA—HEALTH AND WELFARE AGENCY

DEPARTMENT OF SOCIAL SERVICES
744 P Street, Sacramento, CA 95814
(916) 445-7046

October 24, 1980

Mr. Gregory J. Ahart, Director
United States General Accounting Office
441 G Street, N.W.
Washington, D.C.   20548

Dear Mr. Ahart:

U.S. GENERAL ACCOUNTING OFFICE (GAO) REPORT TITLED, AFTER THE PEOPLE'S
TEMPLE TRAGEDY — ACTIONS REQUESTED TO IMPROVE THE CARE AND PROTECTION
OF GUARDIANSHIP CHILDREN

This will provide you with the California Department of Social Services'
comments concerning the findings and recommendations contained in the above
mentioned report. Also attached is a detailed response to each of the
report's findings. Please see Attachment A.

The four major issues identified in the GAO examination are:

1. The circumstances of the placement of foster and guardianship children
   with the People's Temple members who perished in Jonestown, Guyana.

2. Problems associated with the care and protection provided for guardianship children in California.

3. Alleged excessive federal payments made to California for the care of
   guardianship children.

4. Placement of children in foster care homes which also have guardianship
   children.

The first issue in your report concurred with the findings and conclusions
of our own investigation into public and published allegations that 150
foster children died in Jonestown, Guyana on November 18, 1978. Our department's investigation, conducted by the Fraud Prevention Bureau, concluded in
a report entitled, "Investigation Report on People's Temple," published in
November 1979, that no children under the care or supervision of either the
State Department of Social Services or any of the state's 58 county social
services departments died in Guyana. A copy of our investigative report is
attached. (See Attachment B)

The second issue identified by your investigators deals with procedures used
by California's courts and state and county social services departments
relative to the processing of guardianship petitions and the subsequent
monitoring of guardianships after they are granted.

53

In this issue, your staff finds that a lack of protection exists for children placed in court ordered guardianships where the guardians are either receiving no public assistance or the guardian is related to the child.

Your report also finds, without citing any specific instances of neglect or abuse, a lack of consistency by the California courts in ordering home suitability reports from county social services departments. In addition, your report finds county social services departments inconsistent in monitoring nonrelative guardianships and inconsistent criteria being used in conducting the home suitability studies.

In response, we would like to firmly state for the record that neither California nor federal law calls for the continued monitoring of children once they are placed by the courts in the home of a relative or in a home where the guardian receives no public cash assistance.

In this issue, your staff has raised a long-standing, unanswered and potentially volatile social policy issue. In response, I ask you these questions:

o Should not government assume that a relative-guardian will properly care for a child who is their own flesh and blood?

o Should not the government encourage the public to revise the long-standing social policy of allowing children to enter into long-term public assistance dependency, and, instead, actively encourage the integration of the child back into the community by reunifying the family, or if that is not possible, to make him/her a permanent part of a family through the adoption or guardianship process?

At present, our department has no plans to ask the Legislature to embrace in state policy a system of monitoring the homes of legal guardians, who do not receive public cash assistance, or are related to the child.

California's guardianship children are presently protected by the same social welfare and criminal laws which protect all the state's children. This is true regardless of whether or not they are in the homes of the natural parents or in the homes of a legal guardian. Child abuse in California is a crime regardless of where it occurs.

The courts are an independent branch of state government. The executive branch of government, of which the State Department of Social Services is a part, has absolutely no authority to mandate that judges on a consistent basis request home suitability studies be conducted on each and every guardianship petition that comes before them. Our interpretation of the law is that all nonrelative guardianship petitions should receive a home suitability study before the courts make any guardianship decision, and only the Attorney General can force the courts to enforce that law. This apparently has not been done on a uniform basis.

In pursuit of our interpretation of the law, we have asked the California Attorney General to issue a legal opinion and circulate it to all Probate Court judges, spelling out the requirements of the State Probate Code concerning the necessity for a suitability study prior to awarding guardianships. (See Attachment C.) Likewise, we have issued directives to county social services departments

54

reiterating and redefining their role and responsibilities in conducting home suitability studies. These directives also reiterate and define uniform criteria to be used in conducting home suitability studies. A copy of those directives is attached. (See Attachment D.)

The third issue identified by your staff centers on alleged excessive federal payments made for care of guardianship children. Our attached detailed response addresses this question in depth, hence it does not require elaboration here. However, we would like for your to know that it is our belief the federal government should assume its financial responsibilities for guardianship children as contained in Public Law 96-272, and implement regulations to provide Title IV-A money to children living with nonrelated court appointed guardians.

The fourth issue raised by your staff recommends that State Department of Social Services' staff should automatically reduce the licensed capacity of a foster care facility by the number of the foster parents' guardianship children. We disagree. Department of Social Services feels that each case should be determined on its own merits. Existing state regulations require an evaluation of the presence of other members of the household to determine the extent to which these individuals impair or affect the ability of the foster parent(s) to adequately care for the foster children. After a review of the circumstances of a particular foster home applicant or licensee, the presence of another individual (including a guardianship child) can result in a reduction of the licensed capacity. Such a reduction would appropriately be based on the inability of the foster parent(s) to care for a specific number of foster children because of the needs of other household members.

We will take steps to re-emphasize and clarify these provisions of the law to state licensing agencies. These steps are outlined in detail in our attached point-by-point response.

If you should have any future questions concerning this response, please call Laura Williams, Chief of the Audits Evaluation and Financial Appeals Section. Her telephone number is (916) 323-0274.

Sincerely,

MARION J. WOODS
Director

Attachments: 1/

A. Technical Response - Item by item to GAO Report
B. California State Department of Social Services' Investigation Report on People's Temple
C. Letter to Attorney General regarding Suitability Reports for Probate Courts
D. All-County Letter - Providing Direction on Guardianship Suitability Studies
E. Preprint Senate Bill No. 14 Corrective Action - Proposed Legislation.
F. Los Angeles County Welfare Response to GAO Audit
G. Alameda County Welfare Response to GAO Audit
H. San Diego County Welfare Response to GAO Audit

1/Attachment B to H not included as appendix because of the large volume of material.

ATTACHMENT A

CALIFORNIA STATE DEPARTMENT OF SOCIAL SERVICES RESPONSE TO THE GAO REPORT TITLED,
AFTER THE PEOPLE'S TEMPLE TRAGEDY--ACTIONS REQUIRED TO IMPROVE THE CARE AND
PROTECTION OF GUARDIANSHIP CHILDREN

FINDING NO. 1

No children, who were in foster care or under the supervision and care of the
California Department of Social Services, perished in Guyana. However, a few
of the victims of the tragedy who were taken to Guyana without court approval
were Wards of People's Temple members.

GAO Recommendation:

> GAO recommends that the Department of State have the U.S. Passport Service
> adopt policies and procedures which would verify, prior to issuance of
> passports, that where required by state law, guardians have obtained court
> approval to take their wards out of the country.

State's Response:

> Since this recommendation is directed at a federal agency and does not
> affect SDSS, we have no comment.

FINDING NO. 2

Guardianship children in California frequently did not receive all the protection
intended for them by state law because:

Item A. California law is not consistently followed as to when and how preguardianship suitability assessments should be done.

Item B. Although not required, protection (other than suitability reports)
was not made available to some children, i.e., continuing periodic
reviews of guardianships not receiving assistance payments and foster
home licensure investigations on guardianship homes who were foster
care facilities.

Item C. Ongoing reviews of guardianships were not consistent, i.e., the Probate
Court reviewed only cases where financial accountability for the child's
estate was involved; county social services departments were inconsistent
in performing ongoing reviews of guardianship cases receiving assistance
payments.

Item D. Suitability reports do not address the physical well-being of the child.

Item E. State regulations covering assessment and reassessment of guardianships
were inadvertently terminated by the state in January 1980 and/or were
not fully implemented in some counties.

GAO Recommendation:

In fulfilling the federal role as an advocate for the welfare of the nation's children, the Secretary of HHS should direct the Office of Human Development Services to encourage the State of California to:

-- reiterate to state court judges the importance of county social workers in filing suitability reports on petitions for nonrelative guardianship custody,

-- assist the counties in expanding suitability report criteria to more fully address the physical well-being of guardianship children, and

-- reissue regulations specifically covering guardianships and require compliance by county social service agencies.

State's Response:

Item A.   The GAO report concludes the inconsistent application of state law relative to preguardianship suitability reports by county social services departments was caused by: 1) failure of the Probate Court judges to require the reports because of inconsistent court interpretation of the Probate Code, and 2) insufficient time (15 days) alloted to counties to prepare the reports prior to hearing dates.

The Department wishes to clarify that under California statutes, the attorney for the person seeking guardianship is required to file a copy of the petition for guardianship with SDSS. If a suitability study is required, SDSS notifies the county social service agency that such a report must be completed.

This notification process does not always work because of the short time frame between when SDSS receives a copy of the petition and the scheduled court hearing date for the petition. In addition, some court judges have interpreted the Probate Code as not requiring suitability studies in all cases and therefore have not required the study be presented during the court proceedings. We have no jurisdiction over the courts. However, we firmly believe a report should be filed in every nonrelative guardianship case and have been proceeding to process all guardianship petitions received by this Department on that basis. In order to reaffirm this Department's role in guardianship proceedings and to pursue means of encouraging consistent court interpretation in that area, we have taken the following actions:

1.   We have completed and distributed an All-County Letter (Attachment 1) reiterating the requirements of the Probate Code and the need to file such a report. The letter instructs counties on detailed procedures and information to be contained within the report and provides the time frames within which the report must be submitted to the courts. It also instructs counties to notify the court of any delay and to seek postponement of the hearing if necessary to enable them to file the report prior to granting of guardianships.

2. To encourage consistent interpretation of the Probate law by the courts, we have requested the State Attorney General to issue a legal opinion on the pertinent Section of the Probate Code and distribute that opinion to all Probate Court judges. (Attachment 2.)

3. To alleviate the problem of insufficient time alloted to counties for preparation of the studies, the department has sponsored state legislation (SB 14 Preprint) to amend the current 15-day time frame for completion of the studies to allow for 60 days. (See Attachment 3)

Item B. The report states there are no continuing periodic reviews of guardianship cases.

Once the guardianship has been granted the child becomes a ward of the guardian. If the child is not receiving assistance payments, the county social services department has no further contact with or jurisdiction over the child. SDSS and county social service departments have no legal authority to monitor such placements unless, of course, protective intervention is necessary as a result of suspected abuse or neglect.

The report also states there are no continuing foster home licensure investigations of guardianship homes that were previously foster care homes. SDSS regulations contained in Title 22, California Administrative Code, Division 6, Section 80105 (II) excludes from licensing those living situations where care providers are legal guardians (or natural parents) for all of the children in their care. (See Attachment 4.) If a licensed foster care home operator becomes the legal guardian of all foster care children in the home, the home is no longer subject to state licensing requirements. Neither the state nor county licensing agency have statutory authority to continue conducting licensing studies in those situations.

Item C. The report states that ongoing reviews of guardianships are not performed consistently and states that two types of periodic reviews either by the Probate Court, or by county social services departments, could provide ongoing protection.

As noted in the report, annual or biennial court reviews of all guardians are not required by the Probate Code. To effect such a requirement would necessitate a change in the current code. In cases where the child does not receive AFDC-BHI or other services from the California Department of Social Services, this Department has no jurisdiction over the child and any periodic review would have to be conducted by the court establishing the guardianship.

When the child in guardianship placement receives AFDC-BHI payments, the county social services department must complete a routine six-month reassessment of AFDC-BHI eligibility and assure that the needs of the child are being met. SDSS recently completed a statewide survey of foster care cases, reviewing case record compliance for AFDC-BHI six-month eligibility determination. Based on this survey, corrective action is planned for those counties found to be out of compliance with the six-month reassessment mandate.

Item D. The report states that suitability studies should address the physical well-being of the child. The department agrees and has reiterated this requirement which is contained in the Probate Code to the counties in All-County Letter No. 80-59, dated October 1, 1980. The letter requires onsite evaluations of unlicensed homes similar to those conducted for foster family homes. (See Attachment 1.)

Item E. SDSS is in the process of implementing regulations similar to the one identified as being deleted. However, it should be noted that while the regulation which was deleted stipulated that aid payments could not be provided for a child placed under certain circumstances (one of which was guardianship) unless a determination had been made that the home/facility met the physical, social and psychological needs of the child, it did not create the requirement for such a determination. Such a determination is required in Section 30-206.151 of the SDSS Manual of Policies and Procedures. (See Attachment 5.) The Department of Social Services did not intend, in any way, to reduce protection for children in guardianship arrangements. State Assembly Bill 2749 (Statutes of 1980, c. 1166) clarifies state law with regard to children who may be aided under the AFDC-BHI Program, and provides statutory authority which addresses AFDC-BHI eligibility for children living with non-related legal guardians. Specifically, this law requires that the following requirements be met before AFDC-BHI payments are made:

a. The legal guardian must cooperate with the county welfare department in developing a needs assessment, updating the assessment every six months, and in carrying out the service plan.

b. The county social services department must complete the needs assessment, update it every six months and carry out the service plan.

FINDING NO. 3

California received federal foster care maintenance payments for guardianship children who did not meet federal eligibility criteria.

GAO Recommendation:

The Secretary of HHS should direct the Office of Human Development Services to:

Item A. Issue instructions to all the states notifying them that guardianship children are not eligible for federal reimbursement for foster care maintenance payments when responsibility for such children is removed from the State Title IV-A Agency.

Item B. Obtain retroactive adjustments for federal overpayments that were made for guardianship children in California.

Item C. Determine if other states are also receiving federal overpayments for ineligible guardianship children, and if they are, take action to identify and recover the overpayments.

State's Response:

Item A. The state believes this recommendation to be inconsistent with the statements contained in the report defining HHS' role as that of an advocate of children in need of care and protection. We firmly contend that HHS could be instrumental in improving the protection provided to guardianship children nationwide and that action should be taken immediately to achieve those improvements. We also believe that this is the appropriate time for HHS to consider the intent of PL 96-272 which clearly is to encourage the utilization of stable placement for children such as guardianships provide.

As an advocate for all of the nation's children, HHS should ensure that the protection extended to guardianship children includes aid payments as well as services. Children living with nonrelated guardians should be currently eligible for Title IV-A funding. HHS should implement regulations which provide for Title IV-A funding for such children. Currently, federal funding is refused for children living with nonrelated legal guardians under Title IV-A and is not provided for under the proposed Title IV-E.

Notwithstanding the state's contention that federal funding should be made available for all nonrelative guardianship cases, it is the state's position that federal eligibility does currently exist at least in certain guardianship cases where the detention order making a child the responsibility of the county social services department is not dismissed but guardianship is awarded. When this occurs, care and supervision remains with the county social services department and federal financial participation should be available for children meeting all other eligibility requirements.

Item B. The state cannot address this finding directly without reviewing each individual case record for the children for which the alleged overpayments were made and examining the circumstances leading to guardianship status. We would also ask that all action relative to recovery of funds be postponed until HHS has issued instructions to the states as suggested in the GAO Recommendation, Item A; and until such time as the state has had the opportunity to review each individual case found by the GAO to be ineligible for federal funds.

Item C. The state has no comment.

FINDING NO. 4

The health and safety of some children have been jeopardized by placing them in small foster family homes which housed children in excess of licensed capacity.

GAO Recommendation:

The state has initiated action to stop the out-of-home placement of children (including guardianship children) in homes in excess of licensed capacity. However, the Secretary of HHS should direct the Office of Human Development Services to follow-up on and work with the State of California to ensure that federally eligibile children are placed only in licensed facilities that fully meet state health and safety licensing requirements.

State's Response:

SDSS does not agree that guardianship children should always be counted as placements against the licensed capacity of the foster care facility. However, state law does recognize that in some situations the presence of other children or adults in the home affects the care provided to the foster children. Current state regulations for both Small Family Homes-Children and Foster Family Homes (Title 22, California Administrative Code, Section 81005 and Section 85101), require an evaluation of the presence of other members of the household to determine the extent to which these individuals impair or affect the ability of the foster parent(s) to adequately care for the foster children. (See Attachment 6.) After a review of the circumstances of a particular foster home applicant or licensee, the presence of another individual (including a guardianship child) can result in a reduction of the licensed capacity. Such a reduction would appropriately be based on the inability of the foster parent(s) to care for a specific number of foster children because of the needs of other household members.

As an interim response to the GAO findings, the Department of Social Services' Community Care Licensing Division will issue a release to all licensing agencies to reaffirm the importance of these regulations and provide instructions for reducing licensed capacity if it is determined that the presence of other household members impairs the ability to provide care to the foster children. This will be done on a case-by-case basis and reductions in capacity will only occur if the individual case evaluation supports this action.

The long range action plan is to propose new regulations which will more definitively outline those circumstances where a reduction in capacity is necessary by identifying those "other" individuals including adults, who also require a significant amount of care and supervision thereby limiting the ability of the foster parent(s) to care for the maximum allowed number (six) of foster children. Such proposed regulations could result in some circumstances of a greater reduction of capacity than a reduction based on the GAO's suggested mathematical formula of reducing capacity by one person for each guardianship child.

In addition, the regulations will:

1. Require notification to the licensing agency when additional members are added to the family composition;

2. Authorize the licensing agency to reduce capacity based upon these additions to the family's compositions; and

3. Require notification to the licensing agency if members of the household leave when those individuals were responsible for the provision of care and supervision (i.e., if the foster parents become separated).

We believe that these short and long range actions responsibly address the findings of the GAO's Report relative to the issue of considering guardianship children in determining licensed capacity.

(104112)

CPSIA information can be obtained at www.ICGtesting.com
Printed in the USA
BVOW07s1947260514

354513BV00009B/539/P

WORKS HEALEYS
IN DETAIL

WORKS HEALEYS
IN DETAIL

By Graham Robson
Photography by Simon Clay

Herridge & Sons

ACKNOWLEDGEMENTS

If I had not been personally involved in motor sport at the time when the works Austin-Healeys were in their pomp, I doubt if I would ever have got to know so many people, whose memories, and generosity, I hope will make my story credible.

First of all I want to start with a bit of justifiable name dropping and thank the entire Healey family – Donald himself, Geoff, 'Bic' and Geoff's wife Margot – for their help. I must also thank team managers and senior administrators, notably Peter Browning, Marcus Chambers and Bill Price. All of them were helped and encouraged by Eddie Maher and Daniel Richmond (of Downton), without whom the engines of these cars would have been less than formidable.

I must also record just how helpful a number of mechanics and technicians connected with the team have always been – notably Dan Green, Brian Moylan, Doug Watts, and their colleagues from Abingdon.

Next --and this paragraph encompasses my long links through personal friendships and interviews – with almost all the drivers and co-drivers who contributed so much to the results that Healey and Austin-Healey achieved. Listing them all individually would take a whole chaapter, so I will merely say that my first contact was probably with Jack Sears and Paddy Hopkirk in the 1950s, my closest contacts were probably with Rauno Aaltonen, Timo Makinen, Donald Morley, Pat Moss and John Sprinzel in the 1960s, and that many of the 'Old Lags' (including the incredible Willy Cave, who was still co-driving competitively when many of us had given up even trying to stand upright) are still around and able to talk of their experiences. When I tell you that this list of characters should also include Stirling Moss, Maurice Gatsonides, John Gott, Eugen Böhringer, Christabel Carlisle, Steve McQueen (no I never met him), and Alick Dick, the reader will understand that their views have often had to be compressed.

I have received help, not only in the tapping of their memories but also in the way they have provided images commemorating the past, from Kathy Ager, Gary Anderson, Peter Browning, John Chatham, Jonathan Day, Jeff Eakin, Paul Easter, Bill Emerson, Geoff Howard and Paul Woolmer. Along, of course, with ace photographer Simon Clay, and my publishers, Charles and Ed Herridge, without whom this volume would quite definitely not have been completed.

Graham Robson
July 2018

Published in 2018 by
Herridge and Sons Ltd
Lower Forda, Shebbear
Devon EX21 5SY

ISBN 978-1-906133-79-5
Printed in China

CONTENTS

INTRODUCTION

Some works race cars never die. NOJ 393, which had a very eventful career, was finally restored in the 2010s.

What is the connection between a newly launched car sprinting up and down an Italian autostrada in 1946, a team of girls winning the world's most arduous rally, and a Coventry-Climax-engined sports car taking part in the Le Mans 24 Hour race? The answer, simply, is the magic name of 'Healey' – for it was Donald on the Italian autostrada in 1946, an Austin-Healey 3000 on the Liège-Sofia-Liège in 1960, and Geoff Healey's little team preparing the Healey SR for le Mans in 1968.

Of course, much has already been written about the formidable works rally cars, and both Donald and Geoff wrote their own autobiographies – but until now no one has tackled the four-decade story of all the works competition cars that carried a Healey badge, and which achieved so much. I was unbelievably lucky to get the chance to assemble the entire chronicle, and immediately fell to the task, as much of it occurred during my own time 'at the coalface' of this period of motorsport.

Although some of the general story has partly been told before, in many cases the most outstanding individual performances, and some of the most successful cars, have had to be neglected. It wasn't until I began digging deep to research for this book that I realised just how much there was to be covered.

Healey and Austin-Healey enthusiasts alike should be proud of the number of different models that won events both on the track and in rallying. It was not only the 3000s that made their mark. All of the cars were unique and memorable in some way, so I set out to profile each and every works car that was campaigned in a 34-year period.

Although books have been written about the nuts-and-bolts specifications of some of the cars, no previous author has had the chance, the scope or the space to go into great detail about the individual histories of each car, nor to examine the myths and legends surrounding them.

I have been digging into the history of these Healeys and Austin-Healeys for years, but this is the first time I have been able to list every event (International and National) tackled by every car, and to list some of the political events, and even the unspoken deals, involving the cars. I have also been able to follow the rather mysterious ways in which some cars seemed to evolve from one identity to another, or where a new car took on an old identity.

Why did some worthy drivers never get the chance to drive regularly in the works team? Why, on the other hand, did one or two drivers who were not of the highest standard turn up repeatedly in factory cars and not shine? Why were some theoretically unsuitable cars entered for certain events? And why did some cars not appear on events where they might have shone? It's all here. I don't believe anything like such a full story of all the Healey/Austin-Healey works cars has ever previously been told.

PMO 200 first competed in 1958 and was progressively developed by John Sprinzel into this sleek machine.

Registration numbers – a warning

Although the author can think of no more accurate way of identifying which car achieved which speed, which record or which motor sport success than quoting registration plates, this should always come with a caveat.

Even in the 1950s, and especially later as more and more events were tackled in more and more cars, for a whole variety of reasons (financial and in connection with the crossing of international borders among them) it became normal for registration plates to be swapped from car to car. As far as Healey and Austin-Healey were concerned this never reached the heights practiced by BMC in the 1960s and by Ford in the 1970s, but it was by no means unknown.

Geoff Healey made a remarkable admission of one such episode when describing the original high-speed run carried out by the still-secret Healey 100 in Belgium in October 1952: "DMH decided that we could get some advance publicity by combining the speed trials with a test by one of the motoring periodicals. The prototype was not registered, so the number plates off the crashed Mille Miglia Nash-Healey were bolted onto the new car. These were used until the car was properly registered with a different number, which probably confuses many who try to refer to cars by their registration numbers".

GRAHAM ROBSON
June 2018

THE HEALEY DYNASTY

Donald Mitchell Healey was a buoyant character who could smile through any setback – even a shunt with a Westland like this!

No one could possibly have invented a character like Donald Healey. As a non-stop motoring dynamo he was unique. Famous for so many things in his long career, he seemed to be quite ageless. When the Austin-Healey marque was at its most famous Donald was already in his sixties but with the energy of a 30-year-old.

Until his final years in reluctant retirement in Cornwall he was quite amazingly active and never looked back if there were future projects he might influence. He seemed to have been a British motoring icon for so many years that we thought he would always be with us.

Having won the world-famous Monte Carlo Rally in his thirties, one might have thought he would slow down, but to Donald Healey this was just the start of another life. Success, he concluded, simply made him better known – and better able to get further, faster, in his profession. In the late 1940s he

set up his own company. Surely that was enough? Not for this Cornishman. Then after 18 roller-coaster years in harness with BMC and BL, surely it was time to retire? Not Donald Healey – at 72 years of age he went out and helped to take over Jensen and establish yet another new sports car, the Jensen-Healey.

Everything that Donald Healey tackled received his full attention, whether it was designing new cars, re-creating the gardens of a gracious mansion in his beloved Cornwall, experimenting with closed-circuit TV years before the Japanese made it commercially possible, or trying to harness nature with high-tech windmills! He'd been like that since 1915, when he learned to fly, and he was still the same in the late 1970s when casting around for a successor to the stalled Jensen-Healey project.

Most people, I'm sure, will remember him for the BMC Austin-Healeys, first on sale in 1953, and finally dropped by the philistines at British Leyland in 1970. But this was merely one high spot in an incredibly fruitful business life. Not only had he won the Monte Carlo Rally in 1931, but he was Triumph's technical director for six years later in that decade. Before the Austin-Healeys there had been the original Healey sports cars, built at Warwick. After British Leyland had killed off the Austin-Healey marque, he got together with Kjell Qvale to buy Jensen, and tried to reconquer North America with the Lotus-engined Jensen-Healey. Without the Energy Crisis, and without the rampant inflation which followed, the two might just have made it.

Like Henry Ford, Donald Healey became famous in the automobile business without any family backing. Born at Perranporth in Cornwall in 1898, when there was still not a single motor car in this part of the nation, he grew up in a sleepy little country town where his family ran a grocer's shop.

His interest in machines came from what he saw, rather than what was in his blood, and after serving in the Royal Flying Corps during the First World War he set up the Red House Garage in the town. For the next few years the young Healey made his own way, paying his own bills, in motor sport, and moving up from reliability trials to rallies. Having won Britain's first major long-distance rally, the Bournemouth, and

taken impossibly small (832cc) Triumph Super Seven saloons through the snows of the Monte Carlo Rally, he then got his first works drive with Invicta, for whom he won the Monte in 1931. After two more high-profile years in motor sport he turned to Britain's motor industry in Coventry (which in those days was the British 'Detroit'), working briefly for Riley before moving on to Triumph. From 1934 to 1939 he was Triumph's technical director, and in the next 40 years he became one of the British motor industry's most engaging characters.

In all his years at the top, I have no evidence that Donald Healey ever drew a line on paper to design a new car, yet he inspired many famous machines. Although he was an innovator and in many ways a true engineer he was not a designer. He knew what he wanted, which was almost invariably something fast, something elegant, and something sporting – but someone else was always there to interpret his wishes.

At Triumph his supercharged eight-cylinder masterpiece, the Dolomite Straight Eight, was inspired by the Alfa Romeo Monza of the early 1930s but designed by George Rupert Swetnam's team (Swetnam had once worked for Sir Henry Royce) and styled by Frank Warner.

Well-authenticated legend puts the design of the first post-war Healeys in the hands of 'Sammy' Sampietro (chassis) and Ben Bowden (body) with the Riley Motor Co. supplying engine, gearbox and back axle, while Donald's eldest son Geoff had much to do with the layout of the original Austin-Healey 100 and all its developments, along with the Sprite and the Jensen-Healeys which followed. From the 1950s Geoff, who had joined his father in 1949, controlled the complete design office, until the demise of the final Jensen-Healey of 1976, with Donald getting more and more involved in commercial matters and in wheeling and dealing, at which he was an expert.

Along the way the myth evolved that Donald Healey became extremely rich through all these activities, but his son Geoff always made it very clear that this was not so. Too trusting and too nice a man for this, he rarely seemed to get the most out of some opportunities. Then, of course, there were diversions into other activities like his sports boats.

Having joined the Triumph Board of Directors in the 1930s and bought shares to back that appointment, he then lost most of this money when the company struck financial trouble in 1937. Having recovered some of it, he then lost more in 1939 when Triumph called in the Receiver. We know too that there was much more fame than money in the Healey project of 1945-53, meeting the payroll on Fridays often being a real problem. We also know that his meeting with George Mason of Nash Kelvinator not only produced the Nash-Healey model, but also that Nash underpinned the £50,000 ($140,000) bank overdraft which was threatening Healey at that time and helped Healey to recover from a very rocky position.

It was only after BMC started to build tens of thousands of Austin-Healeys every year and the Healey family began to earn royalties on every car made that long-term prosperity was assured. Even then, much money had to be ploughed back into running the compact design and development offices in Warwick. Later in life Donald spent heavily on houses, and on 'why-don't-we?' projects, the final company, Healey Automobile Consultants Ltd, being busy and creative to the last.

No matter where he settled, nor what he tackled, Donald could push, cajole, persuade and inspire a team to produce something new, and to improve whatever existed. Though there was rarely much financial backing, he was always stubborn, always optimistic, and the results were impressive.

During the war, intent on designing a new British sports car, he started work while Hitler's bombs were still falling and was first to the market with a new car, way ahead of Jaguar and MG, in 1946. The pace then quickened. His link with Nash was the first post-war Anglo-US motoring co-operative deal, and his link with BMC (to found Austin-Healey) was simply inspired. Others, for instance, might have yearned to join forces with BMC in a sports car project – Jensen and Frazer Nash both tried – but it was a combination of his effervescent character and his eye for a line in the prototype Healey 100's styling which caused BMC's Sir Leonard Lord to choose that particular car.

As far as BMC was concerned Donald Healey could do no wrong, which explains why Sir Leonard Lord's team let him keep control of the cars bearing his name while BMC built them, why he was allowed to run the racing and record breaking programmes, and why his designers got the job of

Whether young or growing gracefully old, Donald Healey never lost the love for any of the cars he had created. This pose was with a 1935 Triumph Southern Cross – and was taken in the 1970s.

1935 TRIUMPH GLORIA "SOUTHERN CROSS"

developing the little Sprite.

Even so, Healey could be very stubborn. Protective of his name to the last, he would not approve of proposed new MG-designed cars which might have carried his name, and when BMC was drawn into British Leyland he certainly did not approve of what Sir Donald Stokes's marketing men had in mind for the future. In 1970 the parting between Healey and British Leyland was bitter, but there was nothing unique in this. For 'Healey', substitute 'Cooper' and 'Downton', and you may agree that the Stokes management was quite incredibly short of the vision that any team at this level should have had.

Problems, though, sometimes lead to opportunities, which explains how Donald then got together with Vauxhall Motors (for running gear) and Kjell Qvale (the wealthy motor trader from San Francisco) to take over Jensen, and eventually to launch the Jensen-Healey. Most of the money came from California, but most of the ideas came from Healey. If the Energy Crisis had not erupted in 1973-74, and Britain's inflation had not roared ahead for the next few years, this might have been another long-term success story. Unhappily sales slumped, losses mounted, and Qvale eventually closed down the enterprise.

Because the cars had done so much export business and earned so many US dollars, Healey then turned to the British government for aid. To his amazement this was refused (some misguided people in London loaned a mountain more money to DeLorean instead, and look what happened to him), and the company had to close down. Healey never forgave the left-leaning British administration for this – especially as they had already poured money into a loss-making workers' co-operative trying to make obsolete Triumph motorcycles. History now tells us that every penny of those loans was lost, whereas with Healey it would probably have been returned, with interest.

At 78 years of age Donald Healey finally began to slow down, but only reluctantly. In retirement, so called, one of his consolations was that there was now time for him to accept worldwide invitations from the clubs which preserved his cars, and it was only a gradual loss of mobility that eventually caused him to stay in his native Cornwall. The end came in 1988, nearly 70 years after he had started his first business enterprise, but only months after his flow of bright new ideas began to dry up. By any standards he was a unique personality, and his had been an astonishing life.

Donald Healey: Career Profile

3 July 1898: Born in Perranporth, Cornwall. His father was a local grocer.

1914: Joined Sopwith Aviation Company as an apprentice.

1915: Joined Royal Flying Corps (the predecessor of the RAF).

1919: Opened a garage business in Perranporth.

1931: Won the Monte Carlo Rally in a 4½ Litre Invicta.

1933: Joined Triumph Motor Co., soon becoming Technical Director. Famous Triumph products included the supercharged straight-eight Dolomite.

1940: After outbreak of World War Two, joined the Rootes Group to work on military vehicle design. During leisure hours, began designing his own sports car.

1946: Set up the Donald Healey Motor Company, and announced the original Healey car.

1950: Announced the Nash-Healey, which used a 3848cc Nash engine.

1952: Developed the new 100 sports car, which became the Austin-Healey 100 of 1953, manufactured by Austin.

1956: 100 became 100-Six.

1958: Introduction of Austin-Healey Sprite.

1961: MG Midget re-born, a clone of the latest Sprite.

1968: Last Austin-Healey 3000 built.

1970: Last Austin-Healey Sprite built. With Kjell Qvale of San Francisco, Donald Healey bought the Jensen car company of West Bromwich, England, becoming Chairman of the Board.

1972: Introduction of the Jensen-Healey sports car, with Lotus engine.

1976: End of Jensen-Healey production.

15 January 1988: Died, aged 89.

Donald Healey standing proudly alongside one of the many works Austin-Healey cars which he did so much to promote.

GEOFFREY HEALEY: CAREER PROFILE

Too many studies of Donald Healey and the motor cars which bore his name ignore the huge contribution which his eldest son, Geoffrey, made to his post-war enterprises. Although father and son could not really have looked more different – for Geoff was tall, well-built and splendidly moustached, while Donald was small, slim and dapper – they were both fully paid-up petrol-heads.

From 1949, when Geoff came to work for his father in Warwick, the family worked in harness. Donald provided the bright ideas while – if they were technically practical – Geoff turned them into hardware. The inspiration behind the Austin-Healey 100, the Sprite and the Jensen-Healey might have been Donald's, but the engineering, the drawing board graft and the perspiration were all down to Geoff and his tiny team.

Incidentally, if you think those were the only cars ever designed at Warwick in the 1950s and 1960s, you clearly haven't read Geoffrey Healey's splendid book The Healey Story, and the three earlier volumes which he penned. Not only were there Austin-Healey prototypes with 4-litre Rolls-Royce six-cylinder engines, but also mid-engined race cars which competed at Le Mans, lightweight leisure speed boats and much-modified front-wheel-drive Ford Fiestas – while along the way Healey also bought a Ferrari Type 625 single-seater just for fun !

Father and son were perfect foils for each other. Donald, the father, would look over the horizon, work up another ambitious scheme and find the backers to make it happen: Geoff, the son, would then draw up the car, see the prototypes pummeled into shape, and keep the dealers happy. Donald, by that time, would be up and away, two or three schemes further ahead. Geoff, on the other hand, would still be at his drawing board, slide rule in hand, squinting furiously through a haze of pipe tobacco smoke, stroking that luxurious moustache and, if he had his way, placidly sipping away at another foaming pint of beer.

When 'classic mania' hit the British motor car world in the 1980s, several romantics talked about reviving the Austin-Healey marque, and two set out to produce replicas which were very close to the Frog Eye Sprite and the 3000. Because these looked exactly like the old cars, none could carry the famous name until the family had seen and approved them. It was Geoff, not Donald, who assessed the clones, turning down the Big Healey project but giving his approval to the Frog-Eye lookalike.

In terms of Healey-badged cars, one Healey personality could not properly function without the other, and they worked together until the end, through Healey, Austin-Healey, Jensen-Healey and beyond. Neither ever retired – maybe officially, but never in their minds – and both were ever-inventive to the last.

1922: Born in Perranporth, Cornwall, the eldest of Donald Healey's three sons. Eventually moved to Barford with his parents, and became an apprentice at Cornercroft (a motor car accessory business) in Coventry.

1943: Joined REME (the Royal Electrical and Mechanical Engineers) in the British Army, becoming a Captain.

1947: Joined Armstrong-Siddeley Motors of Coventry as a development engineer.

1949: Joined the Healey Motor Co., working with his father as a design/development engineer.

1951/52: Became the principal designer of the original Austin-Healey 100. Soon became Healey's most senior engineer, interpreting all his father's plans and wishes.

1958: Responsible for the concept, layout and design of the Austin-Healey Sprite.

1968: Began concept work on a new sports car which would become the Jensen-Healey of 1972.

1970: After the Jensen takeover, became a director of Jensen Motors. Meantime, set up Healey Automobile Consultants Ltd.

Late 1970s/80s: After collapse of Jensen, worked on many projects, including sports car investigations for Ford-USA, Mitsubishi and Saab, dabbling with new-technology windmills, and even co-operating with the Austin-Rover company for some time.

1994: Geoffrey Healey died.

CHAPTER 1
MONTE CARLO RALLY VICTORY AND THE EIGHT-CYLINDER DOLOMITES

Although this book concentrates on those cars which carried the Healey name it would only tell half the story if Donald Healey's earlier career was ignored, for the events and projects with which he was connected had an influence on what happened after World War Two. It would be wrong to sideline these, as the story of the conception of the original Healey motor car of 1946 could not properly be told without summarising the influences, exploits, and industrial ups-and-downs of the Healey-inspired machines which came before that.

He was always involved in motor sport, in competing at all levels, and in driving the cars which he inspired. The Triumph Super Sevens which he rallied in 1928, 1929 and 1930 were chosen because the family garage business in

Donald Healey's works career with Invicta included this drive in the Austrian Alpine rally of 1931.

Cornwall held a Triumph franchise. Then in 1931 he became a works driver for the first time, driving for Invicta, in whose fearsome 4½-litre Meadows-engined sports cars he not only won the 1931 Monte Carlo rally but also came second in the 1932 French Alpine event.

Early in 1933 came his first direct involvement in the development of new models, which resulted from an approach from Victor Riley. One of the family which controlled the Coventry-based car-maker, Riley was considering buying the financially-troubled Invicta concern and wanted to tap into Donald Healey's experience with that marque. Although that scheme soon foundered, Riley then suggested that Healey might like to consider moving to Coventry to work for his company on the preparation of a team of Lynx tourers for rallying, and also in the final development of its still-secret Imp, Sprite and MPH two-seater sports cars.

This was the break that Healey had deserved for some years although it was to be a brief episode. No sooner had he bought a house in Leamington Spa (just a few miles south of Coventry) into which he moved his family than a chance conversation with Col. Claude Holbrook, managing director of Triumph, also in Coventry, changed everything.

The conversation, I understand, took place at a rest halt during the French Alpine Trial, in which both Triumph and Riley were competing with works cars. Riley and its family owners had already come to Healey's attention, but Donald had already concluded, "I began to wonder how long they would keep going in the face of their apparent lack of financial know-how", so Holbrook's news that Triumph was about to move up-market and launch a new range of Gloria models, in which sports cars would figure prominently, sounded interesting. In great secrecy, Healey was invited to try out a pre-production version of the new range but was not overly impressed by what he found, and suggested that Triumph should get someone on to their payroll – an engineer with the appropriate experience – to put it right.

"Well, we've got to find somebody", Holbrook apparently said, which was Healey's none-too-modest opportunity to put himself in the frame. Within days a firm offer appeared, and within weeks Healey became Experimental Manager of Triumph, this being a new title for a new job which had previously not existed. At the time, indeed, there was no person at Triumph whose official job title was Technical Director, though Gordon Parnell was Chief Designer, so Healey would often find himself reporting directly to Col. Holbrook himself. Even though Triumph twice sank deep into financial swamps, he was to remain there for the next seven years, ending up not only as Technical Director, but as the most senior member of the company, which was finally swallowed up by bankruptcy in 1939/40.

This, it seems, was the period in which Healey's fast-growing expertise in two-seater sports car design, and in which the management and encouragement of a design and development team, became important. Although a car badged as a Healey would not be launched until 1946, it was cars of the 1930s, such as the Riley Lynx/Sprite/MPH family, or the series production Triumph Southern Cross sports cars, which first sowed the seed in his fertile brain.

No sooner had Healey joined Triumph in September 1933 than, just before the opening of the Olympia Motor Show in London, a range of Gloria models, all with Coventry Climax engines of a type which featured overhead inlet and side exhaust valves (the industry knew these as IOE units), was put on sale. There was just one basic chassis design, with two wheelbases, one for small four-cylinder engines, the other for the longer but closely related six-cylinder units, and although 1.1-litre four-cylinder and 1.5-litre six-cylinder cars were both previewed at the same time, it was a year before the first six-cylinder cars reached customers. Four-door saloons and two-door four-seater tourers were available, all with timber-framed coachwork.

Superficially there was nothing exciting about these cars on which Healey could easily work his magic. The 'base' 1087cc engine produced 40bhp at 4500rpm, and there was a Special version with twin carburettors and 46bhp, but right away Healey was allowed to prepare works cars to tackle the 1934 Monte Carlo rally, and also to bring together a package of improvements to the original Gloria tourer, turning it into the Gloria Monte Carlo. The Monte Carlo was based on the Special Tourer model, with rear quarters revised to make the machine more suited to rallying conditions. There were twin spare wheels mounted up against a huge 17-gallon fuel tank, built-in Sessions jacks, and Andre Telecontrol suspension dampers.

Except for the first handful of cars, the Monte Carlo was usually delivered with a 1232cc version of the Coventry-Climax engine, which had twin downdraught Zenith carburettors and produced 48bhp at 4750rpm. The selling price was £325, £40 more than the Gloria Special Tourer on which it was based; here was an indication of the direction in which Healey wanted to push his new type of Triumph.

Donald Healey and his crew with the Invicta in which Donald had won the Monte Carlo rally in 1931.

In the meantime, for the Monte Carlo rally, Healey arranged for two very special new works Glorias to be built in Coventry. These looked ungainly but were undoubtedly effective. The low-slung Gloria chassis frame had been discarded in favour of the old-style, higher, short-wheelbase Triumph Southern Cross types though space was found for the latest 1232 cc Monte Carlo engine. Healey also arranged for enormously fat tyres to be fitted, on 16in wheels, the better to provide a lot of ground clearance for the expected wintry conditions. Jack Ridley drove one car, and Healey himself, accompanied by the then-young journalist Tommy Wisdom, took the other.

The result was a real triumph for Triumph (that was a

During his brief stay with Riley in Coventry, in 1933, Donald Healey influenced the design of smart sports cars of this Imp/Sprite/MPH variety – and some of the characteristics of those cars were later to re-appear on Triumphs.

Early in his career at Triumph, Donald Healey (behind the wheel) helped to finalise the specification of the original Gloria range, this being the 1934-model Gloria Speed type, from which he soon evolved the Monte Carlo variety. His colleague, standing by, is Jack Ridley.

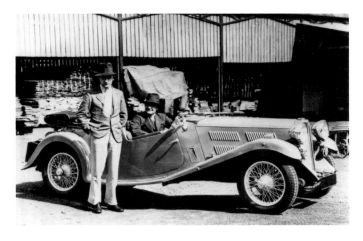

success headline to use, surely?), for after a hair-raising run all the way from Athens in Greece (no motorways in those days, of course, and primitive road conditions), Healey surpassed himself with excellent runs in the two final manoeuvring tests on the promenade in Monaco and ended up third overall, behind two much larger and more costly French cars, while Ridley took sixth place.

The pace of Healey's working life now accelerated, not only because several other new Triumph road cars had to be finalised and made ready for sale, but also because he had somehow persuaded Col. Holbrook, to support the development of an astonishing new supercharged eight-cylinder sports car which was to be called Dolomite. This was such a remarkable diversion from Healey's everyday life that the author thought it appropriate to reproduce an impression

Donald Healey's works Triumph entry in the 1934 Monte Carlo rally was this very ruggedly modified Gloria, in which he finished third overall.

gained from driving a surviving car many years later. This is published in the Appendices. It is difficult to comprehend how a tiny Coventry-based development team could produce this amazing machine. It is rather like expecting Lotus to design and develop a Bugatti Veyron in their spare time – and stay sane.

Sadly, all the work that went into the eight-cylinder Dolomite eventually proved to be fruitless. It soon became clear that there was no demand for such a costly machine in the UK market, and in addititon Triumph concluded that it could not afford to invest in the specialised tooling which would have been required The project was abandoned early in 1936, when the two prototypes and all the spare parts were sold to Tony Rolt to go motor racing and to enjoy himself while the money lasted.

By that time Healey's engineers were heavily involved in expanding the available range of Glorias, for the six-cylinder engine had become available and a smart short-wheelbase two-seater version called the Gloria Southern Cross had also been made ready for sale. This, incidentally, was really the first two-seater production car with which Healey can ever be credited, but very few were ever sold, essentially because when considered against their rivals at MG they were rather too costly, the 2-litre six-cylinder version being priced at £335.

In the meantime Healey had been appointed a non-board Technical Director and had invested money in the company. He was leading the team which was designing a completely new range of engines – a four-cylinder and a closely-related six – which had overhead valves in cross-flow cylinder heads. Both would make their first appearance in the autumn of 1936.

Triumph was now notching up serious financial losses and was selling off the motorcycle side of the business to help balance the books. It was also planning to take over an ex-state-owned factory previously used for the part-manufacture of artillery shells in the 1914-18 war a couple of miles away on the outskirts of Coventry, a move which was completed by the end of 1935.

Clearly the strain was considerable for all concerned, as losses continued to mount (the company lost no less than £212,104 in fiscal year 1936), and in December 1936 it needed an extensive write-down of existing shares and a major injection of new money to keep the business afloat.

Now is time to relate a very mysterious part of Donald Healey's career. At Triumph he lost a good deal of his capital in the financial reconstruction, and he apparently left the company in April 1937 to become the racing and competitions manager of Lucas, whose headquarters were in Birmingham. This is all very strange, for in spite of this appointment being announced in *The Autocar* on 9 April 1937, little more was ever heard of the move. Not only that, but there is absolutely no mention of this episode in his life in his own ghosted autobiography (*My World of Cars*, published by Patrick Stephens Ltd in 1989), nor in any of

Donald Healey, on the left, handing over a Triumph Gloria Six to the British aviator hero Flt-Lt. Tommy Wise (centre). Also in shot are (L-to-R) Maurice Newnham, W.P.Meeson, and A.S.Osborne.

Geoffrey Healey's books. Surely this cannot have been an 'April Fool' announcement …?

In any case, Healey was firmly back at Triumph in October, this time as a full board member, with more influence and control, in a rejuvenated company which was clearly looking to prosper. And so it did for a short period, the company making a £35,000 profit in the first nine months of the 1937-38 financial year, while they were even bold enough to engage in talks about a merger with Riley before that company itself collapsed in February 1938.

Even so, there was little money around for spending on mechanical innovation in Healey's last two years at Triumph, but at least he had the pleasure of co-inspiring the style of the Dolomite Roadster Coupé (Walter Belgrove, who would later style the Triumph TR2, was responsible for the looks), which not only featured the latest fashion for a 'waterfall' grille but also had a hideaway dickey seat. Healey used one such car to win various prizes in rallies and concours but this was too large and too cumbersome a car to use in motor racing.

Unhappily, by this time the war clouds were once again gathering over Europe. The government reacted by increasing taxes to raise money for rearmament, which badly affected sales of cars like the Dolomites, and suddenly money began streaming out of the gates rather than in through them. The factory which had been bought with expansion in mind in 1935 was now found to be too large, so some sub-contract work on aero-engine component manufacture was taken on to keep the workforce busy, but on 7 June 1939 the Official Receiver was called in, Triumph car assembly abruptly ended, and Healey's business life seemed to be in ruins.

It was only then – during and indeed after the awful events of the Second World War which followed – that Healey's thoughts of setting up his own car making concern took shape.

Donald Healey was technical director at Triumph in the 1930s, and among the new cars he saw go into production was the smart Vitesse range, complete with a newly designed 2-litre 6-cylinder engine.

While he was technical director of Triumph in the 1930s, Healey inspired the launch of the smart Dolomite Roadster.

CHAPTER 2
FOUNDING THE HEALEY MARQUE

This was the sturdy chassis frame which Healey laid out to be the basis of all the cars produced at Warwick from 1946 to 1954.

I think it is true to say that if Triumph had not gone to the wall in 1939 Donald Healey might never have set up his own business. If Thos W. Ward, the Sheffield-based steel company which bought the remains of Triumph in August 1939, had been serious about reviving it as a car-manufacturing business, Donald Healey might have stayed on board. And in that case, from 1945 the entire history of Triumph might have evolved in a totally different way – while Healey or Austin-Healey sports cars might never have been invented.

Since this book concentrates on the Healey and Austin-Healey businesses we must not divert too long into what happened to Donald Healey between June 1939 (when Triumph folded) and May 1945 when the European war ended, and when he could once again continue planning his future. It might have been six sometimes frustrating years of toil, but all of it had an influence on what was to follow.

First of all, Donald discovered that it was not just he himself, but other influential characters, who believed that he could run a business or project. No sooner had Thos W. Ward acquired Triumph from the Receiver – the principal asset being the two factories, the modernised Gloria car-assembly plant in Foleshill, and the cramped, traditional, Stoke factory block to the east of the city centre, in Clay Lane – than war was declared, which meant that all tentative plans to resume Triumph car production had to be abandoned. As Donald Healey wrote in his autobiography: "Thomas Ward appointed me as their local General Manager while they continued to look for a customer for the factory. Eventually they sold a portion of it to the Air Ministry at a big profit – more than they had paid for the two factories that Triumph had owned – and retained the car spares and the trading name. War came, and the Air Ministry, through H.M.Hobson, asked me to stay on as Works Manager of the factory, making Claudel-Hobson carburettors for aero engines. So far as I was concerned it was not a very interesting job, though it was, I suppose, some contribution to the war effort."

The only real attraction for Healey in running the newly-established H.M.Hobson factory in the old Triumph works was that his director was to be Laurence Pomeroy (not *The Motor* journalist of the 1940s and 1950s but his illustrious father, who had been Daimler's highly respected technical chief in the 1920s and 1930s. Healey was therefore distressed when Pomeroy died suddenly in May 1941 and almost immediately resigned, taking up another post in Coventry in the Rootes Group (Humber-Hillman) design team involved in the development of military vehicles such as scout cars, reconnaissance vehicles and armoured cars which came to be built in their thousands.

There followed what was one of Donald Healey's most frantically busy, varied and ultimately satisfying periods. Not only was there his day job with the Rootes Group but he also undertook a major reconstruction of his house in Leamington Spa (to install a bombproof but as it transpired rather damp

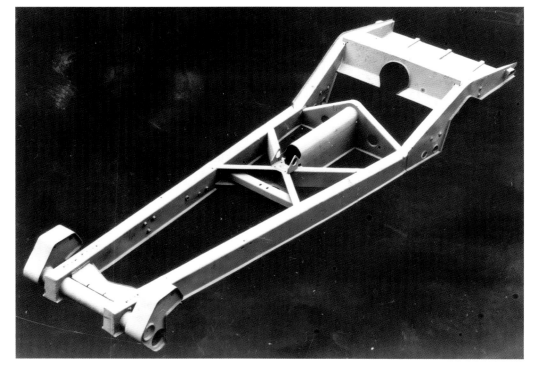

concrete cellar/shelter), and was also commissioned into the RAF Voluntary Reserve, where he took up part-time training duties in the Air Training Corps. Eventually promoted to Squadron Leader, he became a liaison officer arranging flying programmes for newly enlisted cadets at a variety of local RAF airfields. Incidentally, and to emphasise what a close-knit and in some ways inter-mingled 'family' Coventry's motor industry had become, one of those RAF airfields, which was very close to both Leamington Spa and Coventry, was Honiley (on the outskirts of Balsall Common), which after the war would eventually be taken over by Lucas-Girling as a development centre, then sold to Prodrive (who once proposed to set up a Formula One facility there), and finally became part of the ever-expanding Jaguar-Land-Rover concern !

It was during the war, however, that Healey took the first steps towards producing a new sports car of his own conception and, since the old Triumph design team had been dispersed, he realised that he would have to start again from scratch. He had hoped that he would eventually be reunited with his old company, Triumph, which he assumed would be revived, and that his new car might be badged a Triumph, but work on his project could only take shape when he (and a few chosen colleagues) had the spare time to devote to it. To quote from his autobiography: "During my time with Humber I met Ben Bowden and Achille "Sammy" Sampietro. Ben was their chief body draughtsman and Sammy, an Italian who had been released from internment because of his valuable engineering skills and the work he had done pre-war at the Talbot works, was one of their chassis designers". Sampietro had also had much previous technical experience with Alfa Romeo, Maserati, and (for a time) with the noted company of Thomson and Taylor at Brooklands, before joining Rootes via Talbot, a company which had joined the group in 1935.

Donald again: "Later, when the end of the war began to seem likely, the idea of building sporting cars grew stronger and stronger in my mind, and I discussed the possibility with Ben and Sammy. We made plans for the day when we would be free to have a go at it". Too many myths concerning the birth of the original Healey still circulate, but in this case what follows is drawn from an interview I had with Donald Healey many years later.

First of all, it is important to realise that the concept of this car did not take shape around the bare bones of a chosen engine, transmission and rear axle since in 1943/44, when serious concept work began, there was no settled plan or agreement as to who would be building it. First there were discussions as to what should be proposed, these soon crystallizing into using a common chassis with a choice of two-door saloon or open-top bodywork, and next came work on scheming up the new car's proposed layout. As I wrote on a previous occasion, "It was Ben Bowden who struck the first blow, and he did not let any existing traditions get in his way. First of all he schemed out body lines on the wallpaper of his dining room

in Coventry, and later took tracings from the originals. In the meantime, Sampietro, much impressed by Volkswagen and Auto-Union suspensions of the 1930s designed by Porsche, schemed out trailing-arm front suspensions, while alongside him another Rootes employee called Ireland found time to sketch a new chassis frame. All this invention, need it be said, took place in normal weekday working hours, by Rootes employees on Rootes drawing boards!"

Even so, when the trio had any available spare time they would get together in the evenings and at weekends to make more progress, but at this point no engine and associated running gear had yet been chosen, so there was still no question of building any prototype pieces, or of having a fully worked-up design.

Great plans, however, had already been made. Salesman James Watt, a recognised marketing expert who was advising Healey on the project, was once quoted as saying, "Donald and I began to feel that our little team was really getting somewhere, and we now thought we nearly had a good enough design to think about production and that the time had come for us to try and sell our ideas to Triumph. I had already made two fairly successful approaches to Triumph's, and in February 1944 the opportunity arose for another meeting. At first, things seemed most encouraging and they (Ward in Sheffield) genuinely thought that our scheme and ideas had merit. However, Triumph (i.e. Ward) had had a board meeting recently, and I was tremendously downcast to learn that they had decided not to back Healey, mainly for the simple reason that we were not car manufacturers. And so we put aside all thoughts of building our cars at Triumph's…We had begun to call the car 'the Triumph', but when we lost the Triumph deal we just called it 'the car'."

This was a body blow for the burgeoning enterprise, and yet it could so easily have been avoided. But since Ward had taken over Triumph in 1939 as a bankrupt but 'going concern', it had sold off the corporate arms and legs, only later to discover that the body alone did not attract them after all. Therefore it too was no longer interested in being in the

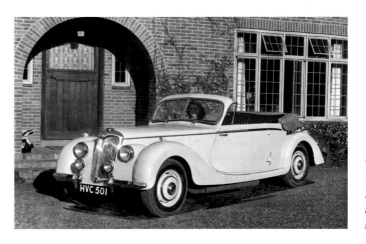

This was the Riley RM of the late 1940s, whose twin high-camshaft 2.4-litre engine was used to power the 'Warwick' Healey, which made its bow in 1946.

The first Healeys were launched in 1946: the Elliott saloon (above) and the Westand Tourer.

The Healey Duncan was introduced in 1948.

motor-car business, and was actually preparing to sell off the remains of the company.

In fact it was a totally specious insult, a lame excuse, to turn down Healey's plans on the grounds that 'he was not a car manufacturer'. He had, after all, directed Triumph's technical fortunes from 1934 to 1939, and had not Ward made him its Triumph general manager for a time in 1939/40?

We can now see what happened to Triumph and its heritage, and we can immediately see how foolish those decisions look in retrospect. Although this is not a part of the on-going Healey story, Triumph was rescued by Sir John Black and the

Standard company, went on to become a thriving part of that company, and even rivalled Austin-Healey in many ways in the 1950s and 1960s.

No sooner had the European war been won than Donald pulled out of his responsibilities in the RAFVR and, together with Bowden and Sampietro, really got down to the detail design of 'the car', which by now Donald had decided should be badged as a Healey. However, before much work on the chassis and mechanical layout could be concluded the project needed an engine. There was never any question of a special engine being designed - it would clearly be far too costly – and yet as the centrepiece of the new model it was vital that a suitable power unit should be secured. According to his son Geoffrey, Donald wanted this new car to have outstanding performance, aiming for a power/weight ratio of 100bhp/ ton, which would make his new car as rapid as any other British car of which he knew. For all the obvious reasons (and particularly in view of the British government's post-war edict that new products should be exported to earn currency) it would also have to be British-made.

Even if they were commercially available to him, it became clear that there were few current British engines which could even come close to satisfying this aim. No engine from an established member of Britain's 'Big Six' (Austin, Morris, Ford, Vauxhall, Standard or the Rootes Group) was even a contender. This really left only two viable candidates – the Jaguar 2½-litre six-cylinder or the 2.4-litre Riley four-cylinder. Jaguar's William Lyons had secured all the manufacturing rights for the ex-Standard engine in 1942, but wanted to retain all supplies of it for his own cars, so this option was also eliminated, almost without discussion.

Healey then made what was probably the best decision, so far, of his business life, by personally approaching Victor Riley, to see if supplies of the Riley engine could be made available. In that the Riley company had recently been absorbed by the Nuffield Organisation, in 1938, this was a remarkably audacious move, but since Lord Nuffield's management had become less and less 'hands-on' as the founder grew older, the Riley family was still being left to manage its affairs, and apparently warmed to Healey's approaches.

According to Healey himself, 'We were designing a car which, as our principal objective, would offer direct competition to the pre-war 2-litre BMW 328, by far the best small sports car of its time', and after a series of clandestine meetings Riley agreed that they could and would supply new engines just as soon as post-war manufacture could start in 1946. Not only that, but Riley also agreed to supply their four-speed gearbox and torque-tube rear axle assembly.

For Healey, quite suddenly, in mid-1945 'the sun came out', for his team could now go ahead with finalising the rest of the design, apart from a mere three major obstacles – one was where to build the production cars, the others being where to secure supplies of the body and how to finance the establishment and growth of the business!

While Sampietro got on with the finalisation of the chassis layout, Donald Healey and James Watt set about inventing a commercial way of building cars. First of all, Donald scoured his list of friends and business associates in the Coventry area, and soon found that Wally Allen (at one time a director of the 1930s Triumph concern, but now a director of Benford Ltd, a maker of concrete mixers) was able to provide a small workshop in one corner of the rackety little Benford factory in Warwick where the first car could take shape. Later, Benfords also made a larger workshop/factory space (a converted military building) available for production to begin, and finally Healey set up a dedicated unit on The Cape, making use of an ex-RAF building with a semi-circular cross-section which Geoffrey Healey described as having a lot of headroom, except at the sides.

In the meantime, the Donald Healey Motor Co. Ltd was set up, with an issued capital of £50,000 (a considerable amount in those days), which was found by the assembling Donald's own money, contributions from his family, other local individuals and James Watt, who became the fledgling company's Sales Director, although at first all he had to sell was promises.

The first models, the Westland tourer and the Elliott saloon, both launched in1946, shared a 102in wheelbase chassis which formed the basis of all Healey cars. It had trailing-link independent front suspension by coil springs, a very effective though expensive system made fashionable by racing cars such as the Auto Union single-seaters of the 1930s. The chassis was a simple and rugged structure with box-section side members and a substantial structure supporting the front suspension. At the rear, the Riley axle was located by a torque tube, Panhard rod and coil springs. The brakes were by Lockheed, with large drums of 11in front and 10in rear. The robust long-stroke four-cylinder 2443cc Riley engine featured twin camshafts set high in the block; in the Riley RMB saloon it had an output of 90bhp, but the modified version Riley supplied to Healey gave 104bhp at 4500rpm, endowing the Healeys with a 100mph top speed and 0-60mph acceleration in around 12 seconds.

The Westland was a two-door four-seat tourer with two-piece windscreen and removable sidescreens; the bodies came from Westland bodies of Hereford. The Elliott was a two-door four-seat saloon with Perspex side windows and the bodies were supplied by a Reading concern whose main business was building shop fronts. Both bodies were in alloy over a timber frame.

Once the tiny new company had started to deliver cars, a competition programme developed almost of its own accord. It was really only limited by the amount of money that Donald Healey could put into various demonstrations, high-speed runs, against-the-clock record attempts and motor racing. These are all recorded, and detailed in the Chapters which follow.

At this moment therefore it is only necessary to summarise the sequence of new model introductions

1946: The first production cars, the Westland roadster and the Elliott saloon, were delivered. 101 Westlands and 64 Elliotts were produced.

1948: Introduction of the Sportsmobile (23 built) and the Duncan roadster (39 built).

1949: Introduction of the two-seater Silverstone. 105 cars built.

1950: The Tickford saloon and the Abbott DHC (replacements for the Elliott and the Westland) were introduced. 224 and 77 respectively were built.

1951: Introduction of the American-engined Nash Healey sports roadster. Built until 1954, a total of 404 were produced, 151 of them with Farina bodies.

1951: Introduction of the Alvis 3-litre engined sports convertible. 25 produced.

All these cars were assembled in the factory in Warwick, but it must be emphasised that Healey always had complete bodies built and delivered by outside suppliers, while engines, gearboxes and rear axle assemblies all came from their manufacturers.

The first big change came in 1953 after the first 20 examples of the Austin-Healey 100 (the BN1) had been built at Warwick. Series production of that car then began at BMC's massive factory at Longbridge, in Birmingham. From 1954, when the last of the Healey Healeys (as opposed to Austin-Healeys) was completed at Warwick, the Cape factory became purely the centre of the company's design, development, and motor sport operations.

The elegant Tickford was the second-generation Riley-powered Healey saloon of the early 1950s.

CHAPTER 3
THE HIGH-SPEED RUNS IN EUROPE

Within months of the initial launch of the Healey motor car, Healey sent this Elliott to Italy, where it achieved no less than 104.65mph on an autostrada.

Until the first overtly sporting Healeys – cars like the Silverstone and the Le Mans-type Nash-Healeys – came on the scene, Donald Healey tried successfully to keep his new cars' potential in the public eye by setting them to achieve remarkable top speeds in high-speed runs against the clock, either in a straight line or on banked circuits. Because it was not possible to satisfy any of these ambitions on British roads or circuits – Brooklands would have been useful but had shut down, and there were no suitable straight roads which could be closed for two-way runs in the UK – Healey looked abroad for alternative venues.

In the late 1940s setting straight-line figures meant (with influence being applied) using either the Jabbeke highway in Belgium or a suitable autostrada in Italy. Amazingly, in spite of the depredations of war, neglect and a lack of funds to make good, these stretches of highway were in reasonable condition.

The only high-speed track immediately available (Monza was not in a suitable condition, and had no banked corners at this time), was the French Montlhéry track, south-west of Paris, a well-known racing circuit since the 1930s which included a 1.58-mile oval with two steeply banked turns. Except for the sometimes questionable state of the track surfaces it was ideal for long-distance record attempts.

ITALIAN AUTOSTRADA, NOVEMBER 1946
The first of these high-speed runs was completed as early as November 1946, when Donald Healey and an unregistered Elliott saloon accompanied the editor of *The Motor*, Christopher Jennings, on what that august personality headlined as a 'High Speed Holiday' starting and finishing in the UK. At the time Healey was still struggling to get any sort of production of the Elliot and the Westland models under way, so with very little money available to publicise their new products, but here was a chance to prove and publicise the new car. As *The Motor*'s road test commented: "Adequate testing of an automobile of this calibre is difficult since there are no tracks or roads in this country where the full qualities of the car can be completely assessed. To cope with this problem *The Motor* decided that the car should be taken on the Continent and given an extended run over a thousand miles or more".

In his 'High Speed Holiday' feature Christopher Jennings noted that the Healey Elliot travelled in convoy with his own Riley 2½-litre, the two cars therefore sharing the same engine, transmission and back axle.

The road test car wore British trade plates (199 NX) though fictitious British plates – the same as used on the original Westland Tourer when launched early in the year – would be used for the official photoshoot after the Elliott's return. The route to and from Italy was by way of Chalons and Zurich to an Italian hotel in Tremezzo, close to Como.

The high speed runs on the autostrada were carried out with the cooperation of Count Johnny Lurani and the Milan Automobile Club and a top speed of 104.65mph was confirmed, which led to Healey claiming, with justification, that at this time the Elliott was the fastest British production car.

JABBEKE HIGHWAY, BELGIUM, JULY 1947

Using a newly-built Elliott, a factory development car, Donald Healey returned to the Continent in July 1947 to take advantage of the closure of the Jabbeke highway (a still-developing autoroute between Brussels and the coast at Ostend) where Lt. Col. 'Goldie' Gardner had recently been setting new figures in his MG record car, EX135 (the Gardner Special).

Healey set out to demonstrate the Elliott's capabilities, not only in maximum speed but also in standing-start acceleration, using commercially available petrol from a Belgian source, and having the run timed by experienced Royal Automobile Club of Belgium officials. To give an idea of how much fuels have improved since those days, the rating 'on the day' was between 70 and 72 Octane!

In glorious weather, on a perfect summer's day, Healey made several two-way runs, the fastest of which was recorded at 110.80mph, with a best one-way run at 111.87mph. On the following day, the same car, needing no re-preparation but running on 16in wheels instead of the 15in wheels used on the first day, averaged 107.136mph for the Flying Five Miles,

followed by a standing-start mile figure of 77.785mph.

If only for a limited period, therefore, Donald Healey was once again able to claim that the Elliott was the world's fastest production car, and with *The Motor*'s Midlands Editor, Harold Hastings, alongside him, the car was given a good clean and tidy up so that it could compete in the Ostend concours that weekend, where it won its capacity class. This was the only time that this particular car was used to demonstrate the performance of the new model.

MONTLHÉRY BANKED CIRCUIT, FRANCE, OCTOBER 1948

Only days after two Healeys (one a Westland Roadster, GWD 43, the other an unregistered Elliot saloon) had competed in the Paris 12-hour race at Montlhéry (see Chapter 4) a small team from Warwick then re-appeared at the Montlhéry banked circuit to make a point. This is how *The Motor* reported on what happened:

"A modest little party, headed by Donald Healey himself, arrived at the Montlhéry Autodrome with a standard Healey saloon, the engine having been sealed by the RAC prior to its departure from England. The intention was to cover over 100 miles in an hour, on the outer piste de vitesse, of course, a performance never before attempted in a production saloon car. Readers whose memories go back to pre-war days will recall the difficulties encountered when attempting to coax a car to equal on Brooklands its normal road maximum,

In an impressive high-speed demonstration run, this works Elliott achieved one hour's run at 103.76mph.

and Montlhéry is little different in this respect. With but little preparation, limited to a check of tyre pressures and a set of clean plugs, the test run was started and completed without incident under the vigilant supervision of the official timekeepers of the Automobile Club de France. The flying-start hour's run was completed at an average speed of 103.76mph, while an hour's run from a standing start was covered at an average speed of 101.7mph".

The only thing not mentioned here (and surely this cannot have been deliberate?) was that the driver was motoring journalist Tommy Wisdom.

PRE-LAUNCH PROVING RUNS – JABBEKE HIGHWAY, BELGIUM, OCTOBER 1952

Before the Healey 100 was officially unveiled and when only one prototype car existed, Donald Healey was anxious to establish some performance figures and gain some good pre-launch publicity. According to Geoff Healey (in *The Healey Story*), this is what happened:

"Although we were able to obtain maximum speed on several stretches of road in the UK, we could only obtain an officially timed set of figures on the other side of the English Channel. DMH decided that we could get some good advance publicity by combining the speed trials with a test by one of the motoring periodicals. The prototype was not registered so the number plates off the crashed Mille Miglia Nash-Healey were bolted onto the new car [this was KWD 947]. These were used until the car was properly registered with a different number, which probably confuses many who try to refer to cars by their registration numbers.

"Gregor Grant had not long set up *Autosport* as a motoring magazine for enthusiasts and concentrated on reporting races. John Bolster was the magazine's Technical and Road Test Editor, and he came to Belgium to carry out the tests, which were conducted on the new Jabbeke-Aeltre motorway, not far from Ostend. The Belgian Automobile Club officially timed the car and recorded a two-way mean speed of 106.05mph with John driving and Gregor in the passenger's seat.

"However, we knew that the car could go faster, and DMH wanted to get 110mph out of it. Back at The Cape we called on Jimmy Harrison to tune the carburettors for maximum power. Jimmy came up with some needles that provided a richer mixture at peak rpm, and Champion suggested we try a spark plug that was one stage colder. We also fitted a tonneau over the passenger's seat and then returned to Belgium. DMH drove and was timed by the Belgian Club at a two-way mean of 111.73mph for the flying kilometre and 110.974mph for the flying mile, with some good figures for the standing start... The engine was a standard production unit and we never removed the head to try to obtain more power".

One should note, incidentally, that this car had left-hand steering and was running on steel disc wheels with both front and rear bumpers in place, while the speed runs were accomplished with the windscreen folded as flat as possible.

A full report, with all the elements of a typical 'Bolster road test' was published in *Autosport*, of 24 October 1952.

This car, incidentally, was later loaned to the editor of *Autosport*, Gregor Grant, so that he could compete in the Lyons-Charbonnieres rally, in France, in March 1953, (where he finished 50th after a mechanically troubled run), but in the author's opinion this did not constitute a 'works' entry.

HIGH-SPEED ONE-HOUR DEMONSTRATION – MONTLHÉRY, 23 OCTOBER 1955

BMC publicists mounted a series of demonstration runs on the Montlhéry high-speed oval in October 1955 when not one but five different BMC models of various marques all set out to achieve 100mph for a flying-start hour's run in what turned out to be frightful weather conditions. The principal reason for this demonstration was to prove just how much faster the new MGA was than the old TF which it had just replaced – and also to show that several BMC cars could achieve and maintain such speeds. The five cars used were:
• Austin-Healey 100M (BN2) – registered ROB 423
• Austin A90 Westminster saloon
• MGA 1500
• Riley Pathfinder
• Wolseley 6/90

This seems to have been a joint enterprise set up between the recently-established BMC Competitions Department at Abingdon and the BMC publicity operation at Longbridge, but none of the five cars chosen had any previous competition history. All, including the Austin-Healey 100M BN2 chosen to take part, were part of the publicity fleet, and none of them had any link with the team at Abingdon. That said, all the engines were carefully prepared and slightly 'improved' by the much respected Morris Engines Development team led by Eddie Maher in Coventry, and each car was signed off by Abingdon's Doug Watts and Tommy Wellman before being committed to the high-speed runs.

It later transpired that 'The Five' should have been 'The Six', but the Morris Isis which had also been proposed would not achieve a consistent 100mph, so was withdrawn even before the cavalcade left for France. The 100M performed impeccably and without problems. Its actual performance – 104.32mph, with racing driver Ron Flockhart at the wheel throughout – was good enough for BMC's purposes, although some knowledgeable observers noted that this was a significantly lower figure than had been expected. BMC, in fact, was almost hoist with its own petard, for in 1953 the company had cheated by choosing to send one of the Le Mans BN1s out for road test, as an 'absolutely standard' machine, by *The Autocar* and *The Motor*, both of whom had achieved significantly better results than a truly standard car could have delivered at the time.

CHAPTER 4
HEALEY & NASH HEALEY – THE RACE CARS

Although none of the original breed of 'Warwick Healeys' was ever developed with works competition in mind, the company occasionally competed over several years in lightly modified road cars. It was not until the rather special works Nash-Healeys came along in 1950 that this policy was modified. Even then the cars used were based very closely on their road-car equivalents, so the results gained in competition proved just how sound the original designs had been.

The story began in 1946, when two factory-owned demonstrator/test/development machines – GWD 42, an Elliot saloon, and GWD 43, a Westland roadster – began to appear in everything from high-speed demonstration runs to endurance rallies and lengthy races. These two cars, followed by others which rather mysteriously were never given British registration numbers while in works competition use, were later backed up by the Silverstone two-seater.

For the record (detailed below) the last works appearance by an Elliot or Westland was in 1949, the first works Silverstone following in the summer of that year, while the last appearance of a works Riley-engined car was at Silverstone in August 1950.

The Nash-Healey programme was altogether more serious and resulted in rather special and significantly faster machinery which appeared in works'guise from 1950 to 1953, culminating in the Le Mans 24-Hour race of June 1953. After that the factory turned its attention to a variety of Austin-Healey models, which are described in a separate Chapter.

What follows is, as far as the author is aware, a complete record of the progress of Riley- and Nash-engined cars up to 1953.

REGISTRATION NUMBER	ENGINE SIZE	MODEL TYPE
GWD 42	**2443CC 4-CYL OHV**	**ELLIOTT**

This hard-working car had already seen much use, had participated in several high-speed demonstration runs, and was effectively one of the company's go-to development and test cars before DMH decided to commit it to a limited number of races.

The first outing came in July 1948 when Tommy Wisdom and Nick Haines (Healey's Belgian distributor) were invited to tackle the gruelling Spa 24-Hour race which, held on the original long road circuit, was almost as important a challenge as the Le Mans 24-Hour itself. In 1948, indeed, it was the most demanding race in the European calendar, as the Le Mans circuit had not completely recovered from the war damage suffered in 1944 and could not yet be used.

History records that the 1948 Belgian race was run in appallingly wet conditions (how many times, in more recent years, have we seen the Belgian GP affected by rain!). Although GWD 42 was a 4-seater saloon car the race organisers saw fit to amalgamate the few saloons which had been entered into the unlimited-capacity sports car class, which immediately set the Healey at a disadvantage. (Their only advantage, it seems, was that Messrs Wisdom and Haines kept dry throughout, while the open sports car pilots got soaking wet!).

In later years Wisdom commented that he completed his driving stints while wearing his favourite tweed suit with a trilby hat, smoked cigarettes, and never donned a crash helmet. In those days there were no safety and regulations to spoil the fun.

Forty cars, some of them pre-war but nevertheless still competitive, took the start at 4.00pm, which was carried out in the Le Mans style with drivers scampering across the track to reach their machines when the flag dropped. The Healey began by averaging more than 70mph, and soon settled into the awful wet conditions, running steadily behind two 3-litre Delages. Then, with only one hour to go, one of the Delages had retired and the class-leading Delage faltered (to quote *The Autocar*'s report: "The Veuillet-Varet Delage, leading the 3000cc class, was showing ominous smoke streaming from its front end, to the marked annoyance of its driver").

With only a handful of laps remaining, in drying conditions, the Healey swept past the Delage, only for the French driver to throw caution to the wind, ignoring the smoke screen the car was laying, and re-take the class lead, eventually beating the Elliot by just 0.78 miles. Only 23 of the 40 starters finished the race. The Healey had averaged 65.36mph, which put it in seventh place overall. It had been a remarkable

performance by a car which was neither super-special nor a dedicated race car.

Two months later the re-prepared GWD 42 faced up to the Paris 12-Hour race, held on the banked Montlhéry circuit, which was a British-versus-French challenge match between two assorted team of eight cars each. Healey provided two cars (the other being GWD 43, the Westland, see below), but even though two top-class drivers tried their hardest, the Elliot retired with three hours to go due to suspected big end failure.

That was the end of GWD 42's works career, as Healey's attention was soon to be transferred to a new high headlamp Elliot and to the still-secret Silverstone two-seater.

Competition Record

1948 Spa 24 Hour race	Tommy Wisdom/Nick Haines	2nd, 3-litre Class
1948 Montlhéry 12 Hour race	Leslie Johnson/Nick Haines	DNF

REGISTRATION NUMBER	ENGINE SIZE	MODEL TYPE
GWD 43	**2443CC 4-CYL OHV**	**WESTLAND**

Healey's first works motor sport roadster was GWD 43, which was the prototype originally unveiled to the public carrying a fictitious registration number early in 1946. Once properly registered, it became one of Healey's most regularly used works cars, taking part in no fewer than five International events in the next three years.

GWD 43 was the original works Westland, which was used in major races and rallies in the late 1940s.

Its first outing was in the French Alpine rally of July 1947, the very first post-war Alpine to be run in France after the war-damaged French roads and in particular the mountain passes had mostly been tidied up. Tommy Wisdom, a great friend of Donald Healey, and his wife Elsie, always nicknamed Bill, were provided with the car for this open-road event which started from Marseilles and finished in Cannes, taking in three long legs, with night halts at Aix-les-Bains and Annecy, totalling 1000 miles. There was an overall running average of 37.5mph, with several speed sections, the passage of Cols which would later become familiar to all Alpine fans (Cayolle, Granier, Monte Revard, Iséran, Galibier, Isoard and Allos among them), and a complete ban on outside service assistance and of tyre changes apart from those being carried on the cars. Some cars eventually finished the event with little more than canvas separating the air in the tyres from the outside world!

The rugged Healey, driven by a very experienced crew who had both been accomplished drivers in the 1930s and during the war soon dominated their 2-3 litre capacity class, and went on to win it by a considerable margin. Of the 61 cars which started from Marseilles, only 27 finished the event, and of the nine British entrants only four including the Wisdoms made it to the end.

The redoubtable Westland gained class awards over each and every speed test and comfortably won the 3.0-litre category. Finally, to rub it in that here was a genuine fully-equipped production car, it was entered for the post-event concours and was judged the smartest of all the open cars. After that it was a case of driving the car all the way back to Warwick – no picnic as many of the Routes Nationales still bore the scars inflicted by armoured and tracked vehicles between 1939 and 1945.

In 1948 Donald Healey himself took the wheel of GWD 43 in the Mille Miglia, with his son Geoffrey as co-driver. Revived after the Second World War in 1947, this was one of the world's most important long-distance races, and in 1948 there were no fewer than 187 starters on the 1000-mile loop Brescia-Rome-Florence-Brescia. The Westland was prepared in full touring guise, with full-width windscreen and the fold-down hood which could be used or not as conditions allowed. Geoffrey Healey, in his first serious outing as a racing co-driver, gave great detail of this event in his Haynes book Austin Healey – the Story of the Big Healeys, mentioning that the Dunlop racing tyres lacked wet-road grip (so Pirellis were hastily purchased just before the start) and that the team were unhappy about the quality of the Girling dampers.

The car was driven the whole way from Warwick to Italy, recorded a flat-out top speed of 112mph with the soft-top erect, and proved to be remarkably sturdy throughout the race. Although the dynamo failed before the car reached Rome, they carried on, as they did after hitting a dog soon after leaving Florence (which damaged a wing, and unhappily despatched the dog), though bodging up repairs took 30 minutes. It was with some relief that they reached the finish in ninth place, which was fourth in the unlimited Sports Car class; the the course had taken well over 17 hours to complete.

Two months later Donald Healey, accompanied by Nick Haines, used GWD 43 to compete in the French Alpine rally, which by that time had re-established itself as the most popular and most competitive of all European road rallies. It followed the familiar layout – starting from Marseilles, night halts at Aix-les-Bains, Lugano and Chamonix, finishing at Nice.

Sixty-one cars started, and in an event whose route included almost all the classic hill-climb tests of the French Maritime Alps, the Healey was ideal for its job, and soon beginning to dominate the 2-3 litre capacity class. Fast and reliable (apart from the punctures which were to be expected on these sometimes unkempt mountain roads), the Healey was still unpenalized on the road sections, and on the final day, descending the Col d'Allos, looked as if it might gain the outright victory which Donald Healey deserved so much. It was then that the crew realised that a Sunbeam-Talbot behind them had suddenly suffered brake failure, crashed badly, and put its crew in peril. Healey immediately sacrificed all chance of outright victory by stopping, turning back to help at the crash scene, and losing 45 minutes before he felt able to resume the route. Even so, he managed to reach the end of the event within time limits and was still able to claim a class victory for his car.

Was it then time to retire this gallant though ageing car? Healey thought not, once again gave GWD 43 a good working over, and entered it in the Paris 12 Hour race at Montlhéry alongside its Elliot team mate. Tommy Wisdom and Norman Black arranged to share the wheel, but even though they had a great deal of racing experience (as did the car by this point in its career!), they were forced to retire when the transmission failed.

So now was it time to put GWD 43 out to grass? Not a bit of it, for in April 1949 Tommy Wisdom and Donald's son Geoffrey Healey took part in the Mille Miglia, in the same car as had tackled the event a year before. The Westland excelled itself yet again, fighting from Brescia to Brescia via Rome against other works teams in the Touring Car class, especially Alfa Romeo and Lancia. After a race-long battle the Westland beat every other car in the class, but only by the tiny margin of one minute 54 seconds over the most competitive Alfa Romeo; it had taken 14hr 24min 3sec to complete the event, and had averaged 68.57mph. This was a creditable way indeed for the valiant Westland to end its works sporting career.

This study, taken while the car was on loan to one of the major British motoring magazines, shows a purposeful, if not beautiful, machine. Note the distinctive badges, all of which had been earned by Donald Healey himself, and the two prominent horns between the lights which were thought essential for clearing the way in certain events.

Competition Record

1947 French Alpine rally	Tommy Wisdom	1st in Class
1948 Mille Miglia	Donald Healey/Geoffrey Healey	9th Overall
1948 French Alpine rally	Donald Healey	1st in Class
1948 Paris 12 Hour race	Tommy Wisdom/Norman Black	DNF
1949 Mille Miglia	Tommy Wisdom/Geoff Healey	1st in Touring Class

REGISTRATION NUMBER	ENGINE SIZE	MODEL TYPE
NOT REGISTERED (Ran on UK trade plates 192 AC)	**2443cc 4-cyl OHV**	**ELLIOTT**

Donald Healey and Geoff Price at speed in the 1949 Mille Miglia.

It is thought that this Elliot is the same one as completed the Flying Hour run at Montlhéry in October 1948. Certainly it was not GWD 42, which was a very early example with the original low-headlamp nose. It was prepared for the 1949 Mille Miglia for Donald Healey and his service manager Geoff Price to drive, where it competed alongside Tommy Wisdom and Geoff Healey in the ageing GWD 43 Westland.

After what almost qualifies as a 'routine' run, Healey and Price finished the closely-fought race in fourth place in the Touring Car category, taking 14hr 50min 50sec. As far as is known this car did not compete again as a works machine.

Competition Record

1949 Mille Miglia	Donald Healey/ Geoff Price	4th in Touring Class

REGISTRATION NUMBER	ENGINE SIZE	MODEL TYPE
JAC 100	**2443cc 4-cyl OHV**	**SILVERSTONE**

Developed to satisfy a demand for a lighter, smaller and faster evolution of the established Healey road cars, the Silverstone was a starkly trimmed and equipped two-seater, with exposed cycle-type wings and a light-alloy body produced for Healey by Abbey Panels in Coventry. Compared with the Westland and Elliott, the Silverstone had its engine/gearbox assembly eight inches further back, there was an anti-roll bar on the front suspension, and there were changes to the rear frame and fuel tank. Inside the driving compartment there were few creature comforts, and although there was a full-width windscreen and a rather basic hood, most buyers ran (or competed in) their cars with the hood stowed and the windscreen folded.

The rationale behind introducing this model was not only to provide a much lighter machine (an unladen Silverstone weighed about 2075lb compared with 2520lb for the Westland), but also to allow it to be marketed in the UK for a (basic) price of less than £1000. However, demand turned out to be limited, and only 105 cars were produced in two years.

This was the short career of the works Silverstones – and I must also note that the Nash-Healeys evolved from the same basic chassis.

The first works entry for a Silverstone came in July 1949, immediately after the road car version of the new model had been introduced to the media and before deliveries had begun. Donald Healey, pairing up with the promising young Leeds-based motor trader Ian Appleyard, entered the French Alpine rally in JAC 100. Appleyard had been hoping to drive his own brand-new Jaguar XK120 NUB 120, which would become world-famous in years to come, but it was not available in time.

The Alpine was everyone's favourite summer rally, for the weather was usually great, the demands of the route, which seemed to use every high pass in the Alps behind the Riviera coast, were unsurpassed, and there was much favourable publicity to be gained by doing well.

With the roads now considerably improved following the damage caused by the Second World War, this Alpine was set to link Marseilles (the start) with Nice (the finish), by way of 1850 miles of stiff climbing, with night halts in Monte Carlo, Cortina in the Italian Dolomites and Chamonix. A measure of the British enjoyment of the event is that there had been 107 entries, of which 64 were British cars.

Right from the start Healey and Appleyard were fighting for the lead, but unhappily lost two minutes at a time control due to being delayed at a closed railway crossing. "We did manage to drive the car under the barrier", Healey later commented, "but the delay cost us a vital two minutes". Ian Appleyard was doing much of the driving and they might have won the event outright except for this delay, for at the end of the five-day trek only one other car, a much-modified Citroen traction avant, had completed the course without penalty, and the Healey's special speed test performances were significantly faster. In the end the Silverstone took second place, only 31 cars having made it to the end of the event.

Within days Healey had entered not one but two Silverstones in the high-profile Production Car Race at the *Daily Express* Silverstone race meeting, one of them being a hastily cleaned-up JAC 100, to be driven by Tommy Wisdom. The second car, driven by Tony Rolt, was unregistered (see below), while there was also a third car in the list, driven by Monégasque racing driver Louis Chiron. Some pundits said this was a works car (which it does not seem to have been); it carried the London registration number GCY 145

Entrants for the one-hour 28-lap race were divided into three classes. The unlimited category was dominated by three works Jaguar XK120s, and the 2.5-litre category was disputed by the Healeys and two Bristol-engined Frazer-Nash Le Mans Replicas. Rolt and Chiron proved to be the fastest of the Healey drivers, while Tommy Wisdom, in JAC 100, finished a steady fifth in class, enough for Healey to claim the Team Prize.

JAC 100 was not used again in International motor sport until April 1950, when Healey allocated it to Tommy Wisdom and Tony Hume for the Targa Florio. Held in appallingly wet

This was the purposeful nose of the original works Silverstone model of 1949 – which was all very well, but the aerodynamic performance was disappointing.

weather (by Sicilian or indeed any standards), this proved to be even more of an endurance test than expected. Because the race was also held in conjunction with the Tour of Sicily on a 675-mile course, both crew members were on board throughout, and it says much for Wisdom's experience and determination that they kept going steadily where many of the other 185 starters faltered.

At the end of a gruelling event, where they were in the car for well over 11 hours on what sometimes looked and felt like the worst of all Sicilian roads, the gallant pair took sixteenth overall (Ferraris, Maseratis and Alfa Romeos dominated the leader board), finished fourth in their class, and were the highest-placed British entry.

JAC 100 then appeared for one last time as a works race car when it was allocated to Duncan Hamilton to compete in the Silverstone Production Car race in August 1950. The event was dominated by Ferraris, Jaguar XK120s and Frazer Nashes and was run to a weird performance/handicapping system. Hamilton, however, thought nothing of this, ploughed on steadily, ran third in the 3-litre category for much of the time and finally overtook the two works Aston Martin DB2s of Raymond Sommer and Reg Parnell to win that category.

Following this, Healey decided to concentrate on the newly-developed Nash-Healey in future, which meant that the Silverstone could be gracefully withdrawn from the scene.

Competition Record

1949 Mille Miglia	Donald Healey/ Geoff Price	4th in Touring Class
1949 French Alpine	Donald Healey/Ian Appleyard	2nd Overall, 1st in Class
1949 Production Car Race, Silverstone	Tommy Wisdom	5th in Class
1950 Targa Florio, Sicily	Tommy Wisdom/Tony Hume	4th in Class, 16th overall
1950 Production Car Race, Silverstone	Duncan Hamilton	8th overall, 1st in Class

REGISTRATION NUMBER	ENGINE SIZE	MODEL TYPE
NOT REGISTERED	**2443CC 4-CYL OHV**	**SILVERSTONE**

Tony Rolt drove this brand-new Silverstone in the Production Car race at Silverstone in August 1949, where 29 cars of all types, the fastest undoubtedly being the newly-launched Jaguar XK120s, circulated for one flat-out hour. As expected, the XK120s and two Frazer Nashes were always up front, but Rolt's Silverstone was undisputedly the fastest 'real' production car, eventually taking fourth place overall and averaging 78.40mph in the process.

As *The Autocar*'s Sammy Davis wrote in his column immediately afterwards, "To me the production car race stood out a mile – it really didn't matter a bit who won. It was just a good practical demonstration."

Tony Rolt's works Silverstone,
battling with a Jaguar XK120,
during the Silverstone Production
Car race in 1949.

Competition Record

1949 Production Car race, Silverstone	Tony Rolt	4th Overall, 2nd in Class

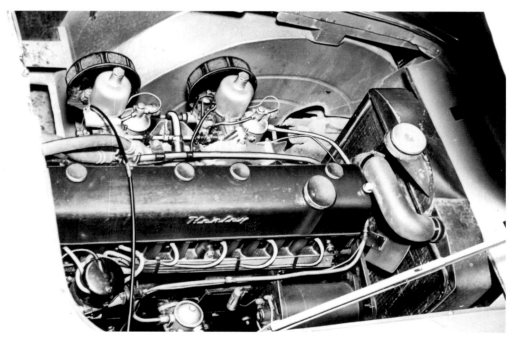

This was the basic engine installation of the Nash power unit, for use in the Nash-Healey.

NASH-HEALEYS – 1950-1953

It was not until 1950 that Healey felt able to build any dedicated race cars, the development of the Nash-Healey car for the Mille Miglia being the first in a programme which went on until 1953. The works Nash-Healeys then competed in carefully chosen long-distance races (sometimes with Donald Healey at the wheel), after which a succession of steadily-developed 100 BN1 and 100S types took over.

The Nash-Healey was really a lineal descendant of the existing Riley-engined models (not least the Silverstone), and was conceived in December 1949 following a chance meeting on board the transatlantic ocean liner Queen Elizabeth between Healey and George Mason, who was President of the Nash Kelvinator Corporation of Detroit. Healey was on his way to Detroit to try to acquire supplies of Cadillac V8 engines to install in Silverstone chassis and mentioned this to Mason. He was surprised to receive a counter offer – which was that if Cadillac should turn him down, then Nash would be interested in supplying their own engines instead.

Healey was flattered by this but had reservations. The Nash engine on offer was an ageing overhead-valve 3.8-litre straight six which was only rated at 125bhp, whereas the Cadillac unit was a newly launched 160bhp 5.4-litre V8, and, to quote

Healey about the Nash engine, "There were various snags, among which was its considerable weight. It was one of the heaviest engines I'd ever been associated with, but it was very robust, and I knew it would never break in any conditions it might have to face in so small a car."

'Small', of course, is only a relative adjective when used here, for such a car. A Nash-Healey would not only be the largest-engined car that Healey or Austin-Healey ever put on sale, but by Nash standards it was indeed quite small. George Mason, in fact, had mused that he would "much like to make a smaller car than the usual run of American cars, and I'd like it to be a sports car".

Based on the existing Healey chassis, the Nash-Healey went into production towards the end of 1950, with all supplies sent directly to the USA for sale on that continent. Bodies came from Panelcraft of Birmingham, Nash supplied the gearbox and rear axle as well as the engine, and front and rear suspensions, like the chassis, were the same as on the previous Healeys.

Donald Healey could see that a properly prepared race car would be faster than any of the Riley-engined cars that they had already raced. Since he was still personally determined to take part in long-distance events such as the Mille Miglia, he encouraged Geoff Healey to keep on improving the cars in the next three years The only feature that could not easily be improved for use in motor sport was the cars' weight.

The first 3.8-litre version of the robust Nash engine had been included in Nash's 1934 product range and been used in all of Nash's own domestic cars after that. As used in the Nash-Healey, and before development by Healey themselves began, independently-recorded British test bed figures for the standard engine revealed that it produced just 103bhp at 3700rpm. By the time 'Sammy' Sampietro had worked at improving the output, the 'Dual Fire' engine featured an aluminium cylinder head, twin SU carburettors and a special camshaft, adding up to a claimed 140bhp (gross) at 4000rpm, which was more often quoted as an honest 125bhp (nett).

As far as motor racing was concerned this all looked very promising, but one related difficulty which immediately had to be tackled was that the three-speed Nash gearbox, which was backed by a Borg Warner overdrive, also included a free-wheel. Because the use of a free-wheel had already been banned by the European sporting authorities, ways had to be found of dealing with this, but it was speedily achieved at Warwick.

In his autobiography Donald Healey insists that the Nash-Healey was not originally intended to be a racing car, but that Nash wanted to demonstrate its pace in a big race, so preparation work had to begin in Warwick. Geoff Healey is reputed to have greeted the news by saying, "It's going to be our biggest job yet – making it handle properly with that great heavy engine in front". Amazingly enough, the completed prototype two-seater was found to handle quite well, and the

problem of dealing with the 'illegal' free-wheel feature was soon solved too.

From this point a steady, if under-financed and rather modest, motorsport programme got under way. As will be clear from the individual histories spelt out below, the cars usually proved to be highly competitive, though so far as most historians were able to discover some cars competed without registration numbers either known or being in place, and more than one car changed its identity over the years.

The build-up began slowly. The original two-seater race car, known internally as X5, which wore a modified E-type Silverstone type of body, was completed just in time for father-and-son Healey team to compete in the 1950 Mille Miglia, which was run in awful weather. Afterwards it was returned to base for a much-modified full-width body to be fitted. The Silverstone front grille was retained. This car, known as X6, took an astonishing fourth place overall at Le Mans in June.

During the next three years, the specification of the works racing Nash-Healeys was consistently improved, though Healey wisely confined their major efforts to entering the Mille Miglia and Le Mans events, where endurance and rugged reliability counted for more than flashing acceleration and sensational roadholding. Although Donald Healey himself took the wheel on the Mille Miglia cars (in 1953, the car's last appearance in the race, he was already 54 years old), he hired seasoned and more active race drivers for Le Mans.

The 1951 Le Mans car (X7) was a closed coupé with an entirely different style with a rectangular radiator grille. It was later badly damaged in a crash in the 1952 Mille Miglia. For Le Mans in 1952, and to replace it, X8 was constructed, with what was effectively a new open-top derivative of the body, and then, for the 1953 Mille Miglia and Le Mans there would be two brand-new and very attractive open-top cars with sleek long tails in which the spare wheel was exposed.

Along the way, both Healey and Nash themselves worked at improving the power output of the engines, increasing the capacity to 4138cc, fitting new carburation and altering the

X-NUMBERS

Because of Healey's sometimes cavalier way of placing the incorrect registration numbers on his cars, in the case of some of the cars covered in this book I have preferred to identify them by the Healey project 'X-number' which Geoff Healey detailed so carefully in his book *Healey, The Specials*. The list of X-numbers applying to the works Nash-Healeys was as follows:

X5	First Silverstone-bodied Nash-Healey engine race car prototype
X6	First prototype, raced at Le Mans 1951, with all-enveloping body
X8	1952 Le Mans car (first version of X114)
X14	1953 Le Mans car, with special style (sister to X15)
X15	1953 Le Mans car, with special style (sister to X14)
X102	Coupé Nash-Healey race car (1951 Le Mans car)
X114	Light-bodied Nash-Healey race car, Le Mans 1952

This was the original type of Nash-Healey road car, which went on general sale in the USA in 1951.

camshaft profiles. This moved the peak up to the region of 140bhp, still not enough to ensure that the cars ran at the head of the field, but the engines were usually very reliable and the cars were competitive.

Along the way there was one little-publicised experimental engine from Healey which raced at Le Mans in 1952, and about which very little detail was every made known. In *The Autocar* post-Le Mans issue of 27 June 1952, the following was stated: "The second Nash-Healey, that driven by the French drivers Veyron and Giraud-Cabantous, was fitted with a special cylinder head with inclined valves and hemispherical combustion chambers, the valves being operated rather on the lines of the BMW design, with additional pushrods to the exhaust side."'

In the late 1970s Geoff Healey told more: "The original race car was being prepared [for the 1952 Le Mans] with a special engine. The limitations of the Nash engine lay in the cylinder head, with its in-line valves and inlet gallery cast in the cylinder head, a design that had no advantages and which was not unlike the head used on the early Austin-Healey six-cylinder engines. Sampietro was still acting as a consultant to us, and with Nash's agreement he was given the job of designing a new cylinder head. Sammy drew up a hemispherical head with valves at an included angle of 90deg. There were six large inlet ports on one side and six exhaust ports on the other, by way of rocker arms and cross pushrods. Prior to the very successful adoption of overhead camshafts, as on the Jaguar, many designers tried to operate hemispherical heads with pushrods. This inevitably resulted in a very heavy head, due to the multiplicity of pushrods and rockers."

We now know that detail design, manufacture and development were allocated to Thomson and Taylor at Brooklands, where the 4.1-litre engine's potential was initially thought to be 190bhp, but the best figure obtained in the very limited time available was 160bhp at 4500rpm. Once installed in one of the proposed Le Mans cars, the extra weight was found to promote an excess of understeer, and the lead drivers (Leslie Johnson and Tommy Wisdom) elected to use the conventional power unit, the new engine being fitted to the other machine, which was crewed by a French duo.

Not a success in its only race appearance, the design was later handed over to Nash in case they felt like productionising it for road car use, but nothing more was ever heard of it. In fact, before the end of 1952, when they had much on their plate to productionise the newly-launched Austin-Healey 100 road car, Healey seem to have decided to wind down their works Nash-Healey race programme. Both of the cars which raced at Le Mans, X5 and X8, together with the special hemi-headed race engine, were sent off to Nash in the USA, and therefore fall gracefully out of this story.

But this was not the end of the Nash-Healey period. Healey set up a 1953 Le Mans visit by a team of the brand-new Austin-Healey 100 Special Test Cars (see Chapter 5), and Nash agreed to support a further season of racing for Nash-Healey machines. This led to the building of two new and very attractive open-top two-seaters, X14 and X15, which appeared in the Mille Miglia and at Le Mans.

Thus ended a four-year works race car programme for Nash-Healeys which, though somewhat hampered by the heavy road-car chassis, and the limited tuning porential of the Nash six-cylinder engine, had brought great credit to all parties.

REGISTRATION NUMBER	ENGINE SIZE	MODEL TYPE
JWD 300 (X5)	**3848/4138**CC	**NASH-HEALEY PROTOTYPE**

Originally completed in time to compete in the Mille Miglia of May 1950, this was the first works Nash-Healey, so much of a prototype that it ran in the Italian road race with a virtually standard Silverstone body, complete with exposed front wheels and wings. To their dismay, the Healeys, father and son, found that this body had an unexpectedly poor aerodynamic shape.

As Geoff Healey later wrote, "It would rush up to 100mph and then cease accelerating". It was good on the mountain passes, but on the long straights small 1100cc sports cars would overtake the 3.8-litre machine. This, allied to the fact that they went off the road at one point, meant that they finished well down, too far behind to be officially classified, but it was later clear that they had been a miserable 9th in their class.

An immediate decision was taken to re-prepare the car for Le Mans, using a very different shape of body, one which would hopefully improve the aerodynamic performance and therefore help the car to make the most of the long Mulsanne Straight. The overall 'envelope' was changed by the use of a full-width body which included fully faired-in front and rear wheels, headlamps in the front fairings, with a small

The Nash-Healey prototype wearing a full-width Silverstone body. Tony Rolt is seen at the wheel at Le Mans in 1950.

streamlining hump behind the driver's head. Two experienced sports car race drivers, Duncan Hamilton and Tony Rolt, were hired to drive.

Against all the odds – time, a lack of finance, and the team's inexperience at Le Mans with this car – Healey achieved a quite remarkable result by taking fourth overall behind the two winning 4½-litre Talbots (which were scantily-disguised Grand Prix cars), and Sydney Allard's 5.4-litre Cadillac-engined Allard. Along the way, when Duncan Hamilton was driving as dawn broke, the Nash-Healey suffered a crash with a Delage, but the car survived, in spite of the back axle having been pushed out of line, which damaged the clutch housing, the flywheel and the exhaust system. Somehow lashed together by Roger Menadue and his team of mechanics, the car moved up to third place after the works XK120 ahead of it retired, but in the final agonising hour it was overhauled by Allard's Allard, which was stuck in top gear. Even so, what a performance: fourth overall, 2103 miles covered, and a fastest lap at no less than 94.3mph.

After nearly two years rest the car was brought out again for the 1952 Mille Miglia, to be driven by Leslie

Johnson (gentleman-racer/business tycoon), and co-driven, with publicity in mind, by Bill McKenzie, then Motoring Correspondent of the *Daily Telegraph* newspaper. For this event it was given the same type of enlarged 4.1-litre Nash engine as was being used by X6 in the same event.

Though McKenzie was a tyro, Johnson (who at one time controlled the destiny of ERA) was a seasoned racing driver and he put in a remarkably steady, forceful and successful drive in the 1952 event, finishing a remarkable seventh overall.

X5 was still not considered obsolete, however, and only a few weeks later, with the French drivers Giraud-Cabantous and Veyron sharing the driving, it competed at Le Mans. As already noted in the introduction to this section, the car was equipped with the very special new engine which 'Sammy' Sampietro had conceived .This engine was rated at 160bhp at 4500rpm but it did not survive the Le Mans race. During the event a rocker shaft broke and the car was forced to retire on the spot. This was the first and last time that the engine was seen in public, for soon after this mishap the car was shipped off to Nash in the USA.

Competition Record

1950 Mille Miglia	Donald Healey/ Geoff Healey	DNF
1950 Le Mans 24 Hour race	Duncan Hamilton/Tony Rolt	4th overall
1952 Mille Miglia	Leslie Johnson/Bill McKenzie	7th overall
1952 Le Mans 24 Hour race	Yves Giraud-Cabantous/Pierre Veyron	DNF

REGISTRATION NUMBER	ENGINE SIZE	MODEL TYPE
LAC 880 (X6)	**3848/4138**CC	**NASH-HEALEY PROTOTYPE**

As a result of the experience gained in 1950 with X5, Healey built up a new car for 1951, the X6, basing it on the same running gear as the X5, but with a sleeker, more aerodynamically-efficient fastback coupé body designed by Donald Healey and his trusted stylist, Gerry Coker. After taking advice from airflow specialists at Armstrong Whitworth in Coventry, this one looked very different from the 1950 car. It had a vee-screen, a lower profile, and a squarer front air intake, while the front end had extra driving lamps built in. As before, Duncan Hamilton and Tony Rolt were hired to drive the car at Le Mans.

By comparison with the eventful 1950 race, Healey's effort

For the 1951 Le Mans 24 Hour race, Healey produced a much-modified coupe body, in which Tony Rolt and Duncan Hamilton finished sixth overall.

at Le Mans in 1951 was at once fast, regular, predictable and reliable for the entire 24-hour period. By daybreak on the Sunday morning the Nash-Healey was in sixth place overall (behind a Jaguar C-Type which would eventually win, two Talbots and two Aston-Martin DB2s). Fifth later on, then fourth, then back to sixth, it finally failed to catch the Abecassis/Shawe-Taylor DB2 by a mere eight seconds. Honour, however, was well and truly satisfied.

For 1952, X6 was re-jigged and re-prepared for the Healeys, father and son, to tackle the Mille Miglia. The car, previously unregistered, was given the regstration LAC 880. Donald would do all the driving, his son being co-driver, cheerleader and otherwise No.2 in the car) but the outing resulted in

mechanical disaster. Let Geoff Healey, from his book on the history of the Austin-Healey, take up the story: "In appalling conditions, we were approaching Rovigo at full speed when DMH attempted to slow the car for a bridge and corner. He shouted to me that something was wrong – the car would neither stop nor steer. He tried all he knew, jabbing the brake pedal and moving the steering wheel. At what seemed the last moment the wheels gripped and he was able to regain some control. We struck the bridge on the exit side where it turned a corner". Happily neither crew member was hurt, though the car was seriously damaged by the impact and quite incapable of going any further. Although it was retrieved it was effectively written off by this accident and was not seen again.

Competition Record

| 1951 Le Mans 24 Hour race | Duncan Hamilton/Tony Rolt | 6th overall |
| 1952 Mille Miglia | Donald Healey/Geoff Healey | DNF |

REGISTRATION NUMBER	ENGINE SIZE	MODEL TYPE
KWD 947	**3848/4138CC**	**NASH-HEALEY**

This was a works Nash-Healey entered with standard body for the 1951 Mille Miglia which went on in much modified form to compete at Le Mans in 1953.

Its first outing came in April 1951 in the Mille Miglia when the Healeys, father and son, took it out to compete in the sports car class, complete with folding soft-top and every possible piece of standard equipment. Not expecting to win, they settled for a full-distance reliability run, especially as the weather was so wet. Eventually they finishing fourth in their capacity/type class, and a very creditable thirtieth overall. The car was so healthy that when it returned to the UK it was promptly entered for the over 3-litre Production Car Race in Silverstone's Daily Express International Trophy, where Tony Rolt took sixth place behind a fleet of Jaguar XK120s.

Clearly this car was a glutton for punishment, for its next outing came only five weeks later when Reg Parnell was entrusted to drive it in the BRDC's Empire Trophy race, held on a tight 3.9-mile circuit on the outskirts of Douglas, Isle of

Man. The race was for road-equipped sports cars of all sizes, and the Frazer-Nash Le Mans Replicas were strongly tipped to succeed. Parnell made a great start from the motorcycle TT grandstand and led the field into the first corner where (as described in *The Autocar*) there was a multi-car accident immediately behind him. Soon, however, he was overwhelmed by Stirling Moss and Bob Gerard, both in Frazer-Nashes, but he hung on gamely until obliged to retire when the gear lever broke away, making further progress impossible.

Soon after this, and with KWD 947 rebuilt more as a long-distance sporting machine than a race car, Geoff Healey took what must have seemed like a busman's holiday by entering it in the Tour de France, the first ever of those beguiling rally-cum-race events, which occupied more than a full week, starting and finishing in Nice but taking in more than 3000 miles of motoring, circuit racing, mountain climbing in the Alps and speed tests all round France. Unhappily the car was forced to retire near La Boule after an accident caused by a skid on someone else's dropped oil.

Competition Record

1951 Mille Miglia	Donald Healey/ Geoff Healey	4th overall
1951 Silverstone Production Car race	Tony Rolt	6th overall
1951 British Empire Trophy	Reg Parnell	DNF
1951 Tour de France	Geoff Healey/Tom Kenny	DNF

REGISTRATION NUMBER	ENGINE SIZE	MODEL TYPE
NOT REGISTERED (X8)	4138CC	NASH-HEALEY RACE CAR

Conceived and built in a tearing hurry, X8 took shape because Healey had an authorised entry for the 1952 Le Mans race and was to have used X6, but after this car was badly smashed up on the Mille Miglia (see above) it was decided to write it off and to build up a brand-new 'cheap and cheerful' race car to take its place.

X8 was designed in a matter of days in May 1952, based on a production Nash-Healey rolling chassis, used a body hastily produced by City Street Metal of Coventry. It used as much of the crashed Mille Miglia car as could be salvaged. Amazingly, it turned out to be lighter than any of Healey's previous works race cars, and even though it had been built in such an insanely short time it proved very reliable when driven absolutely flat-out for 24 hours by Leslie Johnson and Tommy Wisdom.

Once Jaguar's C-Types, which as the 1951 winners had started as hot favourites, had all been eliminated due to overheating engines, the battle settled down to a fight between Mercedes-Benz 300SLs, Cunninghams, Ferraris and Gordinis, but the Healey kept on going, as fast as possible and without taking risks.

At half distance, the Healey was still not on the leader board, but as other cars failed it kept on gaining places. Four hours later it was up into sixth place, and after twenty hours it was fifth, being led only by Levegh's Talbot, two Mercedes-Benz 300SLs and a single Aston Martin. Then in the closing hours the works Aston Martin broke its transmission and the leading Talbot's engine suddenly expired. Suddenly the Nash-Healey was in third place, behind the two surviving 300SLs, and there were to be no more upsets, with the British car completing 2196 miles at an average of 91.5mph – a magnificent result in what had been an under-financed, under-prepared and distinctly 'let's-have-a-go' entry in this prestigious motor race.

Competition Record

1952 Le Mans 24 Hour race	Leslie Johnson/Tommy Wisdom	3rd overall

Tommy Wisdom at Arnage in the Nash-Healey at Le Mans in 1952. Leslie Johnson did most of the driving with 17 hours behind the wheel.

REGISTRATION NUMBER	ENGINE SIZE	MODEL TYPE
NOT REGISTERED (X14)	**4138CC**	**NASH-HEALEY**

Le Mans 1953, with Leslie Johnson's Nash-Healey ahead of the Gatsonides/Lockett Austin-Healey 100. They would finish eleventh and twelfth respectively.

For 1953, the last pair of works Nash-Healey race cars were given this striking new body style. Ignore the registration plate which, as far as this particular car was concerned, was fake.

For 1953 Healey built up two very attractive-looking open-top two-seater Nash-Healey race cars, the first of which (internal project code X14) was ready to race in the Mille Miglia race, where the American John Fitch drove it throughout, accompanied by Ray Willday, a Warwick-based mechanic who had been partly responsible for the construction of the car. For the pre-event press photographs it carried the KWD 947 registration plate, but this one turned up on various works cars from time to time, and bears little significance to the project.

Mechanically, this was an evolution of the now-familiar works race car specification, using a development of the standard Nash (as opposed to 'Sampietro') engine, now with two horizontal Carter carburettors, and a specially fabricated three-branch exhaust manifold. Although a modified Nash three-speed gearbox was retained, for the first time this was mated to a Laycock De Normanville overdrive unit operating on second and top gears, therefore giving the driver five forward speeds to play with.

The sleek, long two-seater body was based on a lightweight steel frame, with all the exterior panels in light alloy, and featured a complete undershield, a full width radiator intake, and cut back sections under the widely spaced headlamps

which encouraged the flow of air on to the brake drums.

Fitch, a highly rated American driver, had no luck at all on the Mille Miglia, where the car suffered from a failed rear axle, subsequently blamed on the type of lubricant which had been used.

Rebuilt and with that problem rectified, the car was entrusted for Leslie Johnson and Bert Hadley to drive at Le Mans, where it plugged gamely on in an event dominated by Jaguar's C-Types (which raised the race-winning average to more than 100mph for the first time), eventually taking eleventh place overall and completing 2218.6 miles, which meant that it had averaged 92.44mph.

Competition Record

1953 Mille Miglia	John Fitch/Ray Willday	DNF
1953 Le Mans 24 Hour race	Leslie Johnson/Bert Hadley	11th overall

REGISTRATION NUMBER	ENGINE SIZE	MODEL TYPE
NOT REGISTERED (X15)	**4138CC**	**NASH-HEALEY**

This, the second of the prettily styled 1953 works Nash-Healey race cars, was only just completed in time for the 1953 Le Mans race. It was near-identical in specification to X14, and was allocated to the same pair of French drivers, Veyron and Giraud-Cabantous, as had driven the 'Sampietro'-engined X5 in 1952. The car had little luck on the event, as the oil pressure soon began to drop due to a defective oil pump which failed and eventually caused its retirement.

The 1953 Le Mans cars used a development of the standard Nash engine rather than the 'Sampietro' version. It had twin side-draught Carter carburettors and a three-branch exhaust manifold.

Oil pressure dropped on X15 early in the race. Healey's crew changed the oil pump but the damage had been done – a big-end bearing failed after only two laps back on the track.

Competition Record

1953 Le Mans 24 Hour race	Pierre Veyron/Yves Giraud-Cabantous	DNF

CHAPTER 5:
100 & 100S WORKS RACE CARS

Bic Healey at the wheel of one of the very first 100S cars which Healey launched in the autumn of 1954. It came with 132bhp and a mainly light-alloy body.

No sooner had Donald Healey formalised the deal with BMC whereby series production of the BN1 100 model and its successors would be centred at Longbridge, with design and development at the Healey premises in Warwick, than he began planning a limited motor racing programme.

After lending the prototype 100, MWD 360, to Gregor Grant for the French Lyons-Charbonnières rally in March 1953, came the serious business of preparing a trio of what the company called its Special Test Cars, which would be followed by speed record contenders of one variety or another.

Work had already got under way early in 1953, with a tiny team under Roger Menadue, and although funds were limited the programme had the backing (both financial and in publicity terms) of BMC. Although the Special Test Cars usually carried registration numbers, these numbers were sometimes switched from chassis to chassis in a rather casual manner, and sometimes – just to confuse the historians – were omitted altogether. In certain cases, therefore, the author has quoted the Healey Motor Company's original Build Number or Experimental Project number.

In the beginning, in 1953, there were four Special Test

This is the first prototype of the Healey 100 chassis, as completed in 1952, which would eventually evolve into the race-winning 100S, and the rally-dominant 3000.

These carried the easily remembered registration numbers OON 439, OON 440 and OON 441.

Work also continued on 'record' cars – some looking standard, some looking extremely special – but their antics were so different that their careers are covered in the next Chapter.

In the meantime, in June 1954 Healey seemed to set themselves against motor racing's establishment by first of all securing three entries for the forthcoming Le Mans 24 Hour race, then very publicly withdrawing them at a later stage. Now, looking back many years, it seems that three cars were more than part prepared to start in the 1954 race, but one wonders if the statement put out by Austin-Healey at the time was part of a strategy to divert attention from their possible shortcomings in the race.

To quote *The Autocar*'s then Sports Editor, John Cooper, "The officially announced reason for the Austin-Healey withdrawal is that the firms concerned [there were other pre-race withdrawals] are taking a stand against the present trend of sports car racing in which prototype vehicles, not necessarily bearing any resemblance to normal production sports cars, are allowed to take part.

"That is all very well (and I shall return to that controversy later); but the fact remains that the Le Mans regulations have been unchanged in this respect for some years. The Austin-Healey team was entered with full knowledge of the regulations and their implications: and for the decision to be taken suddenly, within a few weeks of the race... is surely somewhat discourteous, if nothing more, to the organisers of the race."

Donald Healey responded immediately to this criticism of what his company's decision, and in a long letter to *The Autocar* (published on 11 June 1954) justified his actions

Cars – three of which were used in the Mille Miglia and in the Le Mans 24 Hour race, and one of them (to be covered in Chapter 6) becoming the 'standard-bodied' record car seen at the Bonneville Salt Flats in 1953 and 1954. These cars were dedicated for use as race, test and development cars, but one of them, NOJ 392, which had raced at Le Mans, was pressed into service as a 'standard road car' for road test by *The Autocar* and *The Motor* only three months later!

All the Special Test Cars, and three prototype 100Ss, were kept busy until mid-1954, after which Healey turned its attention to preparing for a production run of 50 of the 100S models, and to building and preparing for entry in major sports car races one or more of the three works 100Ss.

NOJ 392 AS A 'STANDARD' ROAD TEST CAR

One of the minor BMC 'scandals' of the early 1950s involved an Austin-Healey 'Special Test Car' – NOJ 392. Production of BN1 road cars did not truly get underway until June 1953, and the technical press did not get its hands on to a road test car until September. Amazingly, this apparently 'standard' BN1 carried the registration number of NOJ 392 – which just happened to be the same identity as carried by the works 100 which Johnny Lockett and Maurice Gatsonides had raced in the Le Mans 24 Hour race three months earlier.

At the time, *The Autocar*'s published performance figures looked slightly optimistic, but not a word explained why this seemed to be, if nothing else, the rebuilt version of the Le Mans race car? BMC did not explain, or even try to justify this, and the specialist press, which was more docile and inclined to 'toe the party line' in those days than it later became, never commented either.

By the time the BN1 had been accepted as a 'classic' the author made haste to point out certain anomalies, and I am indebted to my fellow historian Bill Piggott for emphasising these in words of his own. Bill pointed out that the car was significantly lighter than a production-line BN1, that it was still using the Austin-supplied engine (with more than 100bhp), retained the carburettor and cold air intake box of the race cars, and wondered 'whether the magazines' road testing staff were really aware of how much NOJ 392 differed from the production vehicle...'

In a way, of course, this eventually rebounded on BMC, for when the time came to submit road test cars of the then-new 2.6-litre/six-cylinder 100 Six, it made the disappointing performance of that car even more disappointing ....

by pointing out that the rules had been changed to allow specially developed 'single-seaters' to take part, which would have rendered cars like the Austin-Healey 100 totally uncompetitive: "...to keep pace with our competitors I found that the cars would have to have such radical alterations as special high-compression cylinder heads and multiple non-British carburettors, multi-pad type disc brakes with complicated servo systems and special wheels to suit, close ratio gearboxes and axle ratios quite unsuitable for normal use. The bodies would have to be converted to virtually single-seater shells. The resulting car would bear no resemblance to our production model..."

Strangely enough (or was it?) no mention was made in this letter of the special cylinder head developed for the Le Mans Nash-Healey of 1952, nor of the fact that the Special Test Cars used hand-built four-speed gearboxes while production BN1s had very different three-speed boxes. Nor, for that matter, did he spell out the many 'prototype' modifications which had been made to the cars he entered for the 1954 Mille Miglia, in the hope that they would be waved through and accepted by the very sporting authorities in Italy.

The fact is, however, that this withdrawal (which was temporary, for works cars were back at top level from November of the same year) did no favours to Austin-Healey, in that much of public and official opinion seemed to be against the reasoning, such that the entire team had to work hard to get back into the media's good books before the 'works 100S programme was gradually run down in 1955/56.

In the last year, however, considerable work was done on the specification of the works cars, not only to make the engines more powerful but also to make the cars lighter. These changes were ready in time for the last appearance of OON 440 and OON 441 in the 1956 Sebring 12 Hour race. As far as engines were concerned, two twin-choke Weber 45

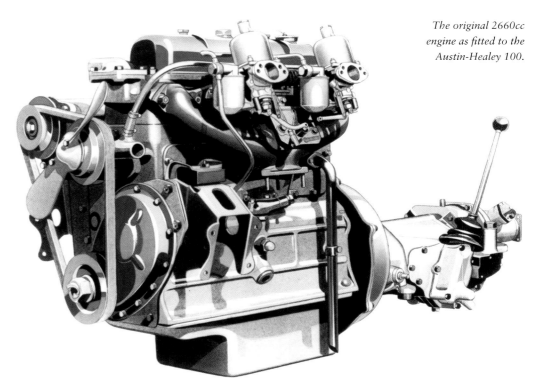

The original 2660cc engine as fitted to the Austin-Healey 100.

DCOE carburettors took the place of the original twin SUs, the result being a peak output of 145bhp at 5250rpm and more mid-range torque. Tubular exhaust manifolds were used in place of the standard cast iron manifolds. Stronger front suspension components were fitted, and various steel body panels were changed to aluminium, the result being that these cars weighed only 1790lb, almost 100lb lighter even than the 'standard' 100S production race car.

This is a summary of what was achieved between 1953 and 1956:

The 100S used four-wheel Dunlop disc brakes as part of its normal specification. This shows the front-end installation, and also shows off the centre-lock hub arrangements.

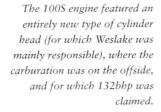

The 100S engine featured an entirely new type of cylinder head (for which Weslake was mainly responsible), where the carburation was on the offside, and for which 132bhp was claimed.

REGISTRATION NUMBER	ENGINE SIZE	MODEL TYPE
MWD 360	**2660CC 4-CYL OHV**	**BN1**

In its own modest way, this was the car which kick-started the Big Healey's competition career. It was the very first Healey 100 (once falsely identified as KWD 947), used in the high-speed runs carried out on the Jabbeke Highway in Belgium in 1952.

Already well used as the original (and only) working prototype in the winter of 1952/53, it was prepared in a real hurry for *Autosport*'s editor, Gregor Grant, to drive on the Lyons-Charbonnières rally in France, on which he was accompanied by Peter Reece, who was one of the brothers who ran a thriving Ford franchise in Liverpool. The engine seems to have been a close relative of the Special Test Cars' unit – larger bore 1.75in. SU carburettors and double valve springs being mentioned in Gregor's later report. It was a virtually standard (if hand-built) machine and it suffered badly from the awful post-winter condition of many French roads. Damage was caused to the rear damper mountings, the hand-brake linkage and the anchorage of a rear leaf spring because (in DMH's own words): "When all was going well, they were confronted at high speed by a cavernous pot-hole. Unable to dodge, they crashed over it and a rear damper mounting mounting snapped off".

It was a miracle that the car managed to stagger to the finish, well down the field. With damaged bodywork underneath. Gregor, a peerless story teller, no doubt dined out on his experiences for some time to come.

MWD 360 did not compete again at the International level of motorsport.

Competition Record

1953 Lyons Charbonnières rally	Gregor Grant	50th Overall

REGISTRATION NUMBER	ENGINE SIZE	MODEL TYPE
NOJ 391	**2660CC 4-CYL OHV**	**BN1/100S FROM 1954**

Along with its sister car NOJ 392 this was one of the first three Special Test Cars, two of which were built up in the spring of 1953 and entered for the Mille Miglia. It carried the evocative and special chassis number SPL 224B. Construction began early in 1953, at the same time as the short series of

The two 100 BN1 cars which raced at Le Mans in 1953 featured engines modified to have special air cleaners, and other details.

pre-production road cars were also taking shape, based on what would become 'standard' chassis frames and body structures, except that all the exterior panels were made from an aluminium alloy called Birmabright, which contained a tiny percentage of magnesium. Writing in the 1970s, Geoff Healey pointed out, "Bodies built in this alloy are strong, light and strongly resistant to corrosion, and for these reasons they are to be found on Land Rovers and many boats".

The 2660cc engine was specially built, slightly tuned, and test-bed proven by Austin engineers at Longbridge, producing 100bhp at 4500rpm (which compared with the nominal 90bhp at 4,000rpm which was then quoted for all the BN1 road cars. Differences for the race-car engines included the use of Austin Champ-type crankshafts made of EN40 nitrided steel, slightly different camshaft profiles, double valve springs and a lightened flywheel.

Backing these engines were special clutches, driving through gearboxes modified from what BMC knew as the 'taxi cab' variety, with four forward speeds (not the three speeds of the normal BN1 road cars), and overdrive, apparently arranged only to operate on top and third gears. These, along with

NOJ 391 was the 'doppelganger' which actually raced at Le Mans in 1953, when it finished fourteenth, driven by Maurice Becquart and Gordon Wilkins. The car which went through pre-race scrutineering was NOJ 393, but that car then suffered an open-road crash on the way back to the team hotel, after which NOJ 391 (the spare car) was retro-fitted with NOJ 393's scrutineered and tagged components, and raced!

features such as special light alloy bumper bars, aluminium radiators, and Nash-Healey type twin trailing shoe front brakes emphasise the way that these really were 'Special' Test Cars.

First used as a demonstrator at the 1953 Geneva Motor Show in March 1953, then subjected to a long European run (which also included a holiday for Geoff Healey and his soon-to-be-wife Margot), NOJ 391was returned to Warwick and made ready to compete in the 1000-mile Mille Miglia The start point, Brescia in the north of Italy, was reached by driving the race car all the way from Warwick.

In the race itself NOJ 391 was driven by Bert Hadley with Squadron leader Bertie Mercer as his co-driver. Unhappily the throttle linkage came apart less than two hours after the race started and could not be repaired at the roadside so the car had to be retired.

What followed next at Le Mans was reassuring for the car's makers while at the same time almost unbelievable. In summary, NOJ 391 was taken to Le Mans, where it was intended to be the 'spare' car to back up NOJ 392 and NOJ 393. After pre-race scrutineering NOJ 393 was crashed and NOJ 391 was fitted with major components from NOJ 393,

including the engine, gearbox and other items which had already been sealed by the officials, and then competed in the race as NOJ 393.

Naturally it did not carry any registration number on the event, but it went on to finish in an extremely creditable 14th place. According to the very detailed internal post-race report which was circulated to Healey and BMC after the event, it was almost entirely reliable throughout, recorded a top speed of 119mph (running without a windscreen fitted, merely a small aero-screen ahead of the driver), and covered 2101.4 miles, which equated to a running average of 87.55mph.

During the race, the transmission became stuck in overdrive, and the decision was made that the car should carry on like that. This paid off, though the clutch was on its last legs when the race ended. Some engine misfiring was noted, this eventually being pinpointed as due to a supply problem from the big fuel tank towards the end of a long stint, when it was almost empty.

Back in the UK and once again in Le Mans trim, the car was entered for the Goodwood 9 Hour race, where it was driven by Johnny Lockett and Ken Rudd. Still with Le Mans gearing, this could never be other than a demonstration or reliability run, so the two experienced drivers treated it as such, circulated without flaw for the entire nine hours, and ended up in a very creditable tenth place (from 17 finishers).

Two weeks later Rudd was allowed to run the car in the very picturesque Brighton Speed Trials (where the sprint course was laid out on the straight sea-front promenade), but as this involved no more than taking 31.77 seconds to cover half a mile from a standing start it barely qualifies as a works run!

For the next year or so, this car was used for testing, for some development work and for loans to friends of Healey. For the French Alpine rally of 1954 it was lent to Raymond Flower, a British businessman/entrepreneur usually based in Egypt, though there was no on-event backing for the car. In a typical Alpine and with his 'Over 2600cc' class dominated by much faster Jaguar XK120s, Flower struggled to be competitive and towards end of the event on the Col de Cayolle he put the car off the road, which broke a track rod, making the car barely (but only barely) driveable to the end. His third place in class put him well down towards the bottom of the field. 79 cars had started the event but only 37 made it to the finish in Cannes.

This phase of the car's life came to an end in September 1954 (not 1953, as claimed by other sources) when, loaned to French driver Roger-André Bouchard, for him to compete in the Tour de France, it crashed into a truck on the very last speed section before the end of the event at Nice. Tragically, Bouchard was killed in the impact, and his female co-driver later died in hospital

Eventually, after the wreckage had been released by the French authorities, it was stored at Warwick for a short time. It was later completely re-bodied and refreshed with a 100S body, engine and other details, and was effectively re-born as a 100S, though never raced as such, and was eventually sold to a customer in the USA in November 1955.

Competition Record

1953 Mille Miglia	Bert Hadley/Bertie Mercer	DNF
1953 Le Mans 24 Hour race	Marcel Becquart/Gordon Wilkins	14th Overall
(raced in this event using much of the crashed NOJ 393's sealed and marked equipment)		
1953 Goodwood Nine Hour race	Johnny Lockett/Ken Rudd	10th Overall
1953 Brighton Speed Trials	Ken Rudd	Finished
1954 French Alpine Rally	Raymond Flower/Ernest McMillen	3rd in Class
1954 Tour de France	R-A. Bouchard/Mlle Y Morel	DNF

REGISTRATION NUMBER	ENGINE SIZE	MODEL TYPE
NOJ 392	**2660CC 4-CYL OHV**	**BN1**

NOJ 392 was one of the two 100 BN1s which raced at Le Mans in 1953 (driven by Johnny Lockett and Maurice Gatsonides) where it finished twelfth. Healey then brought the car home, refreshed it, and offered it to the British magazines as a 'standard' road car. Here it is, parked outside The Autocar's *offices in London.*

Compared with NOJ 391 above, NOJ 392 was virtually factory-fresh when it was driven off from Warwick to Brescia and the start of its first event, the Mille Miglia, where it was to be driven by ex-motorcycle racer Johnny Lockett and 'Jock' Reid, who was Roger Menadue's second-in-command in the Healey experimental shop.

As on NOJ 391, the throttle linkage on NOJ 392 failed on the fast run down the east side of Italy, but fortunately Reid was able to cobble up a temporary repair reinforced by Roger Menadue at a 'pit stop' further around the route, but this was in vain as the hard-worked car suffered from clutch failure within an hour or so of the finish of the event.

NOJ 392 was then made ready for Le Mans where, in stark contrast to its sister cars, it completed an almost faultless weekend, driven by Johnny Lockett and Maurice Gatsonides, finishing in a creditable 12th overall. It had completed 2151.7 miles at a running average speed of 89.65 miles.

NOJ 392 wore No. 34 at Le Mans in 1953 and finished 12th overall.

The car was still in such good condition that almost immediately after the race Geoff Healey and his wife Margot took it away for use as holiday transport, where it reputedly covered at least 1500 more troublefree miles.

Then, as already detailed, NOJ 392 was taken back to Warwick, given a spring clean and loaned to both *The Autocar* and *The Motor* for full road tests of what the magazine editors were assured was a perfectly representative and therefore standard road car – which it most assuredly was not.

NOJ 392 then continued to be used as a development and test car – particularly of disc brakes –and it was not used again as a full-blown 'works competition car. Eventually it was retired and used as Roger Menadue's transport for some time.

Johnny Lockett at the wheel of NOJ 392 at Le mans in 1953, when the two team cars ran in almost normal road-car tune.

Competition Record

1953 Mille Miglia	Johnny Lockett/'Jock' Reid	DNF
1953 Le Mans 24 Hour race	Johnny Lockett/Maurice Gatsonides	12th overall

Then road tested by both *The Autocar* and *The Motor*, reputedly as a standard road car.

Looking almost exactly as it was when raced at Le Mans in 1953, NOJ 392 was immaculately restored in later years. However, when the car actually raced, the number plate was carried under the front bumper (though it was in front of the bumper when later subjected to road test by the press). When prepared as the a magazine road test car, it had front and rear overriders fitted.

The cabin and dashboard look remarkably stock, but for race car use the overdrive switch was moved from its normal position on the fascia panel to being clipped to a steering-wheel spoke.

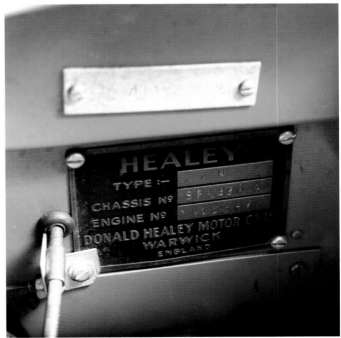

As fitted to NOJ 392 for racing at Le Mans, two 'chassis' plates tell their own story.

The 2660cc engine was specially built, slightly tuned, and test-bed proven by Austin engineers at Longbridge, producing 100bhp at 4500rpm (which compared with the nominal 90bhp at 4,000rpm which was then quoted for all the BN1 road cars). Differences for the race-car engines included the use of Austin Champ-type crank-shafts made of EN40 nitrided steel, slightly different camshaft profiles, double valve springs and a lightened flywheel.

After its racing and road testing career, NOJ 392 then wase used as a development and test car – particularly for disc brakes.

There was plenty of space in the boot of NOJ 392, the spare wheel being carefully mounted above the line of the rear axle.

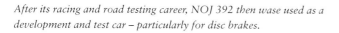

REGISTRATION NUMBER	ENGINE SIZE	MODEL TYPE
NOJ 393	**2660CC 4-CYL OHV**	**BN1/100S (1954-55)**

As has already been made clear in the summary of NOJ 391's race car career, NOJ 393 was the third of the three Special Test Car race cars, built up unhurriedly in the spring of 1953 to the same 100bhp/4-speed specification as NOJ 391 and NOJ 392, then driven to France to take part in the Le Mans 24 Hour race. At this point it was much the freshest of the three cars, for both of the others had already competed in the Mille Miglia.

What followed was both farcical and heart-warming, as Geoff Healey himself has noted: "Unfortunately, when one of our drivers, Gordon Wilkins of *Autocar* was driving one of the cars back [to the team hotel] after lunch, he was struck by a semi-comatose French lorry driver who proceeded out of a side road without any warning." The damage was considerable, so Healey elected to run the spare car NOJ 391 in its place, but the race organisers vetoed this proposal. Accordingly: "All the appropriate parts had to be transferred to NOJ 391. This rebuilding work was carried out by Roger, myself, and whichever of the mechanics…"

The real NOJ 393, therefore, was not raced in 1953, and after a lengthy sojourn as Healey's development car on the four-wheel Dunlop disc brake programme it was updated to become one of the two 100S prototypes. According to the records which still exist, it then ran at Sebring in 1954 with no registration plates and with Dunlop centre-lock disc wheels, but because in later years Geoff Healey could not recall exactly which car was used in that race one cannot be categorical about that.

Whatever, the result achieved in the Sebring 12 Hour race of 1954 was a real triumph, for against a stellar cast of full-house racing two-seaters, including Ferraris, Lancias, Cunninghams and Aston Martins, Lance Macklin and George Huntoon, an experienced American sports car racer, brought the gallant car home in third place, beaten only by a remarkable 1.5-litre Osca driven by Stirling Moss and Bill Lloyd and the single surviving 3.3-litre Lancia.

For Austin-Healey this was an outstanding performance, not only because the car was so demonstrably descended from a series-production sports car but also because it was clearly heavier and less accelerative than most of its rivals. Even so, by starting at a pace which they reckoned they could maintain throughout the 12 hours on this airfield circuit in Florida, Austin-Healey were always up among the leaders, and as the fastest cars gradually fell out they found themselves running in fourth place at half distance. Soon one of the leading Lancias retired with a broken oil pipe which ruined the engine, and Macklin and Huntoon found themselves third. For a time they

NOJ 393 is reversed into one of the scrutineering bays at Le Mans in 1955.

were even hoping to annex second place, but in the closing minutes the engine broke a rocker arm and was reduced to three cylinders, and the car had to ease back, finally finishing third at a running average of 70.5mph. This success gave the company a good excuse for naming the production run which was to follow – those 50-off cars being named '100S' where 'S' stood for 'Sebring'.

After a considerably lay-off, while other cars in the works fleet were raced, NOJ 393 was one of the two cars which travelled to Mexico to take part in the Panamericana Road Race of September 1954. Along with its sister car OON 439 it was flown to Cherbourg, shipped on to the Queen Mary for New York, then transferred to a Mexican Coast Lines ship.

The race started from Tuxtla Gutierrez and took the form of five long public road sections on Mexican highways totalling 1910 miles before ending at Ciudad Juartez, there being night halts in between the stages. After such a long and in its own way exhausting trek just to get the car to the start point, it must have been frustrating beyond belief to find that soon after the start the engine began to misfire, and even before the end of the first day it suffered complete ignition failure and was stranded in the wilderness. The fault was a minor one in the ignition circuit– and Healey made very sure that it would never occur again.

Donald Healey, however, was never likely to miss the chance of more motor racing and to have a good time as well, so instead of the car being taken back direct to the UK it was diverted to Nassau in the Bahamas for the Speed Week, which was more of an excuse for a series of parties with a motor race or two thrown in than the other way round. Lance Macklin was delighted to take part in 'work' of this kind, finishing sixth in the 100 Mile Bahamas Cup event, and 25th in the 200-mile Nassau Trophy event. The car finally made it home to Warwick by the end of1954.

The truly tragic end to this car's front-line sporting career

NOJ 393 in unrestored condition.

The sad remains of NOJ 393 shortly after the accident. It was impounded by the French authorities and did not get back to Warwick for many months.

then came in June 1955, when it was entered for Le Mans with Lance Macklin and Les Leston as drivers. Beautifully prepared, with an engine developing 140bhp and the ability to lap the French circuit at more than 100mph, it settled down to circulate with what looked like great reliability.

This, though, was a race which had been forecast to be a head-to-head match between three works Jaguar D-Types and three works Mercedes-Benz 300SLRs – both types being considerably faster than the 100S. Unhappily, after only two-and-a-half hours of flat-out racing, at a moment where Mike Hawthorn (D-Type) and Pierre Levegh (300SLR) were about to pass the crowded pit area and Macklin's 100S at the same time, Hawthorn suddenly elected to make for his pit, Macklin flinched to get out of his way, and Levegh's 300SLR struck the 100S in its rear quarter and was catapulted into the grandstand, where it instantly caught fire and utter carnage ensued.

The 100S ended up against the pit wall and was severely damaged in the crash, which resulted in it being virtually destroyed around the rear, but miraculously Macklin was quite unharmed. The car itself was virtually written off but amazingly it was eventually rebuilt back in Warwick and sold off.

This is not the place to begin to ascribe blame for the accident, but one should note that the wreckage was impounded by the French police for well over a year before being repatriated to the UK, and both Lance Macklin and Healey themselves were both totally exonerated from any involvement in the horrifying events.

It goes without saying that this car was never again raced by Healey.

Competition Record

1953 Le Mans 24 Hour race   DNS
The car was due to be driven by Marcel Becquart and Gordon Wilkins but was involved in an accident on the open road during the post-scrutineering build-up, its important components (and theoretically its identity) then being transferred to NOJ 391 for the race

1954 Sebring 12 Hour	Lance Macklin/George Huntoon	3rd Overall
1954 Carrera PanAmericana Road Race	Lance Macklin	DNF
1954 Bahamas Speed Week, Nassau	Lance Macklin	6th Overall
1955 Le Mans 24 Hour race	Lance Macklin/Les Leston	DNF

REGISTRATION NUMBER	ENGINE SIZE	MODEL TYPE
OON 439	**2660CC 4-CYL OHV**	**100S (PROTOTYPE)**

During the winter/spring of 1953/54, Healey not only converted two of the surviving Special Test Cars to prototype 100S specification (NOJ 391 and NOJ 393), but also built three new works STCs which were true prototypes of the forthcoming 100S product line. All three of these cars were intended for use in a full works motorsport programme but, as already noted, this strategy was rather blown off course by Donald Healey's growing distaste for the way that some rivals were beginning to treat the regulations, and by his seemingly abrupt decision to withdraw the team cars from the Le Mans 24 Hour race.

Even so, they started their season with a full three-car entry in the Mille Miglia, one of Healey's favourite events. OON 439, the first of the new-for-1954 race cars, was allocated to a team favourite, Tommy Wisdom, who took along as his co-driver Mortimer Morris-Goodall, recently appointed Healey's 'on-event' team manager, a position which proved to be short-lived.

All three cars prepared for the 1954 Mille Miglia (OON 440 and OON 441 were the other two) had been prepared to take part as Grand Touring cars and had already been homologated accordingly, which meant that they arrived at the event complete with normal 100-type windscreens, Universal Laminates hardtops and sliding screens in the doors. This was all very well except that the scrutineers refused to approve them in this class and in this condition. One excuse apparently made was that a car which had recently performed so well in the Sebring 12 hours and had proved to be a match for Italian racing sports cars like the 3.3-litre Lancias would have to run in that category in Italy! Fortunately Healey had brought along the aero screens which might otherwise have been used and rapidly made a pre-event change.

Sadly the Mille Miglia outing for this car was short-lived, for the engine broke a valve spring, which meant that retirement was inevitable.

Its next outing came months later, when it made the long trek across the Atlantic and down the eastern seaboard of the USA, to contest the Mexican Panamericana road race. Details of this event and of the efforts Healey had to make to get this car and NOJ 393 there at all have already been noted. For this event Healey hired the rising US race driver Carroll Shelby (this was years before he invented the AC Cobra), who had already become involved in the Austin-Healey record runs on the Bonneville Salt Flats. His co-driver/riding mechanic was Roy Jackson-Moore.

Shelby, a great fan of this race, started very well and after the first of the five days had been completed he was already

in fourth place overall, but soon after he left Oaxaca on the second morning he hurtled round a corner to find rocks strategically placed in the middle of the road "that spectators had placed strategically to 'liven up' the sport", as Geoff Healey later wrote. Unable to avoid the rocks, Shelby's car hit them and plunged off the road. Shelby himself was injured in the crash (but recovered soon afterwards), while the car had to be trucked back to civilisation.

OON 439 was not seen again in public for some months while it received a rebuild, and then, as something of an afterthought, it was prepared for Donald Healey to drive in the 1955 Mille Miglia. This was to be one of his very last appearances in a competition, and he would be accompanied by Jim Cashmore, one of his most trusted race car mechanics. In truth Healey was not expecting to match the speeds that he

OON 439 was one of the handful of works 100S cars prepared at Warwick, and was the only one of this group which tackled racing and rallying.

hoped that his team-mate Lance Macklin could set in OON 441, but he was really acting as 'spares' on the hoof' to help Macklin if trouble struck his car.

In the Mille Miglia OON 439 ran once again with the full 100-type windscreen in place. Although it completed the 1000 miles there was a delay after DMH had apparently grounded the car's sump on a railway crossing even before the start of the event, which meant that co-driver Cashmore had to apply some 'magic tape' to seal the crack, and several extra stops were needed on the event while more oil was poured into the engine. The result was that although the car completed the course the organisers did not list it as it was deemed to be outside their time limits.

Surprisingly, after the Healey Motor Company's official running down of 100S racing activities, Marcus Chambers's newly opened works BMC Competitions department was persuaded to run OON 439 in a rally, the four-day/four-night Liège-Rome-Liège marathon of August 1955. Apparently it was the new team captain John Gott's idea in the first place, though he was not to drive the car himself in that event.

The car was road-equipped as far as was reasonably possible – it was apparently the only one of the 1955 team cars ever to be fitted out with a proper windscreen, side-screens and a soft-top; thus equipped Donald Healey had used it in the Mille Miglia earlier in the year.

It was much the most powerful rally car yet to be sampled at Abingdon. Hopes were high, especially as the team had persuaded Peter Reece and Dennis Scott to take part. Both of them were experienced rally drivers, mostly when using works Ford Zephyrs. But the outing was not a success. Only hours after the evening start from Liège, near Idar Oberstein in Germany (just to the east of Luxembourg, and north of the Saar territory) that the car crashed and took no further part in proceedings. To quote Marcus Chambers from his autobiography *Works Wonders*, "Dennis Scott had crashed the Healey at a corner on the way out of [Idar Oberstein] – he apparently went straight on instead of turning to the right, and landed in a wood. Dennis and Peter abandoned the car to seek help and on returning found that both the clocks and the spare wheel had been stolen. They returned rather sheepishly to Spa the next day".

Carroll Shelby completing the first of five days in the Pan-Americana Road Race of 1954. At this stage he was running in fourth place overall.

Competition Record

1954 Mille Miglia	Tom Wisdom/Mortimer Morris-Goodall	DNF
1954 Panamericana Road Race	Carroll Shelby/Roy Jackson-Moore	DNF
1955 Mille Miglia	Donald Healey/Jim Cashmore	DNF
and finally, as a rally car:		
1955 Liège-Rome-Liège	Peter Reece	DNF

REGISTRATION NUMBER	ENGINE SIZE	MODEL TYPE
OON 440	**2660CC 4-CYL OHV**	**100S**

This, the second of the new-for-1954 100S prototypes, was completed in time to be entered for the 1954 Mille Miglia, where it ran in the same mechanical specification as OOM 439 and OON 441. For reasons never fully spelt out the car was driven by the Monégasque racing driver Louis Chiron, who was 53 when he took up this drive and had been racing at Grand Prix level since the end of the 1920s. His most recent success had been winning the Monte Carlo rally in1954, driving a Lancia Aurelia GT.

Chiron's drive in OON 440 was short, if not sweet, for between Ravenna and Pescara, only three to four hours after the start, on the high-speed roads down the eastern flank of Italy, the car began to suffer a hydraulic leak affecting the rear brakes and he was obliged to retire.

Although the car was still relatively fresh, Austin-Healey's pre-event withdrawal from the Le Mans 24 Hour race which was to follow (already discussed in the lead-in to the Chapter) meant that it did not appear again during the rest of 1954, for it was its two sister cars – OON 439 and OON 441 – which were sent off to tackle the Carrera Panamericana later in the year. Its next outing was not to be until the Mille Miglia of 1955.

George Abecassis had made himself available to the company at a late stage to drive, but there is considerable confusion as to which car was actually used in the event. According to the 'official' record, it was OON 440, though Geoff Healey wrote in his book The Healey Story, written in 1994: "At the last minute George Abecassis declared that he was free to join us and so the old nail, SPL224/B [the project number for the original Le Mans100, NOJ 391], was fitted with the plates of OON 440 for him to drive."

NOJ 391, however, had been badly damaged in a crash in the 1954 Tour de France (see the entry for NOJ 391) and would eventually be reborn as a 'new' 100S and sold off to a private owner in the USA in 1955. Originally NOJ 391 was a green car, whereas the Mille Miglia car was red, so what are we to conclude? The author proposes to treat the 1955 Mille Miglia entry as being the genuine OON 440, and let the pedants argue about the rest.

For the 1955 Mille Miglia, therefore, the car started with George Abecassis driving, solo incidentally, and his run proved to be a real triumph, for even though he ran out of fuel after failing to stop at a scheduled refuelling point, he finished a rousing eleventh overall, the best place ever achieved by a 100S on the Mille Miglia. This achievement, however, was quite overlooked in after-event analyses of it, for they were dominated by all the headlines Stirling Moss made by winning in the Mercedes-Benz 300SLR. Moss, incidentally, completed the route in 10hr 8min, whereas the gallant Abecassis took 12hr 22min.

After a long lay-off, the car was prepared for the 1956 Sebring 12 Hour race, where Roy Jackson-Moore was paired with Forbes Robinson. Unhappily it was one of the 'new-for-1956' features – the tubular exhaust manifold – that let the side down, for after eight hours of flat-out motoring the manifold broke. Escaping hot exhaust gases damaged the nearby starter motor and soon forced retirement. The same failure befell OON 441.

Competition Record

1954 Mille Miglia	Louis Chiron	DNF
1955 Mille Miglia	George Abecassis	1st in Class, 11th overall
1956 Sebring 12 Hour race	Roy Jackson-Moore/Forbes Robinson	DNF

REGISTRATION NUMBER	ENGINE SIZE	MODEL TYPE
OON 441	**2660CC 4-CYL OHV**	**100S**

Here was the third of the three 100S prototypes (OON 439, OON 440 and OON 441) that were built to take part in the major 1954 and (as it transpired) 1955 sports car races. It became Lance Macklin's favourite car and seemed to have most of the stories to tell.

Like its sister cars it turned up at the start of the 1954 Mille Miglia ready to run as a 'fully-equipped' road-going car, complete with full-width 100-type windscreen, a hardtop and sliding sidescreens but (as explained in the OON 439 section), the scrutineers obliged the team to re-equip (or de-equip!) the cars – which meant that the car had to run in stripped down state with a low-line plastic windscreen and no other weather protection.

Macklin elected to drive without a co-pilot and soon settled to drive at his own pace, which was nevertheless faster than almost every other British entrant. By half distance there was some clutch trouble, but this was soon sorted out at the Austin-Healey 'pit-stop' in Rome. Picking up place after place in the second half of the event, which involved tackling the major passes between Rome and Brescia, he climbed from 35th place to 31st, then – before the finish – to 23rd overall.

If this does not sound outstanding, please note that there had been 380 starters in this stupendous motor race, and that in the last 83 miles OON 441 averaged 89mph. In the end, the Austin-Healey finished fifth in the unlimited class, one which contained the winning Lancia and three V12 Ferraris.

Soon after this Austin-Healey officially withdrew (temporarily, thank goodness) from motor racing, though this did not deter Macklin from driving OON 441 again in the future. The next most outstanding performance came in March 1955 when Healey sent him and Stirling Moss to contest the Sebring 12 Hour race in Florida. This event had been won outright by Moss in 1954 so his appearance in a 100S in 1955 was received with real interest.

No fewer than eight Austin-Healeys were entered in this race, but there was never any doubt that the Moss/Macklin entry was much the most competitive. In the early hours Moss was at the wheel and was always on or close to the leader board. By half distance, the car was approaching sixth place overall, which was where it would stay for the rest of this gruelling race. Sixth overall, by the way, meant that it was only headed by the race winners Mike Hawthorn and Phil Walters in a Cunningham-entered Jaguar D-Type, two 3-litre Ferraris, and two 3-litre Maseratis.

Soon after the Sebring outing the car was returned to the UK, where Macklin then drove it in the British Empire Trophy race held at Oulton Park. However, as this was a race for out-and-out sports racing cars, including Jaguar D-Types, Aston Martin DB3Ss and Lister-Bristols, he had no chance of a high rating and finished in 14th place.

The Mille Miglia, held only weeks later, was a much more serious affair in which Healey had entered all three of the OON cars, and OON 441 was allocated at his request to Lance Macklin. Unfortunately it was not to be his weekend for although he started a spirited battle with Ron Flockhart (in the privately owned/privately entered 100S, OJW 303) it all went wrong after about two hours when Macklin misjudged his approach to one corner in a town, slid off, and ended up perched atop the straw bales. Once back on the road he resumed his battle with Flockhart, which lasted for more than half-an-hour before Flockhart, leading into another tortuous section, put the privately-entered 100S off, flew over a bridge, and dropped into a river. Macklin stopped to help his friend and rival, losing a lot of time before he could carry on, then lost more time when the throttle linkage came adrift. This required him to use the celebrated ignition key on-off trick to control the engine and caused even more delays, such that he ended up well down the field.

Macklin went on to use this car, sometimes as a quasi-private entry, in British events during the summer. Then, during the winter, it was refreshed and updated for Lance and the up-and-coming British driver Archie Scott-Brown to drive in the 1956 Sebring 12 Hour race. Unhappily the car suffered the same mechanical breakdown – a broken exhaust manifold – as OON 440 and had to be withdrawn, which brought its works career to a close.

Competition Record

1954 Mille Miglia	Lance Macklin	5th in Class
1955 Sebring 12 Hour	Stirling Moss/Lance Macklin	6th overall
1955 Empire Trophy Race, UK	Lance Macklin	14th overall
1955 Mille Miglia	Lance Macklin	2nd in Class
1955 Sports Car Race, Silverstone	Lance Macklin	17th overall
1955 Daily Herald Trophy, Oulton Park	Lance Macklin	12th overall
1956 Sebring 12 Hour	Lance Macklin/Archie Scott-Brown	DNF

CHAPTER 6:
THE RECORD CARS AT BONNEVILLE SALT FLATS AND MONTLHÉRY

Even the 200+mph streamliner needed fuel from time to time. This was an early proving run at the MIRA test track in Warwickshire.

Donald and Geoff Healey were obviously the guiding lights behind the competition programme from 1953 to 1956, but they needed support to make it happen. With the late Geoff Healey's approval (he once told me, 'I'd rather you quoted my words than made mistakes of your own') I quote him here: "The original suggestion that we should go after speed records came from Captain G.E.T. Eyston, several times holder of the World Land Speed Record, and a director of C.C. Wakefield, the manufacturers of Castrol oil. George, DMH and Len Lord discussed and agreed on a record breaking programme as an expansion of

the competition work already in hand".

The aim was to use progressively improved and modified versions of the new 100 BN1 model, and after a great deal of discussion in which George Eyston was a keystone, Healey decided to concentrate its efforts on the legendary Bonneville Salt Flats in Utah, which might have been remote from the UK – several thousands of miles away, in fact, well on the way across the USA towards San Francisco – but which to many car-buying speed-freaks of the day were at the very centre of the universe. With Eyston lending his enormous experience and his influence with the local dignitaries, the Healeys could get on with the engineering and operation of the cars.

They were interested in taking new records in FIA International Class D (2001-3000 cc), whether as short sprints or in endurance motoring, which would stretch all the way up to 24 hours if the cars would stand it. The Salt Flats were ideal for this sort of ambition, as there was not only the opportunity to go flat out for several miles in one direction, but there was also a regularly used ten-mile circular track for the endurance work. It also helped that George Eyston persuaded BMC to get MG back into the groove, so that

on two occasions – 1954 and 1956 – they arranged joint assaults, and could use the same team of AAA (American Automobile Association) officials as time keepers and circuit verification authorities.

As the following details will show, works Austin-Healeys appeared on the Flats in 1953, 1954 and 1956 before common sense suggested that there was no further point in breaking their own records, so the motorsport emphasis turned further towards circuit racing and (through BMC's own Competition Department) international rallying instead.

Chassis Number	Engine Size	Model Type
SPL 227B (NOT REGISTERED)	2660CC 4-CYL OHV	100 BN1

The first car to go to the Bonneville Salt Flats in search of new speed and endurance records was chassis number SPL 227B, the fourth of the 1953 Special Test Cars (and therefore a sister to NOJ 391, NOJ 392 and NOJ 393). All those cars occasionally swapped number plates – at least one publicity picture (shown in *The Autocar* on 18 September 1953) shows NOJ 391 with right-hand-drive and running with extra driving lamps, captioned "Mr Donald Healey at speed … at Bonneville, USA," which was certainly not the case.

Like the other cars, this fourth machine was built a few weeks before genuine series production of BN1s had begun, so with the aid of Jensen Motors it had an especially lightweight structure, whose body contained many BB3 (Birmabright) aluminium panels.

Visually this record car looked almost standard, except that it had left-hand-drive, had its standard windscreen removed and replaced by an aeroscreen, and featured a small streamlined headrest behind the driver's head. A light alloy tonneau cover was fitted above what would have been the passenger seat. To ensure that the engine would not overheat in the sometimes startlingly hot temperatures of Utah in September, the outer sections of the front grille were removed. At the same time a pair of cooling ducts (for the engine bay and, not least, to blow ambient air directly to the driver's feet and lower body) were fitted, with their intakes on each side of the truncated grille. As originally tested in the UK it had wheel spats covering the rear wheel arches but these were abandoned before the actual record runs began.

Because the regulations covering such runs were relatively flexible, Healey made several important mechanical modifications. The engine was probably the very first example of what would become the Weslake-inspired 100S power unit, featuring an entirely new cylinder head; even then it was quoted as producing 131.5bhp at 4750rpm as against the standard engine's 90bhp. To keep it well supplied with fuel and to make sure that the car would need to stop only at three-

hour intervals, it was fitted with a massive 25-gallon fuel tank. What was known as the four-speed 'taxi' gearbox, as also used on the works Le Mans cars (described in Chapter 5), with Laycock overdrive, was employed, allied to a 3.65:1 final drive ratio, while Dunlop provided special 16in tyres and centre-lock spoked wheels.

Before any endurance running was attempted Donald Healey went out to see what the car's straight-line speed actually was, finally leaving it at 142.64mph for the flying mile. Five days later, and using the accurately laid out ten-mile circular track, a team of drivers set out to keep the car running for, they hoped, 24 hours. All was well at first. The car settled down to run at around 125mph and broke many records – then a connecting rod broke and wrecked the engine. Incidentally, in the post-event PR message put out to the specialist media, BMC claimed, "Rain and storms caused the run to be abandoned after 18 hours." This was believed, with sympathy at the time, but when Geoff Healey came to write his acclaimed books in the 1970s the real story emerged.

The same car returned to the Salt Flats in 1954 with an improved 100S type of engine which produced 141bhp when bench-tested at Longbridge before fitment to the car. The intention was to use it solely on the ten-mile circular track, and to run for up to 24 hours with a change of drivers every time it had to return to base for refuelling.

This attempt was totally successful, and apart from a pre-planned tyre/wheel change after 12 hours there was nothing but refuelling, driver changes and routine maintenance to be done. The car seemed to be absolutely as healthy at the end of 24 hours as at the beginning. It had averaged 132.23mph, which means that 3173.5 miles had been covered,

If the runs had not been carried out on the super-corrosive surface of hardened salt in Utah, the car would no doubt have been preserved for later exhibition and demonstration, but it was returned to Warwick and put into store. Two years later in 1956 it was revived for a final flourish at Bonneville (see below).

Competition Record

1953 record runs, Utah	Donald Healey	142.64mph straight line
1953 endurance runs, Utah	Donald Healey/George Eyston/	Up to 127.00mph for 17 hours
	Bill Spear/John Gordon Benett	
1954 endurance runs, Utah	Donald Healey/George Eyston/	132.23mph for 24 hours
	Carroll Shelby/Mortimer Morris-Goodall/	
	Roy Jackson-Moore	

REGISTRATION NUMBER	ENGINE SIZE	MODEL TYPE
NOT REGISTERED	**2660cc 4-cyl OHV**	**100 BN1**

When Healey set out to break International records in 1953 with the very special car SPL 227B (described above), they also arranged to take two totally standard production models from the existing stock of BN1s already in the USA, and use them to set a series of American stock-car records. Apart from careful preparation at the Salt Flats venue and the use of 15in wheels and special tyres run at no less than 50psi, these cars were totally standard.

During Healey's stay in Utah in September 1953 a whole team of drivers – Donald Healey, George Eyston, Bill Spear, Jackie Cooper (a Hollywood-based actor), Roy Jackson-Moore, Mortimer Morris-Goodall and John Gordon Benett – all took turns at the wheel on the ten-mile circular track. The car circulated reliably for almost 30 hours, by which time it had broken a whole raft of records up to distances of 5000 kilometres/3100 miles, almost all of them with recorded speeds between 104 and 105mph. It was a remarkable performance by a machine which counts as a works car but was as near to standard as could be arranged.

The 'stock car' – chosen from a stock pool to be absolutely standard – set some astonishing long distance endurance records at Bonneville in September 1953, which incuded a 30-hour stretch at 103.93mph.

The 1953 'Endurance car' which set a hatful of long-distance records at the Bonneville Salt Flats – up to 123.75mph and up to 15 Hours.

Competition Record

1953 record runs, Utah	Donald Healey/George Eyston/Bill Spear/	Up to 105mph over 5000km
	Jackie Cooper/Roy Jackson-Moore/	
	Mortimer Morris-Goodall/John Gordon Benett	

CHASSIS NUMBER	ENGINE SIZE	MODEL TYPE
SPL 261B (NOT REGISTERED)	**2660CC 4-CYL/2639CC 6-CYL**	**MODIFIED 100 BN1**

This was the supercharged 'sprint' car, built and briefly used in 1954. The basis of the standard car is still clear – but for 1956 much wind-tunnel work by BMC boffins produced an improved but less smart version of the same car. Behind the car are (Left to Right) Eric Vale, Roy Jackson-Moore, 'Mort' Morris-Goodall, Donald Healey, Louis Michelin.

As completed at Warwick in August 1954, this was the 'streamliner' in which Donald Healey aimed to beat the 200mph mark.

After the successful visit to the Salt Flats in 1953 with the BN1 SPL 227B the resourceful development team at Warwick, led so exuberantly by Geoff Healey, not only decided to do even better while using that same car but also evolved a very different contender. Carrying the chassis number SPL 261B, this new Special Test Car was sent to the USA. It was a specially developed and startlingly styled streamliner, still with the four-cylinder 100S-type engine, though now supercharged and with 224bhp at its disposal.

The car was based on the standard BN1/BN2 type of chassis, with left-hand steering. Gerry Coker had worked on the exterior style in a successful effort to reduce aerodynamic drag; the result was also startlingly good looking Although the central section of the body was clearly the same as the road car, both front and rear extremities were longer, there was a plastic bubble over the driving seat, with no provision for a passenger alongside, and there was a large stabilising fin behind the bubble. Almost all of the body shell was in light alloy, and the aerodynamic qualities of the radical new shape were assessed in the Armstrong Whitworth wind tunnel in Coventry.

All the work on the 2660cc engine was carried out at BMC's Longbridge plant, though with supervision from Healey at Warwick. The compression ratio was reduced from standard to make allowance for the use of a Shorrock supercharger, and the engine was finally released for fitting with a rating of 224bhp at 4500rpm. No existing BMC gearbox could cope with this sort of power output, so it was backed by a five-speed David Brown transmission (of DB3/DB3S type), and rear axle being of the normal Austin-Healey 100/100S variety but with a very high final drive ratio of 2.47:1.

In fairness it must be admitted that this streamlined car had a troubled time at Bonneville in 1954, all of it connected with the engine and its fuel mixture settings. Finally, however, DMH achieved a two-way average speed of 192.62mph for the flying mile. On the following day Carroll Shelby drove the car for one hour on the ten-mile circular track, this time averaging 157.92mph. Honour was satisfied, and the car returned to Warwick in triumph.

Two years later in 1956 Austin-Healey secured BMC's backing to revisit Bonneville, this time using the about-to-be-launched six-cylinder C-Series engine, and with visual and aerodynamic changes made to the 1954 car. These attempts were made before the launch of the BN4 so they were based on the existing (and about to become obsolete) BN1/BN2 structure. The rare pictures reproduced here show how effective the changes made to the 1954 shape were, and what excellent and painstaking detail work went into them.

In the winter of 1955/56 much of the team's effort had gone into development of what they christened the 'sprint' car, which remained faithful to the style and packaging of the 1954 car (which had been stored for a time, and at one time might have been permanently dismantled) as the basis of its shape. This time around, though, the early 100S-type engine of the 1954 example was discarded in favour of a modified version of the brand-new six-cylinder BMC C-Series power unit (which would soon power every new 100-Six and 3000), and there were a number of detail aerodynamic changes.

It's worth recalling that although the original 1954 car was based on a standard left-hand-drive Austin-Healey 100 BN1/BN2 chassis and running gear, for 1956 it was once again totally re-shaped to produce as wind-cheating a profile as possible. Indeed, compared with the original, the 1956 version of this 'sprint' car was demonstrably much modified, making it even more difficult to recognise it as a production-car-based machine. In particular, the outer shell now looked more completely slab-sided than the 1954 car had done (on which the standard car's 'styling crease' linking front and rear wheel arches had been present), while both the nose and the tail were considerably lengthened and more sharp-pointed than before.

Due to its high-speed exposure to salt-blasting at Bonneville, the 1954 car became as badly corroded as the 1953 record car had been and was eventually scrapped completely (Geoff

Healey confirms this in his books), so an all-new right-hand-drive body was built up for 1956. Visually, the overall style of new machine was clearly developed from the 1954 example, of which scale models had originally been tested in the Armstrong-Whitworth wind tunnel. This time it was BMC's (formerly Austin's) tunnel at Longbridge that was to be used, and Austin's own Dr John Weaving was closely involved. However, this can only have been of questionable merit, as one-time BMC employees have recently confirmed that the BMC tunnel was strictly of the 'low-speed' variety. Even so, Dr Weaving made some minor changes to the basic design, reducing its frontal area to reduce drag, while he also insisted that there should no longer be a tail fin as he was convinced, and later proved right, that the finalised car would be directionally stable without needing one. Instead the cockpit was enclosed in a plexiglass 'bubble' and backed by a lengthened fairing. It was noticeable, too, that the side of the car was reshaped, to eliminate the styling crease, and to shave away the bulge up and over the rear wheels.

Considering that this was a new design of engine, the work carried out by the engineering team was courageous, to say the least, especially as space was at a premium, particularly because the latest car's bonnet line was so low. The engine was supercharged, and along with other tuning carried out at Morris Engines in Coventry it was finally rated at 292bhp at 5090rpm. In spite of Dr Weaving's work to provide as low-drag a body shape as possible, the exhaust stacks all pointed upwards and out into the fresh air ahead of the cockpit. If more time had been available no doubt a fairing would have been added around them.

The record runs at Utah on the 13-mile straight course,

As prepared for record runs in 1956, the streamliner was fitted with a supercharged C-Series engine, in which the six exhaust stubs protruded out of the bodywork.

With Geoff Healey at the wheel, the 1956 streamliner being readied for high-speed trials at RAF Gaydon in Warwickshire.

The 1956 streamliner is pushed from the workshops in Longbridge after wind-tunnel testing.

across the salt were originally started on 9 August 1956, as ever with Donald Healey at the wheel of the car, but there was immediate disappointment when the drive chain to the supercharger failed, the engine suffered major damage, and a rebuild was needed. On the other hand the standard Austin back axle (which was being asked to cope with 292bhp, don't

After Longbridge's aerodynamic experts had made their recommendations, the 1956 record car proved it could exceed 200mph.

forget) survived, if only because full-throttle acceleration was not used when starting the high-geared car from rest.

A painstaking rebuild of the engine involving a complete stripdown and re-work of the pistons (no spares were available at first, and the Morris Engines workshop was thousands of miles away) led to a re-run on 21 August. This time DMH started out quite determined to top 200mph, but as Geoff Healey notes in Austin-Healey, "Before the measured mile had been covered on the return, the familiar bang was heard. This time DMH coasted the car for as long as possible".

Amazingly, the time keepers confirmed that the car had recorded 203.76mph on that run. Nothing daunted, DMH realised that the engine was not totally destroyed and completed the return run at a slightly slower speed. The final two-way average, as confirmed by the United States Auto Club, was 203.11mph, which would have been considerably higher if the engine had stayed in one piece.

And after that? Very little, it seems: the two 1956 record cars, Endurance and Sprint, were shipped back across the Atlantic, brought home, spent some time being admired in public, and were found to be so badly afflicted by salt corrosion that they were unceremoniously scrapped. Which means, I guess, that if anyone pops up today claiming to have discovered the remains of either car, they will not be telling the whole and unvarnished truth.

Competition Record

1954 Bonneville Salt Flats, speed achievements	Donald Healey	192.62mph
	Carroll Shelby	157.92mph for one hour
1956 Bonneville Salt Flats, speed achievements	Donald Healey	203.11mph

REGISTRATION NUMBER	ENGINE SIZE	MODEL TYPE
NOT REGISTERED	**2639CC 6-CYL OHV**	**HYBRID BN1/BN4 PROTOTPYE**

For its final long-distance record attempt, at up to six hours, in 1956 Healey prepared a specially modified car which was still recognisably based on the shape of the production car, but had shapely front and rear body modifications styled by Gerry Coker. As explained by Geoff Healey many years later, "For the six-hour car we took the 1953/54 endurance car, SPL 227B, and extended the nose and tail sections beyond the wheel centres. The wheelbase remained unchanged from the original four-cylinder figure of 90 inches."

Not only was the long-nose/long-tail car more aero-dynamically efficient than the standard road car but it was pretty too, with a droop-snoot nose incorporating a small radiator intake to which had Coker added a cut-out of the

forthcoming 100-Six 'wavy' radiator grille. Under the skin there was right-hand steering, a 100S rear axle and gearbox, while the car also used Dunlop centre-lock disc wheels of 100S type.

The novelty, however, was the use of a prototype version of the big 2639cc C-Series engine which was about the be launched in the 100 Six BN4. For this particular car, however, Eddie Maher and Morris Engines had worked wonders on the rather disappointing lump which was to power the road cars. Not only did it use a six-port version of the cylinder head which would not appear in public until the late autumn of 1957, but it was built up like any long-distance race or rally engine would be, having a compression ratio of 10.2:1,

This was the long-nose/long-tail derivative of the 100, as used for 'endurance' runs at Utah in 1954. The original '200mph' streamliner is in the background.

For 1956, further wind-tunnel work was carried out on the long-nose/long-tail 'endurance car' – though the faired-in cockpit was not used.

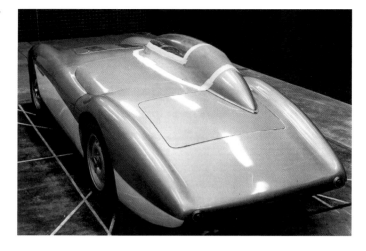

This long-nose/long-tail 'endurance car' was taken to the Utah Salt Flats in 1956 to attack endurance speed records at up to 6 hours. Based on the 1953/1954 car, it had a highly-tuned six-port prototype C-Series engine, and lapped for hour after hour at more than 150mph.

special camshaft profiles and triple dual-choke Weber 40 DCO3 carburettors – all intended to run on a very special fuel mix of ⅓ methanol, ⅓ benzole and ⅓ petrol. All this helped to produce 156bhp at 5500rpm and would provide much experience for future derivatives of thte road cars in homologated form.

On 14 August 1956, the car's first run in anger, Carroll Shelby had no sooner settled in to a lengthy stint than the engine faltered and was found to have a faulty valve-to-head seal. Other faults were discovered in the casting, and although a complete and careful rebuild was immediately tackled, it was thought that this endurance engine was not likely to last indefinitely.

Two days later, on 16 August, and very early in the day so as to take advantage of cool air for a time, the second run was made, first with Carroll Shelby at the wheel and, after the first pit stop (at 500 miles), with Roy Jackson-Moore taking over. The car settled down to lap consistently at 150mph and more until, after some two hours at the wheel, Jackson-Moore detected an overheating engine, stopped for a quick splash and dash of cooling water and 'Wonderweld', after which the run continued with every member of the crew – drivers, technicians, publicists and, not least, the Healey management – keeping their fingers firmly crossed.

In fact the car carried on, lapping at 140mph and more for some time, until the six-hour record was achieved, but soon after this the cylinder head gasket failed, the car coasted to a halt, and no further progress was made. There was no question, however, that big steps had been made in just two years, for in 1954 the 'endurance' car had achieved 133.21mph, while in 1956 it had achieved 146.07mph.

After this event, and a starring appearance on the Austin-Healey stand at the Earls Court Motor Show in October 1956, a period of storage followed. Subsequent examination then showed that salt corrosion had taken hold of a number of vital structural panels, which led to a decision to strip the car of any remaining useful parts and then scrap what remained. No trace now remains of this car.

Competition Record		
1954 Bonneville Salt Flats	Carroll Shelby/Roy Jackson-Moore	Up to 153.58mph for six hours

REGISTRATION NUMBER	ENGINE SIZE	MODEL TYPE
VOK 490	**2639CC 6-CYL OHV**	**100-SIX BN4**

Here was a works car which qualifies as a one-off wonder specifically prepared to attack a series of long-distance/endurance records. It achieved its purpose and thereafter was not used again by BMC. Its purpose was to run at the Montlhéry banked circuit, near Paris, for up to seven days, the aim being to beat a 100mph running average at a series of intermediate points and at setting several International Class D (2-3-litre) records which appeared to be ripe for the taking.

Inspired by the Cambridge University Automobile Club and led by Gyde Horrocks – familiar names which had been involved in setting Austin A35 records at Montlhéry in 1957, this attempt was generously supported by George Eyston and the Castrol oil company. Because the BMC works team was involved, and the university students aimed to make it happen during their summer vacation, September 1958 was chosen for the attempt.

This was a brand-new left-hand-drive car with a factory-style hard top and wire-spoke wheels which may have carried a Warwickshire registration number, but was prepared at Abingdon alongside the team's rally cars. Dunlop racing tyres were used and the car ran without bumpers or any sort of roll-over protection.

Its 100-Six-type six-port, six-cylinder engine was carefully-prepared by Eddie Maher's development team at Morris Engines in Coventry and incorporated all the features of the latest Sebring race engines recently adopted by Healey at Warwick. This engine, with approximately 150/160bhp available, was mated to an overdrive gearbox with a 3.9:1 final drive ratio. Another feature which was to prove useful, was that Pye of Cambridge provided a 'car-to-pit' radio communication system so that the drivers could keep in touch with the pits during their long stints at the wheel.

Although the car soon proved that it could run consistently at lap speeds of more than 110mph (the very best lap was at 124mph), this record attempt was by no means uneventful – though it was ultimately successful. It started well and a running average of 100mph was soon achieved, but soon after one of the drivers had spun the car on a flooded part of the banking the clutch began to slip, and it was decided to call a temporary halt to repair the car.

After the re-start everything went well until after about 30 hours of running when the rear leaf springs began to break up. A rapid rally-style pit stop saw the rear springs changed, and in spite of the clutch tending to slip as the car got away from standing starts, the run continued and after more than four days and nights the final new record (at 10,000 miles) was set. The run then had to be curtailed because the team's short-term tenure of the Montlhéry facility was about to end.

Although VOK 490 was not used again by Abingdon as a front-line competition car, it was soon sold and was used by private owners in British motor racing events for many years.

An enthusiastic young team from the Cambridge University AC set a whole raft of new International Class D records at Montlhéry in 1958, using VOK 490.

Competition Record

1958 Montlhéry	Marcus Chambers/Ray Simpson,/John Taylor/ Tom Threlfall/Gyde Horrocks/Rupert Jones/ John Clark/Bill Summers	Class D records of up to 98.73mph and 10,000 miles

PROJECT NUMBER	ENGINE SIZE	MODEL TYPE
EX219 (NOT REGISTERED)	**948CC 4-CYL**	**MG PROTOTYPE**

The EX219 record car was effectively a rebuild of the MG EX179 car of the mid-1950s.

for it was not until 1959 that EX179 was taken out of store at Abingdon, dusted off and prepared to run at Utah as EX219, badged as an Austin-Healey! Visually it was of course near-identical to the EX179, but BMC's publicists made every attempt, short of telling untruths, to convince the willing-to-be-duped media that this was a new car. Even Geoff Healey, who eventually called EX219 a 'so-called Sprite' in print, went along with this subterfuge for a time.

In September 1959, at the Bonneville Salt Flats with which the team was now totally familiar, EX219 was set to attack existing International Class G records for 750-1100cc cars. Fitted with a supercharged 948cc engine producing 86bhp, and with the driving shared by Tommy Wisdom, Ed Leavens and Gus Ehrman, this car turned the ten-mile circular salt track for hours at more than 140mph, finally breaking ten endurance records at up to 138.75mph.

After a stressful rebuilding session in which a hotter 98bhp engine was fitted, plus replacement clutch, the car attacked more sprint Class records and finally achieved 146.95mph in the hour, with five other International records along the way.

After this EX219 was retired from motorsport and now forms part of the magnificent museum collection at Gaydon.

The last of the so-called Austin-Healey record cars was titled EX219 and when unveiled in 1959 was badged as an Austin-Healey, but it was immediately clear that it was an MG, a substantially re-engined EX179, a record car which had been built by MG engineers at Abingdon. In several different forms EX179 had been used on the Bonneville Salt Flats for record-setting purposes.

The original EX179 of 1954 had used a prototype of the MGA chassis, complete with left-hand steering, an 84bhp 1.5-litre MG TF type of engine, and a sleek all-enveloping body style (not unlike the legendary EX135 that Reid Railton had evolved as early as 1938). Re-developed for use in 1956, using a much-modified BMC B-Series engine of the type fitted to the MGA, and with right-hand steering, it was changed further in 1957 to run with two different types of A-Series 948cc engine, one being normally-aspirated, the other fitted with Shorrock supercharging.

The 'Austin-Healey' side of this story now begins in earnest,

Tommy Wisdom at the wheel of EX219, discussing the design with MG's principal development engineer, Alex Hounslow.

Competition Record

1959 Class G records Bonneville Salt Flats	Tommy Wisdom/ Ed Leavens/Gus Ehrmann	Records up to 146.95mph

EX219 – ITS PEDIGREE

The cute record car which did so much to give the early Sprite sporting pedigree a boost was born as an MG, and only changed its name at a late stage. This is why:

Deep breath time. In 1954, even before the BMC Competitions Department was officially opened up, the MG engineering team designed a new, sleek, single-purpose, record car, coded EX79, which was meant to produce an astonishingly high top speed on the Bonneville Salt Flats in the USA. The basis of this car was a prototype MGA chassis frame copiously drilled to lighten it, originally set up with left-hand-drive, the 'passenger-seat' area was full of fuel tank, and the body style was very much inspired by the avowedly efficient EX135 shape which Reid Railton had evolved for an earlier MG in the late 1930s. Maybe MG nor its designers did not then plan that this new car would have a five-year life, but that is what happened, and its career is complex enough to deserve to be itemised:

1954
As rather breathlessly described in *The Autocar* of 27 August 1964, EX179 was powered by an MG XPEG engine of 1,466cc (which had just been phased in to the MG TF production car, so a bit of good publicity was being sought), and in this case was tuned to produce 84bhp at 6000rpm. One fascinating little detail was that there was no exhaust system as such, for the four individual 'down-pipes' from the cylinder head actually poked vertically up out of the body shell, but were cut off neatly at their exit point to minimise aerodynamic drag. Three different final drive ratios were available– 2.88:1, 3.125:1 and 3.33:1.

The well-known circular track on the Salt Flats (which was also used by Austin-Healey) was pressed into service and, when driven by George Eyston and Ken Miles, the new car set a whole batch of longer-distance speed records at up to 153.69mph, this car maintaining more than 120mph for a twelve hour endurance run.

1956
Two years later, with the new MGA ripe for positive publicity, Abingdon re-worked EX179 considerably. Calling it a 'two-seater MGA with a special body' (which it most assuredly was not!), it was kitted out with a lightly modified prototype Twin-Cam engine producing less than 100bhp, which would finally be put on sale in 1958, and was converted to right-hand-drive. The same type of exhaust through holes in the bodywork top panel was retained, but because of the layout of the new twin-cam engine, these had to swap sides too!

Cleary this was a very efficient body shape, for with the Twin-Cam engine installed it could reach 170mph and keep up to those speeds for hour after hour. Ken Miles and Johnny Lockett were the drivers on that occasion, where they took no fewer than sixteen international 1.5-litre class records, while maintaining 141.71mph for twelve hours, and sprinting at 170.15mph for a ten mile lap.

1957
Still more was available from this plucky little car. In 1957, Abingdon dusted off EX179, which had been on display and (as they say) 'in warm storage' for the winter, to send it to Bonneville again, this time with a supercharged version of the small A-Series engine. Although the Sprite was not yet ready, the intention was there, so for John Thornley's team there was much to be achieved with that amazing little power unit, with an assault on Class G (751cc to 1,100cc) records in mind.

EX179, therefore, had its twin-cam engine stripped out, and replaced by a choice of two 948cc engines, the normally aspirated version producing 57bhp and the Shorrock-supercharged unit a very conservatively-rated 73bhp at 5500rpm.

Tommy Wisdom and David Ash collected a mountain of records with the unblown car at up to 1417 miles for 12 hours, at 118mph, while David Ash and Phil Hill took records at up to 132.62mph in the blown type.

1959
Finally, when it was becoming positively ancient by record-breaking standards, EX179 was re-born – still under MG's control - as Austin-Healey EX219, where Messrs Wisdom, Ehrman and Leavens pushed it all the way up to 146.95mph.

CHAPTER 7:
100-SIX AND 3000 IN RALLYING

The 3000's front disc brake installation (with calipers by Girling) should be compared with the Dunlop installation previously used on the 100S chassis (see page 39).

Almost all the celebrated works Big Healey rally cars were prepared at Abingdon, but the Competitions Department did not begin considering such a programme until after Geoff Healey's tiny motor racing department had committed a 100-Six to rallying. The car in question, UOC 741, started life as a publicity car, and was then prepared for rallying, initially in journalist Tommy Wisdom's hands, before (still in Wisdom's hands) it competed in the 1957 Mille Miglia. Wisdom would also use it in the 1958 Monte Carlo rally before it was finally handed over to Abingdon, where Jack Sears was the first to rally it.

This was the 'prototype' of all the Abingdon fleet, the design progressively upgraded in the years which followed. Apart from the usual careful attention to the welding of the chassis and internal body structure, one initial modification was to make provision for larger lever-arm (Armstrong DAS10) rear dampers to be fitted, which meant the fabrication of new bracketry on the chassis.

According to Geoff Healey, this is what happened in 1958: "Marcus Chambers, then heading BMC competition, had been persevering with the more mundane BMC vehicles in competition, and quickly saw the potential of the car. He rang me and persuaded me to lend him the car for some rallies. We were also able to let him have drawings and specifications of all the special parts and equipment used. Syd Enever (MG's chief designer) redesigned the rear springs to reduce the stress under load and produced the legendary 14-leaf rear springs that were to contribute so much to the success of the 6-cylinder cars. With the departure of UOC 741 to Abingdon our involvement in rallies was greatly reduced."

At this point it is important to stress that it was Geoff Healey's team at Warwick which had already developed the four-wheel disc brake installation which was to make so much difference

Although rear-wheel disc brakes were never used on 3000 production cars, they were homologated for use in the works competition cars.

to the capability of these cars. It was speedily homologated and featured on all 100-Six and 3000s rallied from 1958 on.

Although Group 3 homologation normally made no provision for disc brakes to be approved as an alternative to drums (or front disc/rear drum on the 3000), the FIA regulations stated that if such a kit had been put on sale, and sufficient numbers sold, then approval would follow. But just how many four-wheel disc kits were sold? Enough, BMC staff would say with wide eyes and an innocent expression – and both the RAC and FIA inspectors believed them. This was just the first of many innovations which gradually turned the basic car into a formidably special competition car.

For BMC at Abingdon, however, the era of the works Healeys had only just begun. For the next eight years these machines were always the most charismatic of the cars on the strength, and they were still being improved in 1965 when their rallying career was finally cut off. The author has dug deep into his archive and unearthed the following material which he once assembled to give a flavour of the period: "In the 1950s and 1960s the works Austin-Healeys were near-mythical creations. Those rally cars might have looked almost standard, but were so special that grown men would go misty-eyed when they watched them, and speechless when they listened to their high-speed passage on a special stage. While it was agreed that ten years later the Mk 2 Escorts had always made spine-tingling sounds, it was the Big Healeys which were the first rally cars to be recognised by the sound of their

This is how much of the works pre-event planning took place in the late 1950s – Left to Right: Tommy Wisdom, Ann Wisdom, Pat Moss, Willy Cave and John Sprinzel.

approach, some seconds before they could be seen. It was that sound, more than the performance, which was so dramatic. You only had to stand up close to one on the start line of a rally stage, listen to the beat of the engine, and be hooked. It was a unique noise – a cross between the bubble of a seething cauldron and an emptying bath, a growl from a rather tetchy lion and the drone of a Merlin-powered Spitfire. Men like me – and there were legions of us – heard it, loved it, and never grew bored with it."

MARCUS CHAMBERS

Marcus (nicknamed 'Chub' or 'The Poor Man's Neubauer' because of his bulky build and obvious authority) already had a great background in motorsport before starting the Austin-Healey rally programme in 1958. Having served as racing team manager at HRG in 1947 and 1948 (he had driven for the team at Le Mans in 1938 and 1939), he later opened up the new Abingdon Competitions Department under John Thornley's overall control.

Starting from scratch, he gradually turned the BMC team into a formidable rallying force. Taking good advice wherever it was offered (and most particularly from John Gott, 'the rallying policemen', who was his Team Captain) he never let work get entirely in the way of good living. He gradually built up his on-events service support operation and went out on as many events as possible, but whenever he had to choose between standing outside at a control or service point in the cold and rain, or enjoying a good meal with fine wine, the meal often came first.

It's easy to forget that Marcus had to control a big team on events which were often much more far-flung than in the modern era, and that mobile phones, satellite navigation, GPS, fax machines and computers had not been invented. His organisation – and it really was an organisation – coped by planning meticulously before the events, relying on his drivers to make many of their own decisions, and by using the telephone network of whatever country he was in; some of those telecommunications systems were still unreliable, and caused no end of headaches.

In the seven years that he ran the BMC team he nurtured a lot of new driving talent. His biggest find, no question, was the remarkable Pat Moss, who with her good friend and co-driver Ann Wisdom proved to be an ultra-fast driver – not just a good lady driver, but an ultra-competitive 'bloke' too. He also encouraged Jack Sears to be a top-line rally driver (until, that is, Jack defected to circuit racing), hired the Morley twins in 1959, and caused David Seigle-Morris to defect from the Triumph team.

Not only that, but when he decided to move on in 1961, taking up a post in the retail motor trade, he was personally involved in choosing Stuart Turner as his successor. Marcus came back to motorsport in 1964, running the Rootes Group's fortunes from 1964 to 1968, which included a Hillman Hunter victory in the London-Sydney Marathon.

This was the neatly laid-out cockpit of a works Healey 3000, dating from 1961, when the original type of gearchange was still in use.

The 1964 and 1965 BJ8-type works rally cars were all equipped with this type of fascia/ driving compartment. Note the overdrive switch fixed to the gear lever knob.

These cars – and in a decade there were only 28 of them – were the ultimate in Austin-Healeys, the very best that the works Competition Department at Abingdon, could devise while staying within the regulations. In detail, if not in basic layout, they were just about as different from a road car as was possible.

It helped of course, that dedicated characters like Marcus Chambers, Bill Price and Stuart Turner could read every word of the FIA regulations and usually find a way around what was intended. It was at Abingdon that they learned how to boost the power, how to get weight out of the chassis, how to keep the wheels on the road and, above all, how to build in the rock-solid reliability that 1960s rallying demanded.

Works Healey drivers knew that almost every component of their car was different, and special. The body/chassis unit had all-aluminium skin panels, while much of the engine, all of the gearbox and most of the suspension were changed. Plus the seats, the electrical wiring, the overdrive and -- of course -- the performance!

At first glance the Big Healey didn't look suitable for European rallying. For motor racing maybe, but for European rallying not at all. Events were getting tougher, and rougher, when the original Austin-Healey had very little ground clearance and many minor failings. Then, of course, the 'bumble bee' syndrome set in. 'Bumble bee?' According to the scientists the bumble bee was not built for flight and couldn't possibly fly – but since no one ever told the bumble bee, it carried on flying anyway.

By 1957 the Austin-Healey was not even a contender as a rally car, which was when team boss Marcus Chambers and his top mechanic Doug Watts got involved. So far, Marcus's BMC rally team had been active for three years with little success in other cars, all of which lacked performance. Then one day they inspected a Healey which Geoff Healey had already prepared, thought it could be rock-solid when carefully built, and sensed the potential which might be locked away. In the next eight years three parts of the BMC empire – Abingdon to build and run the cars, the Healey company to carry on designing new pieces, and the BMC Engines Branch to work on the engines – would transform the car.

Once the original 3000 appeared, with a 2.9-litre engine and disc front brakes, there was real progress. Month by month, phase by phase, component by component, and with a build-up of sheer experience, the 'powder-puff car' (which is how it was once described by cynics) was turned into an unbreakable 'tank'. Unless it was physically abused by being hurled off the road, or badly handled by its drivers (did I hear the name of Timo Makinen mentioned?), it was turned into the standard projectile by which every other European rally car of the day was measured. "Easy really," Marcus Chambers once told the author, with a very wry smile, "all we had to do was to make it faster, stronger, better-handling, and suitable for every possible surface".

According to the FIA regulations of the day, one could homologate a raft of extra equipment if at least 100 sets had already been made and sold. One could also beef up the chassis and fit lightweight skin panels all round. The Abingdon team pushed those allowances to the limit – and then some. Further, if they didn't think they would be rumbled by a vigilant scrutineer, they made other changes as well. Straight-cut gears in the transmission, or even ratios which were not normally available – easy. Extra air outlets from the engine bay – why not? Aluminium cylinder heads to 'reduce weight' – of course ! Body changes to accommodate twin spare wheels – necessary!

And more, and more, and more....

It was by beefing up the engines that the real transformation was made, and it was BMC's Morris Engines Branch who did the work. Early works 3000s with standard-looking BN6 engines probably had no more than 160bhp. For 1960 they got three SUs, and for 1961 the extractor exhaust system arrived, by which time there was 180bhp at the flywheel. Within months a triple dual-choke Weber carburettor set-up had been developed, and along with a new aluminium cylinder head, and an overbore to 2968cc, helped produce up to 210bhp. These days, they say, further developed engines produce up to

C-Series Engine – A Difficult Birth

Although Donald Healey was unfailingly loyal to his paymasters at BMC, his chief technical designer, son Geoffrey, never hid his scorn for the original C-Series engine which he was obliged to use when the 100-Six and its successors were developed. In short, he found the original C-Series less powerful, less economical, larger and heavier than the dear old four-cylinder 2.6-litre engine which had proved to be such a success in the BN1, BN2, 100S and a variety of record cars.

This story started in 1952, soon after Austin had absorbed the Nuffield Organisation to found the British Motor Corporation (BMC). Within weeks BMC's chairman, the ruthless Leonard Lord, had decided that all future BMC cars would rely on one of three 'corporate' new engines – the tiny A-Series (which would figure in the original 'Frog Eye' Sprite), the B-Series (which among other cars powered the MGA and MGB), and a newly-engineered six-cylinder C-Series, which was to be launched in 1954 and would be fitted to the Austin-Healey 100-Six and its successors.

The A-Series already existed: it was about to power the new Austin A30, the B-Series was an evolution of the A40 power unit, and only the C-Series was to be completely new. Development of the C-Series began under the leadership of the Morris Engines design team at Cowley, and its initial destination was the forthcoming Austin A90 Westminster, Morris Isis and Wolseley 6/90 saloons. This big new engine was to be manufactured at the Morris Engines factory in Coventry, where the faithful 2.6-litre four-cylinder engines used on existing Big Healeys were already being made.

With an original capacity of 2639cc, the C-Series was almost the same size as the 2660cc unit used in the Austin-Healey BN1/BN2, but there were really no advances to be claimed for the new design as the four-bearing block/crankcase and the cylinder head were both in cast iron, the entire unit being much heavier than the old 'four'. Not only that, but for obscure reasons the inlet passages of the first engine were cast into the head itself (there being no separate inlet manifold as such), and engine tuners like Geoff Healey and Morris Engines' Eddie Maher both found the engine difficult to tune. As originally set up for the A90 Westminster there was only a single downdraught Zenith carburettor and a claimed peak output of 85bhp, while the Wolseley 6/90 version had twin SUs and 95bhp.

It wasn't an inspiring new engine, so when BMC insisted that a replacement for the BN2 should not only be a trifle longer, with 2+2 seating, but also that a version of the C-Series engine should be used, Geoff Healey was not amused., and though he kept this to himself until

after the BN4 went public he was then openly critical, until his persistent nagging saw the BN6 take its place at the end of 1957.

This is an extract of what he had to say in his book Austin-Healey, which was published in 1977: "Our tests in October 1955 showed the 6-cylinder car to be 3½mph faster, but nearly all its acceleration figures were worse. This period saw some quite bitter arguments between the Austin and Morris sections of BMC over the new engine's uninspiring performance... We and Austin were pretty blunt in our criticism of the Morris-designed unit, and Austin works manager Geoffrey Rose was mainly responsible for making Morris carry out the necessary engine modifications and quelling the outbreak of tribal warfare."

Healey, in fact, were always disappointed by the performance of the 2639cc version of this engine, even though it was significantly improved by the adoption of a new cylinder head from late 1957 and the arrival of the BN6. They would far rather have worked on the 'light six' alternative offered from BMC Australia, or even applied a productionised version of the tough and capable 100S 'four'.

Not that BMC's top management were too concerned about this, for they had other new models in mind for the new C-Series. First there was the Morris Isis sedan, from 1956 the Austin A90 became the A95 along with a more powerful version called the A105, while in 1957 the Riley 2.6 saloon appeared, replacing the Pathfinder and its 2443cc Riley twin-cam engine that had powered the original Warwick Healeys of 1946-54.

Next, in mid-1959, BMC achieved what turned out to be a real breakthrough. They dumped the 2639cc engine in favour of the larger 2912cc derivative and used it in the Austin-Healey 3000 along with new Pininfarina-styled saloons variously called the A99 Westminster, the Wolseley 6/99 and the Vanden Plas Princess 3-litre. BMC had clearly learned lessons by studying the art of badge-engineering, for these three models were all based on the same trendily styled four-door saloon shell. Just two years later, when faced with stiffer opposition from Ford's latest Zodiac models, all these saloon cars received an uprated 120bhp power unit.

To their joy, both Geoff Healey and Eddie Maher found that the simple increase in cylinder bore from 79.37mm to 83.36mm seemed to make all the difference to the potential of the enlarged engine, so for the next five years there were steady increases in power output to be enjoyed. From 124bhp in 1959 to 132bhp in 1961, and finally to 148bhp in 1964, this engine urged the Big Healey to the performance levels which it had always deserved.

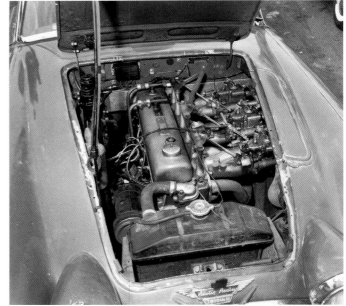

For 1962, BMC homologated a triple Weber carburettor installation for the works 3000 – and included a removable panel in the body shell above the carburettors.

By the end of 1961 the works 3000s had added a three-SU carburettor installation, a tubular exhaust manifold and the definitive 'centre-change' gearbox to their specification.

A works 3000 fitted with the homologated triple Weber engine installation provided a real 'bonnetful' – so the fact that these power units were very reliable was a great relief to the mechanics!

280 or even 300bhp.

Aluminium heads? According to the regulations, BMC should have sold 100 of these before they were approved for use, but only a handful existed in 1962. Protests? No one bothered, because the opposition were all up to similar tricks. As Marcus Chambers once so eloquently put it: "We had long felt that we needed a car with long hairy legs to stride over the mountains, and great lungs with which to rush up the hills; this seemed to be it".

All this was matched by more work on the chassis: seam welding and double-skinning the structure, placing the exhaust silencer in line with the front wheels so that it could follow the same ruts and avoid damage, raising the front suspension to give more ground clearance, and eventually improving the rear suspension by reshaping the rear chassis rails and thus allowing more axle movement (this was tried out before it went into production in the Mk III road cars – an homologation cheat once again), and more direct steering.

At this point it is worth recalling the sequence of events which helped transform the Big Healey into the formidable competition that it became :

Although road-car versions of the six-cylinder Healey (100-Six and 3000) had chrome-plated grille filling the front aperture, works rally cars often looked startlingly different, with outer segments of the grille removed and with ducting added behind the outside line of the bodywork, this being done to allow even more cooling air to enter the engine bay, and incidentally to find its way towards the front wheel arches and the hard-used brakes.

In fact, works rally cars first ran without full-width radiator grilles in the French Alpine rally of 1958, where ambient temperatures in summer were high, the original grilles being rather crudely chopped out at the sides of the aperture. It was on the same event, incidentally, that they ran without bumpers and with low-mounted extra driving lamps. However, because detail regulations differed from event to event, even as late as 1960 they could still sometimes be seen with standard full-width grilles.

Side exhaust outlets (under the passenger door) were first seen in 1959, this system being arranged so that tail pipes did not have to be routed all the way to the back of the car, under the line of the rear axle, and below the line of the main chassis members, as they did on production-line cars. Not only did this save a significant amount of weight, but it also eliminated the possibility of that part of the exhaust system being damaged, or flattened, by the rough roads which were an increasing part of the current rally scene.

For 1960 a cockpit cooling scoop was fitted to the scuttle ahead of the base of the windscreen, though this never seemed to be as efficient as it promised to be. Later, the characteristically shaped, moulded glass-fibre boot lid (which allowed two spare wheels to be carried inside the shallow boot) was first used on cars built for the French Alpine rally of 1960. This proved to be

The final version of the works 3000 featured a massive fuel tank, a bulge in the boot lid (to allow for a second spare wheel to be carried), and usually rallied with all the kit on show in this Autocar *test car.*

so useful that it was immediately standardised in the Abingdon build specification, for Appendix J regulations allowed such a non-functional change to be made without insisting that minimum quantities had to be sold first.

From mid-1960, too, a simple air vent flap was fitted to the rear of the hardtops, just ahead of the line of the rear

Vents in the front wings helped to channel hot gases from the engine bay of later-model 3000s.

Simply equipped, purposeful, and utterly functional – this was the rear view aspect of the 1960s-type works 3000. Because the event regulations usually allowed it, the rear bumpers were removed, the reverse lamp was probably illegally over-powerful (but the police never seemed to be worried by this), and the flip-up ventilator in the roof of the hard top was an efficient way of keeping the cockpit cool.

window, this aiming to reduce the sometimes searing heat inside the cockpit. Romantics would hope that these were special designed, but the truth is more prosaic – they were sub-assemblies actually lifted from one of BMC's current light-commercial vehicles.

The next visual change occurred in May 1961, when cars for the Tulip rally featured triangular hot air outlets in the front wings, behind the wheel arches. Freely acknowledged to have been copied from those used on the Mercedes-Benz 300SL (and finalised after a good deal of ad hoc open-road testing), these helped maintain a cooling flow of air through the engine bay: since a six-branch fabricated exhaust manifold had recently been adopted, under-bonnet temperatures were significantly higher than before. Apparently these vents were developed using cut-and-test methods by Abingdon technician Cliff Humphries.

There was more to come. From the first few months of 1962, new Big Healeys in the 37ARX - 77ARX sequence were fitted with a long, slim, detachable panel in the bonnet surround (the shroud, as some experts call it) on the left (passenger/co-driver) side of the car. This first appeared on the Tulip Rally of 1962, to coincide with the introduction of engines using three twin-choke Weber carburettors, and was intended to allow easy access to those instruments, which were immediately under that point of the bodywork. This modification was later applied to many older Austin-Healeys when they were fitted with Webers.

Extra headlamps, in nacelles ('frog-eye' Sprite-style) let in to

the bonnet shroud on each side and just ahead of the bonnet opening, were first seen on the 1962 RAC rally and were only intermittently seen on cars in 1963, but became a standard feature on all cars prepared for the 1964 and 1965 seasons. These were fitted to provide a conventional headlamp dipping facility, for at this time the main headlamps had been fitted with Lucas quartz-halogen bulbs which were only originally available in single-filament form. Naturally the wiring looms had to be modified to suit.

The very first works cars to have wind-up windows and the wrap-around windscreen were the 1964-build BJ8s (ARX 91B and ARX 92B), and of course the final cars also built in 1964 and 1965 (BMO 93B, BRX 852B, DRX 257C, DRX 258C and EJB 806C). Because of yet another reshuffle of FIA Appendix J regulations, those cars were usually obliged to run with front and rear bumpers in place (though not on the 'bring-anything-you've-got' Spa-Sofia-Liège marathon, where BMO 93B won outright in old, old-fashioned, no-bumper condition).

Except for the never-rallied 1967 prototype-specification car, prepared for the RAC rally which was cancelled less than 24 hours before the start, the last visual change came in the autumn of 1965, for the RAC rally – the last event in which a works Healey was to start. Then, two cars, DRX 258C and the brand-new EJB 806C, were equipped with high-exhaust installations under a shortened passenger door. This involved a major carve-up of the structure of the bulkhead, the body sill, and of course of the passenger door itself.

Structurally, because the box-section chassis frame was welded up to the steel inner body structure on initial manufacture at Jensen, it was impossible for the mechanics at Abingdon to carry out a total strip-down to a 'chassis only' condition. Even so, after every tough event as much as possible of the car – its outer panels, doors, hardtop and of course all its running gear were taken off for refurbishment or repair.

As the later team manager Peter Browning has commented: "Certain cars were individually developed over quite a long period... Unlike the works Minis, very few Healeys were re-bodied to appear again, perhaps with new registration numbers. Generally, the cars kept their identity and were regularly rebuilt, some albeit upon new chassis frames. Once a works Healey was pensioned off it was either written off (the chassis being too badly damaged to be of use) or, if the car was still basically sound, it would be sold to a private owner."

As the years progressed, strengthening panels or reinforcements were added on the front cross-member, to beef up the front lever-arm shock absorber mountings, around the steering box mounting brackets, under and around the rear of the chassis frame, and where larger Armstrong rear shock absorbers had to be supported.

In addition, with rough events like the Liège or RAC rallies in mind, a considerable amount of extra plating would be added to the underside of the main chassis members, and of course the skid shielding under the engine and gearbox would need to be be very strong.

When Abingdon first began using the 100-Six, in standard form the 2639cc engine was rated at 117bhp and virtually no optional equipment was homologated for the car. Even when the 3000 was homologated in mid-1959 the 2912cc engines were only equipped with two SU carburettors on a special inlet manifold, and we may guess (though nothing was revealed at the time) that they had about 150-160bhp.

For mid-1960, however, and strictly according to the FIA's 'freedoms', an alternative carburation system was homologated with three 2in SU H8 carburettors – and it was with this engine, which produced up to 180bhp, that Pat Moss and Ann Wisdom recorded that amazing outright victory in the Liège-Rome-Liège rally of September 1960. A six-branch tubular exhaust manifold was added to the specification from early 1961, this also adding a small but unspecified increase in torque and perhaps peak power.

The next big change came early in 1962, when BMC re-homologated its rally car on the basis of the 3000 Mk II road car, which had its own different triple-SU set-up, and could therefore take advantage of the 'alternative carburation' freedom to homologate triple dual-choke Weber carburettors.

This was the moment at which an aluminium cylinder head was also homologated. According to the regulations, BMC should already have sold 100 such heads by the time approval was granted, which most assuredly had not yet been done, but none of their rivals ever complained in case some of their own transgressions were picked up and paraded against them. Many aluminium heads were then sold in later years to make everything totally legal once again.

The combination of Webers plus aluminium cylinder head produced a very torquey 210bhp, and saw the C-Series engine at the peak of its works development, for no further major improvements were made in the 1962-65 period. However, in modern times, by the use of modern materials (and with the relaxation of homologation restrictions in many classic events) a good deal more horsepower has been released from this basic design.

In the early 1960s, if ultimate power rather than a four-day/multi-thousand-mile endurance tune had been required, then more power could have been produced – and was indeed, produced for circuit racing by the Warwick-based race team – but since Abingdon was determined to produce engines which would (theoretically, at least) easily last through a major international rally, this does not seem to have been done. Although rev-limiters were not fitted the drivers were always instructed to use 6000rpm as the absolute limit. The only recurrent, infuriating and seemingly random failure was the Lucas distributors, which were still failing as much in the mid-1960s as they had been in 1959.

In spite of all this work and of the efforts to improve the road-holding, as a competition car the Big Healey was a bulky and unruly beast which required brave drivers. Only a

few – Timo Makinen, Donald Morley, Rauno Aaltonen and that remarkable lady Pat Moss – truly mastered the car, while others (including Paddy Hopkirk) accepted that it was going to frighten them.

Pat Moss always underplayed her efforts: "If the Big Healey started to weave you had to catch it straight away: two or more snakes and it was Goodbye and Goodnight." Team driver Peter Riley once described its habits graphically to the author, using a cricketing term: "From the start line, on full throttle, the only trouble was that the car insisted on taking off to mid-off." On another occasion, after a test drive he commented: "We set off and I was fairly horrified. Every time you lifted off it dived left, every time you accelerated it dived right. Clearly the axle location needed sorting. But Lord, how it went. A daunting machine, and our admiration for Pat Moss went sky high."

Everything else was developed for 'go', and not for 'show'. The purpose of the big four-wheel disc brake kit was obvious, the hardtops were always fitted to make the cars bearable on long events (and to provide marginally more protection in the case of roll-over accidents), the front grilles were removed to improve cooling, the moulded GRP boot lids were there to allow two spare wheels to be carried and the vents in the front wings were ideal for extracting hot air from the engine bay.

Then there were the Microcell-shaped bucket seats, the detachable shroud panel above the Weber carburettors, the padded covers over the extra driving lamps, the removal of bumpers (when this was allowed by the regulations) – and at the end of the cars' competition life, the raising of the exhaust system. All this explains why preparation of new rally cars took ages, and the rebuild of those battered on a long, rough event took even longer. It was nothing for an ill-used Big Healey to return to Abingdon and need three months or more to be brought back into shape.

So how was the preparation job tackled? Amazingly, by just a single mechanic working on his own. When a brand-new car was involved (and there were very few of those) it was ordered up and came through 'the system' by being assembled on the lines at Abingdon, literally across the yard from the Competitions Department. At this point one of Abingdon's most experienced mechanics would be allocated the job, told how many weeks (rarely months, by the way) he could have, and would be left to get on with it. His first priority was to strip the new machine, discarding parts such as steel panels, standard gearboxes, rear drum brakes and standard seats before beginning the painstaking preparation job. And why not start from a bare shell? The author once asked this question and got the rather pitying response that, by taking delivery of a complete car, which had just been assembled a few yards away on the production line, every odd little item was at least there, on the spot, and did not have to be sourced from the parts book.

Although there was a rudimentary preparation and build sheet, most BMC mechanics were left to their own devices –

which often meant calling up the chosen driver for a particular car or event and asking for his views. Except when needing extra muscle for jobs like manoeuvring engines in and out or getting the back axle into place, expert spanner-men like Den Green and Bryan Moylan could, and usually did, build up the car on their own.

Then it was up to the 'Superstar' driver to deliver – and the record shows that they often did. Yet sometimes something broke or, more likely, the car went off the road or battered itself into submission on the ever-roughening tracks used in European events at the time. On occasions like that it was better not to look underneath the body to see what sort of punishment had been inflicted. When a chassis was bent it was thrown away, and a rebuild took place around a new one. Otherwise the rebuild job was carried out and the car had to suffer it all again. Works cars rarely completed more than a

handful of events in two seasons before being discarded, some then being sold to private owners, others being ceremonially scrapped out.

Make no mistake: from 1960 to 1965, after which new FIA regulations finally killed it off, this was the best and most charismatic rally car in the world. It looked dramatic, it sounded magnificent, it was driven by the world's best – and it never gave in to any rival. Occasionally, just occasionally, Porsche encouraged the use of Carrera 2 and Carrera 2 Abarths, but the Healey usually had the beating of them. Sometimes, on tarmac, brave souls would appear in Ferrari 250GTs, but they wasted their time. There were times when race-prepared Alfa Guilia GTZ Tubolares could match the Healey – until, that is, they broke down.

The Big Healey, in fact, set new standards which others could not match until it had gone. And we all still miss it.

100-SIX IN RALLYING

UOC 741, an ex-Healey car, was handed over to Abingdon by the Healey company at Warwick in 1958, appearing for the first time in the 1958 RAC rally, where racing driver Jack Sears and Peter Garnier, sports editor of The Autocar, struggled without success against very wintry conditions. This was an event which proved to be a battle for sporting survival, and to visit all the controls, which the Healey did not, was essential to success. In the meantime Abingdon was learning rapidly about the Big Healey and its rugged structure. Only weeks later the same car/crew combination performed splendidly on the hill-climbs and speed tests of the Tulip rally before the fuel pump and the distributor drive both failed and the car had to retire. As Jack Sears later recalled: "I remember how impressed I was with the tremendous pulling power of the engine. The factory was sufficiently encouraged to run this car again for Peter and me in the 1958 Tulip rally. Although the car retired towards the end with a broken distributor when we were lying second in class [behind a Mercedes-Benz 300SL, so no shame in that!] and tenth overall, we managed to achieve some very fast times on the special stage hill-climbs. This convinced BMC that the car had class-winning potential, and that they should continue development and embark on a full programme of events". How many more times in the years to come would a C-Series engine suffer from distributor problems? Was there some kind of vibration problem that was never solved?

For the first full team effort, the French Alpine rally of 1958, BMC entered no fewer than five 100-Six BN6 models. No other works BMC cars were prepared for that event but there was a tremendous rush even to get them to the start line, as Marcus Chambers later explained:

"We had at one time hoped to enter five Twin-Cam MGAs but for a number of reasons this was not possible [the launch of the Twin-Cam had been delayed, only being unveiled the week after the Alpine rally] and at the last minute we decided

to enter the same number of Austin-Healey 100-Sixes.

"Owing to the change in our plans there was little time to carry out much testing or to do any of our own development work, although we had been lent the duo-tone green demonstrator [UOC 741] from the Donald Healey Motor Company. This car had most of the chassis modifications which had been developed by Geoffrey Healey and was fitted with Dunlop disc brakes on all four wheels.

"As we only had three cars of our own, in addition to the Healey Company's demonstrator we had to borrow another demonstrator from the Austin Motor Company. This car was red and black and was normally used by the Vice-Chairman, Mr George Harriman. He very sportingly released it for this event and we allotted it to Nancy Mitchell. The three other cars were bright red, a colour which I consider lucky and which has since come to be regarded as the BMC team colour. These were captained by Jack Sears, Pat Moss and Bill Shepherd. The green car naturally went to John Gott, who had a preference for this colour."

This was almost the usual full-strength BMC team. The experienced hands, including top policeman John Gott and race driver Jack Sears, could not wait to get their hands on a car which promised to be powerful enough to deal with the big hills, tight timing and sinuous roads of this classic rally. In fact these cars were still only at the beginning of their lengthy evolution process, and although they put up a brave show, vividly captured on film by the Shell Film Unit, their first appearance was not a great success. They experienced the usual (and frankly, expected) teething troubles of a newly-developed competition car, including John Gott's car losing a wheel complete with hub and Pat Moss's suffering clutch slip after a 'helpful' journalist had tied up an engine breather pipe at a service halt, causing oil to be diverted to the wrong places, while Jack Sears's car suffered accident damage following a brush with another competitor on the Croce Domini pass in the Italian Dolomites.

Even so, Bill Shepherd performed well, winning a Coupe des Alpes for an unpenalised run and taking seventh overall, while Pat Moss and Nancy Mitchell finished first and second in the well-publicised Ladies Award category. It wasn't quite the fairytale start that everyone had wanted, for this was the event in which Ken Richardson's works Triumph TR3As appeared for the first time with a 2.2-litre engine, this being just enough for them to win the capacity class. This was the first and only time that a TR3A ever beat a Big Healey in a straight fight.

The promise of the new cars was certainly there, as the early-event pace of Jack Sears's car (PMO 203), and Bill Shepherd's Coupe-winning performance (in PMO 202) had confirmed. With more power – naturally the drivers all wanted more power! – and with ever improving reliability, these could become formidable fighting machines. The true Big Healey era, an eight-year programme, had now begun.

Following the encouraging Alpine rally performance, Abingdon's mechanics made haste to repair four of the same cars to compete in the Liège-Rome-Liège. Abingdon was still – and always would be – short of fully-prepared rally cars which could be spared for practice and reconnaissance tasks, and when one of the ex-Alpine rally machines (the original car, UOC 741) could not be repaired in time after its Alpine adventures, John Gott was asked to drive an MGA Twin-Cam instead.

On what turned out to be the first of a series of ultra-demanding, ultra-fast and ultra-car-damaging Liège events, the 100-Sixes performed magnificently, for Pat Moss took fourth place overall, beaten only by a very special Alfa Romeo Giulietta

Coupé and two Porsche 356s, and also won her capacity class. Three of the four-works Austin-Healeys finished, which meant that they lifted the Team Prize too.

There were only two more chances for the 100-Six to prove itself at International level, the first being the 1959 Tulip, whre PMO 202 was entered for Pat Moss and PMO 203 for Jack Sears. Compared with previous years this started from Paris and turned out to be much tougher than before, not only because of the number and nature of the speed tests but also because of a more challenging time schedule. Pat Moss started well before crashing her car near St Agrève in central France, but Jack Sears put in a tremendous drive to take eighth overall and win his capacity class. It was on this event, incidentally, that outright victory went to the Morley Twins, driving their own Jaguar 3.4 saloon (DJM 400), and this was the impetus that led to them being invited to join the BMC works team, of which they were members until the end of 1965 and the end of the Austin-Healey 3000 era.

Only a few weeks later Pat Moss competed in the hot, dusty and rough Greek Acropolis rally, but on a road section where co-driver Ann Wisdom was driving the car it left the road and was severely damaged.

And that was the end of 100-Six's short works career, for the 3000 then took over from the French Alpine. Of the three PMOs, PMO 201 and PMO 202 were both sold off almost at once, never again to rally for the factory, while PMO 203 filled in a short gap in Abingdon's programme by being up-engined and thus converted to a 3000 for use in the 1959 Liège-Rome-Liège and the Portuguese events.

REGISTRATION NUMBER	ENGINE SIZE	MODEL TYPE
OOM 439	**2660cc 4-cyl OHV**	**100S**

As described in Chapter 5, this Healey-prepared 100S was used just once as a works rally car and only completed the early hours of the 1955 Liège-Rome-Liège rally before being crashed.

Competition Record		
1955 Liège-Rome-Liège	Peter Reece/Dennis Scott	DNF

REGISTRATION NUMBER	ENGINE SIZE	MODEL TYPE
UOC 741	**2639cc 6-cyl OHV**	**100-Six BN4**

As will be detailed in the next Chapter, when it started its competition life as a rally-cum-race car, UOC 741 had already worked hard for the Healey company before it was decided to re-work it for rallying, the first event chosen being the Italian Sestriere rally of February 1957.

It was the doyen of British motoring journalism, Tommy Wisdom (a long-time friend of Donald Healey), who persuaded BMC management to loan him the car. Tommy himself specified the changes he wanted made for this hard-top BN4, which included a roof-top swivelling spot-lamp.

Tommy Wisdom drove UOC 741 on the 1958 Monte Carlo rally – Big Healey development as a works machine was only just beginning.

Healey themselves rarely built rally cars, but the interior of UOC 741, as prepared for the 1958 Monte Carlo rally, was very neat and purposeful.

At first no improvements were made to the engine or the overdrive transmission, which meant that with little more than 100bhp available the car was not likely to be a potential winner. Tommy took with him his daughter Ann, who was already in the BMC works team as Pat Moss's co-driver, but success eluded the Wisdom family in the Sestriere. However, Tommy apparently put in a very thoughtful and valuable report suggesting what might be done to make a promising car better, and saw that Marcus Chambers at Abingdon got a copy too.

The same car was then re-prepared with a prototype BN6 engine, whose much better and deeper-breathing cylinder head made it a more formidable proposition. It finished honourably in the 1957 Mille Miglia, the last time the event was run, when Tommy Wisdom and Cecil Winby, who worked for the Brico piston company in Coventry, took 37th place out of a field of 365 cars.

Yet it would still be some time before the works' competitions department took much interest in this particular car or model. Accordingly its next appearance (after pre-event preparation at Warwick) was in the 1958 Monte Carlo Rally, when Tommy Wisdom borrowed it yet again. In an event which has now gone down in history as being the worst weather Monte of all time, UOC 741 was eventually eliminated in the blizzard.

Jack Sears and Peter Garnier drove the car in the 1958 RAC rally, held in March. There was so much snow, and so many impassable roads in the hills of the Lake District and Wales, that it was often a case of completing the route rather than being fast anywhere. UOC 741 started from Hastings, met up with the Blackpool starters at the Prescott hillclimb, then set off for the wintry wilderness of Wales where the chaos began. In spite of clouting a stone wall at one point, Sears set up fastest class time on no fewer than ten of the special tests (sprints, hillclimbs and manoeuvring challenges) but was later handicapped by a broken third gear. Commenting after the event in *The Autocar*, sports editor Peter Garnier wrote with some bitterness of the difficulty of completing the route and of having to miss controls: "Jack Sears and I, in the Austin-Healey, were held up for 45 minutes on the Rhayader stretch, 32 minutes on Bwlch-y-Groes, and 20 or so minutes on the approach to Hardknott...." Under the circumstances, finishing 52nd overall was nothing to be ashamed of.

There was similar anguish following the Tulip rally, where the Sears/Austin-Healey combination was demonstrably fast, often setting top-ten times on the hillclimb tests that were a speciality of this event, only for him to be robbed of a fine finish when the distributor drive failed.

UOC 741 was then pressed into service for the French Alpine rally, allocated to John Gott who had at least as much 'Alpine' experience as anyone in the strong team. Not that this helped, as Bill Price notes in his monumental history of the BMC team: "John Gott crashed his car and found that he had lost a wheel; in fact, while he and his co-driver were still sitting in the car, the wheel landed on the roof, after

bounding some way up the mountain side. The splined hub had sheared." Perhaps this explains why so much work was needed to rectify the battered car, and why it was never again used in the works team.

UOC 741 competed as a BMC works car on the 1958 Tulip rally, driven by Jack Sears. It was fast and promised much, but unhappily was let down by an engine distributor failure.

Competition Record

1957 Sestriere rally	Tommy Wisdom	10th in Class
1958 Monte Carlo rally	Tommy Wisdom	DNF
1958 RAC rally	Jack Sears	5th in Class
1958 Tulip rally	Jack Sears	DNF
1958 French Alpine rally	John Gott	DNF

REGISTRATION NUMBER	ENGINE SIZE	MODEL TYPE
PMO 201	**2639CC 6-CYL OHV**	**100-SIX BN6**

One of three brand-new cars prepared at Abingdon for International rallying, it was always allocated to Pat Moss. It was the first time she had ever driven a Big Healey; until then she was more used to driving much less powerful Morris Minor 1000s (although, in fairness, I should also note that until quite recently she had been using a Triumph TR2 as her ordinary road car, and that of course she had already rallied the MGA).

For Pat, to drive PMO 201 in the French Alpine rally of 1958 was a really encouraging start to her relationship with

Big Healeys, for it was clear that although, as she always insisted, she found the car difficult to drive, she was also formidably fast and on a par with the pace of her male team colleagues.

From Marseilles and back to Marseilles, by way of Brescia and Megève, this Alpine was tough by any previous standards, and the still-new Healeys were having to face the well-developed works Triumph TR3As, which, for the first time were using 2.2-litre engines, but until well after the halfway mark it looked as if Pat and PMO 201 might be the

PAT MOSS

Everyone loved Pat Moss. Did we ever find anyone with a word to say against her? Although she arrived in rallying with the patronising tag 'Stirling's little sister' hanging around her neck, within a couple of years she had shown just how fast, tough and capable she was going to be as a rally driver. Within five years of joining the BMC team, she had not only become a credible lady rally driver, but had actually won the toughest of all rallies – the Liège-Sofia-Liège.

A relative latecomer to rallying (she had spent her earlier years competing in showjumpings, at which she was also adept), she started at BMC driving an uncompetitive MG TF on the 1955 RAC rally, though her next drive was delayed until the Monte Carlo of 1956. After graduating to Morris Minor 1000s and MGAs, she got her first chance to wrestle with the Big Healey (a 100-Six) on the French Alpine of 1958.

By that time there was no doubt that this slight, devastatingly pretty and outwardly insecure young woman had become an established member of the team. Although she seemed to be scatterbrained to a fault (many was the time when she left her handbag behind at a hotel, restaurant, or rally service point !), and liked to trade on the 'wide-eyed innocent' reputation which developed over time, she was nevertheless ferociously competitive, with great endurance and a real will to win.

A heavy smoker – it took its toll in later years – and seemingly hyperactive, she liked to be busy-busy and was apparently interested in anything that life had to offer. Her rallying partnership with Ann Wisdom (the daughter of Fleet Street's motoring doyen, Tommy Wisdom, a successful driver of works Healeys himself) was a great success.

Once she came to terms with the Big Healey (she always said it frightened her, but so did Paddy Hopkirk – and they both won events in the cars) she was often as fast as all but the two Flying Finns. Though broad-shouldered, with enough body strength to cope with these big cars, Pat was strictly the sort of active, sport-loving lady who disarmed most men with her charm – yet she could also become depressed if the cars were not always in good health.

Each of her cars got a nickname: (her Liège-winning Healey, URX 727, was soon known as 'Uurrxx', her long-lived Morris 1000 was 'Granny', while a singularly unlucky Healey 3000 was always known as 'The Thing'. And of course she had her own foibles about equipment. Like Big Brother Stirling she liked her car registration numbers and competition numbers to have a 7 in them and disliked the number 13. So it was something of a miracle that her Liège victory was achieved in a Healey carrying the event number 76, of which the numerals add up to 13.

Having met the mountainous Swedish rally driver Erik Carlsson on events, he and Pat rapidly became an item and married in 1962. For 1963 both were courted by Ford, who offered big financial incentives which BMC could not match. Pat took up that offer though Erik did not. Later Pat moved on to drive for Saab and, later, Lancia, but she was never seen as an icon for those teams, not in the same way that she had always been at BMC.

fastest Healey finisher, and could even win the capacity class.

Unhappily 'the case of the knotted breather pipe' then intervened. On the final leg, south of Megève, Pat stopped for some hurried service at a non-scheduled moment, found herself running out of time, and left the engine oil breather pipe hanging loose. Rushing to get back in her car, she asked a 'friendly British journalist' (later identified as Britain's Joe Lowrey of *The Motor*) to close the Healey's bonnet for her, which he did, but not before 'helpfully' tying a knot in the pipe. Within minutes the crankcase pressure began building up, oil leaked out through the rear crankshaft seal, and the clutch began to slip. Once the BMC mechanics had discovered the problem, the repair took seconds, the oil leakage was stopped, and the clutch slip gradually eased. This, though, was enough to cause Pat to slip back down the running order, and instead of winning the capacity class, she was overtaken by the works Triumphs. To win the Ladies' Prize, and to finish tenth overall, only went part of the way to easing her disappointment.

Pat and PMO 201 made up for it all in the gruelling Liège-Rome-Liège which followed in August. Tougher even than the French Alpine had been, this was a 3,000-mile marathon which did not allow a single overnight rest halt for the crews, set target average speeds higher than any other European rally dared to consider, and was enough to make even big strong men quiver at the challenge. To quote Bill Price's recollection: "The heat was fierce, and the Healey with its low ground clearance took a terrible beating on the rough roads. Heat in the cockpit was excessive and the dust poured in through the side-screens and every other hole and crack." The rally involved a lengthy passage of Germany before visiting Italy, Yugoslavia, Italy again, and France. It was in Yugoslavia, on a testing, high-average-speed dash from the Italian border at Tarvisio to Kopvrinica, Solin on the Adriatic coast, Rijeka and Kranska-Gora, where much of the physical damage was caused. It was no wonder that of the 98 cars that started the event only 22 finished when the route returned to Belgium, the miracle being that three were 100-Sixes, two of them in the top ten.

As the event progressed, and after the really rough stuff was over, team manager Marcus Chambers became increasingly worried about Pat's health, and counselled her to ease up somewhat but aim to reach the finish. Pat, just as stubborn then as she was in later life, took no notice. After the rally she found a photograph of her car in action and sent it to him, with the signed inscription: "To 'Sir', who said 'Slower' from Faster and Faster".

PMO 201 then required a lengthy lay off and re-preparation during the winter and spring of 1959, when Pat was driving other, mainly smaller-engined works BMC cars, the two were reunited for the 1959 Greek Acropolis rally in May 1959, the only works entry in a Big Healey. It was not to be a successful outing as the car crashed out at an early stage. Once again, to quote Marcus Chambers: "It transpired that Ann [Wisdom] had been driving and Pat was asleep when the crash occurred. The Healey had been running in a high-speed convoy of Greeks who knew the road and the conditions. They had come to a tightening left-hander which went downhill. Ann had over-corrected and the car had spun and rolled down a steep grassy bank into a cornfield. They had been helped back onto the road by the others, but the timing had slipped and the car was in no fit state to go on".

It was an ignominious way for this pioneering works Big Healey to reach the end of its factory-backed career, but it was soon made roadworthy again and was driven all the way back to the UK, where it was eventually refurbished and sold.

In its very first rally, the 1958 French Alpine, PMO 201, a works 100 Six, was driven by Pat Moss

Competition Record

1958 French Alpine rally	Pat Moss	4th in Class, 1st Ladies
1958 Liège-Rome-Liège	Pat Moss	4th Overall
1959 Acropolis rally	Pat Moss	DNF

REGISTRATION NUMBER	ENGINE SIZE	MODEL TYPE
PMO 202	**2639CC 6-CYL OHV**	**100-SIX BN6**

The second of the new Abingdon-built 100-Sixes, PMO 202, ran with the same specification on the 1958 French Alpine as its sisters, PMO 201 and PMO 203, and was allocated to the Scots driver Bill Shepherd, who had been a driver, sometimes a co-driver, for Marcus Chambers's team since mid-1956.

Described as the toughest French Alpine so far held, the 1958 event was a real car (and reputation) breaker, for only 25 cars finished out of 58 starters, with only seven not penalised on the road sections and therefore winning a coveted Coupe des Alpes – though even those had to be 'invented' following the news that the organisers' set average speeds had been too difficult for everyone at one stage .To BMC's delight one of those was Bill Shepherd's Austin-Healey 100-Six, which enjoyed a faultless run on the event so graphically caught on film by a Shell film unit.

As already noted (see PMO 201, above), this event was fast and furious, used most of the high, demanding and tortuous passes in the French Alps and in the Italian Dolomites, and required real grit and determination by the crews to keep a clean

Gerry Burgess and Sam Croft-Pearson contested the 1958 Liège-Rome-Liège in PMO 202, finishing tenth overall.

sheet. Shepherd, along with his co-driver John Williamson, battled through the five-day event against the works Triumph TR3As, ceding class victory to Keith Ballisat's 2.2-litre car at a late stage, but still finishing extremely strongly and gaining the last of those Coupes.

PMO 202 was then one of four 100-Sixes prepared for the gruelling Liège-Rome-Liège, in which Pat Moss took a startling fourth place in PMO 201. This time PMO 202 was driven by Gerry Burgess/Sam Croft-Pearson as Bill Shepherd was not in the team on this occasion. By finishing tenth overall in such a taxing event, in spite of never having rallied an Austin-Healey before, Burgess's sturdy performance was quite overshadowed by Pat Moss's virtuoso display in the sister car.

After it had then spent the winter resting while Abingdon got on with competing in 'winter' rallies in cars like the Austin A40 and the Sprite, PMO 202 was refurbished for Pat Moss to drive in the Tulip, an event in which Jack Sears produced a magnificent performance in PMO 203. Pat had not driven this particular car beforehand and would probably have preferred to forget what happened on the Tulip, for on the very first night of the event, which had started in Paris, this (according to historian Bill Price) is what happened: "Pat was not very happy with the handling or braking. Near St Agrève the car skidded off the road head-on into a bank. The starter motor shorted out, and was making an awful noise until Pat and Ann disconnected the battery". By the time they were retrieved (by Marcus Chambers, no less, in a chase car), and the rally car had been dragged back on to the road from the rock cliff which it had embraced, the only solution was to arrange for it to be returned to Abingdon for a major rebuild, whereafter it was sold to Bill Shepherd.

Competition Record

1958 French Alpine rally	Bill Shepherd	7th Overall
1958 Liège-Rome-Liège	Gerry Burgess	10th Overall
1959 Tulip rally	Pat Moss	DNF

REGISTRATION NUMBER	ENGINE SIZE	MODEL TYPE
PMO 203	**2639**CC (LATER **2912**CC) **6-CYL OHV**	**100-SIX BN6**

By now the most experienced of the 100-Six rally drivers, Jack Sears was allocated the third of the new machines, PMO 203, for the French Alpine rally of 1958, his co-driver on this occasion being Sam Moore. Like the other team members (see PMO 201 and PMO 202, above) Jack found the 1958 Alpine very demanding, but on the speed sections was as fast as hoped. Second fastest outright at Monza to a gullwing Mercedes-Benz 300SL was a good start, but his progress was somewhat hampered when he met a works Ford Zephyr head-on at high-speed after one of them had taken a wrong turning and was rapidly returning to the junction which mattered. This caused delay, the loss of tempers, and some damage to the 100-Six. The tracking was put out and the off-side front wing was crumpled, one result being that Sears was late at the next control. Later still, and to help Pat Moss out of trouble, there was quite a bit of shuffling around of wheels, tyres and tread patterns, with Pat the real beneficiary. Just to show that he had not lost his will to win, though, Sears then set fastest time in the final speed test on the J.P. Wimille circuit in Marseilles. His

Driving PMO 203, Jack Sears put up a fine performance with a first in class in the 1959 Tulip rally, which suggested that a fully-developed Big Healey could be formidable on future events.

reward in the end was that he finished eleventh overall, the third best placed of the works 100-Sixes.

Its next assignment was for the 1958 Liège-Rome-Liège, where it was allocated to Joan Johns, who was relatively inexperienced on such powerful cars but who had driven works Austin Westminsters and co-driven other cars for Marcus Chambers in previous years. Her co-driver was Sam Moore, who had accompanied Jack Sears on the recent French Alpine rally. As it happened it would be the last time that she was hired as a front-line driver for the team.

This was an unlucky outing for the pair, for although they started in high spirits from Liège, almost as soon as the route led the cars into Yugoslavia, at Tarvisio, the 100-Six skidded off the road near the Predil Pass and damaged the steering so much that it was thought wise to retire. Even so, as Marcus Chambers later reminded us in his memoirs, BMC mechanics based at Tarvisio soon sorted out the steering, which allowed the rejuvenated car and its crestfallen crew to act as a chase car (or 'spares on the hoof') for the rest of the event – in which Pat Moss, in PMO 201, of course, finished a remarkable fourth overall.

There was then a long lay-off for this machine, which did not appear again until May 1959, when Jack Sears, with Peter Garnier of *The Autocar* as co-driver, tackled the Tulip rally. On an event which saw the Morley Twins winning outright in their own Jaguar 3.4 saloon, Jack put up a great performance, for the route was much more demanding than usual for the Tulip, the time schedule being particularly brisk in some sectors. The record also shows that the engine of this car was giving trouble in the early hours of the event – sparking plugs and their behaviour being a particular problem – and that it was Tak's gullwing Mercedes-Benz 300SL that was going to give Sears the most trouble, especially as Pat Moss's car was eliminated after a crash.

Things gradually improved for the Sears and Garnier, however, first of all when the 300SL holed its sump and therefore wrecked its engine. Thereafter Sears led his class and began to dominate the category until finally, on the speed test at the Zandvoort F1 circuit, the 100-Six showed that when driven by Jack Sears it was near unbeatable. The rush for outright victory was close but much affected by the usual complex Tulip Rally performance handicap, so although Sears and the Big Healey convincingly won their capacity class, they could finish no higher than eighth overall, with five slower saloons, an excellently driven works TR3A and a Porshe 1600S ahead of therm. All in all, only a handful of cars (including Sears's one) completed the road section without incurring time penalties.

Rebirth as a 3000

PMO 203 was then re-worked, updated, given a new 2912cc engine and reborn as a works 3000, though this was only a temporary strategy on the part of the BMC works team. In its

STUART TURNER

Turner's best-selling autobiography was titled *Twice Lucky*, but few observers thought there was much luck about his glittering career and the way that it evolved over the years. Not only did he enjoy six remarkably successful years at Abingdon from 1961 to 1967, but in later years (from 1969 to 1990), he was one of the top decision-makers in Ford Motorsport too.

After completing his National Service in the RAF, Turner returned to his native Stone, in Staffordshire, and trained rather unenthusiastically as an accountant. At the same time he took up rallying, always as a co-driver, eventually becoming the most successful in the country.

Having won the BTRDA's National co-driver award on three occasions in the 1950s and become the observant editor of his local motor club magazine, where he was famous for his mordant humour, he branched out even further by tackling European events. He become instantly famous in November 1960 by navigating the giant Swede, Erik Carlsson, to victory in the British RAC International rally, and became the first Rallies Editor ('Verglas') of *Motor Sport* as well.

He always insisted that he was surprised to be offered the job of BMC Competitions Manager in 1961, and he took to it with alacrity and great skill. Although he always admitted that he could not have arrived at a more favourable time – the Mini-Cooper was new, and the Healey 3000 was still approaching maturity – he introduced an atmosphere of ruthless purpose to a still improving team.

Within a year, some of the Old Guard of drivers and co-drivers had been eased out, though he made sure that Pat Moss remained. Other new arrivals included Timo Makinen, Rauno Aaltonen (the original 'Flying Finns'), and Paddy Hopkirk and, eventually, deep-thinking co-drivers such as Tony Ambrose, Paul Easter and Henry Liddon. Yet even he could not persuade Pat Moss to remain at Abingdon, for she left after accepting a big financial offer from Ford at the end of 1962.

It was under Turner's control that the team got down to more serious technical development, to working with Dunlop, refining its reconnaissance and pace-noting expertise, tightening up its service procedures, and being more aggressive with new homologation and the way that a professional team should be run.

By pushing every aspect of this job to the limits – not least by a careful study of homologation and event regulations – Stuart was able to optimise the performance of an already very capable team. As an experienced rallyist, not just as a good manager, of course he always had the confidence of his drivers, who performed better than they might have done for anyone else.

Everyone was surprised when he abruptly decided to leave BMC at the beginning of 1967, saying that he thought he no longer wanted to climb mountains, stand at the side of the road getting soaked, and have to answer to his bosses for the vagaries of event organisers.

This was the moment when he handed over to Peter Browning, in as smooth a transition as could be wished. Even so, after spending just two years with the oil company Castrol (latterly as publicity manager) he had yet another change of mind, was seduced back into the sport by Ford-UK, and spent the next two decades running motorsport and public affairs at that company.

new make-up, and now sporting a white hard top instead of its original black top, PMO 203 then tackled the Liège-Rome-Liège, but although Gerry Burgess was invited to drive it and to improve on his sturdy result in the 1958 event this was not to be.

It was one of those events that hard-pressed team managers prefer to forget. On this occasion five works cars – four 3000s and Pat Moss in an Austin A40 Farina – started the event, but only a single survivor, Peter Riley in SMO 744, made it the finish. As Marcus Chambers later wrote: "The 1959 event was not a great success for BMC; we were only saved from complete disgrace by the achievement of Peter Riley". Gerry Burgess crashed PMO 203 but there is very little remaining evidence of what happened or where. This was Burgess's last drive for the BMC team but it certainly did not break his spirit: three months later he took a works Ford Zephyr out on Britain's RAC rally and won the event outright.

Repaired after the Liège mishap, PMO 203 was used just once more before being sold to the British private owner Bobby Parkes. Pat Moss, having decided that she could become European Ladies Rally Champion with a suitable solid finish in the Portuguese Rally, trekked all the way down to the Iberian peninsula as the only 3000 entry from BMC. But it all went wrong. The event itself was a thoroughly unsatisfactory affair, with very little speed work involved, and where the results seem to have been settled by performance in a single driving test. Pat and her 3000 did not shine, the result being a lowly 53rd overall, but they were given the Ladies Award as a consolation. By this time in rallying, Pat was widely considered to be the equal of any man, and almost shrugged off ladies prizes.

According to Stuart Turner, who wrote Pat's biography, it was this and other shortcomings of the event that caused her to lose her patience and "She vented her displeasure with a demonstration drive in her Healey. The final test had been a short street circuit of two large blocks of houses, lined with pavements and lamp-posts. Pat took the Healey out and gave a perfect display of opposite-lock control with power-slides around the right-angle corners. It was a rare, very rare moment of Pat being a hooligan".

Competition Record

1958 French Alpine rally	Jack Sears	11th Overall
1958 Liège-Rome-Liège	Joan Johns	DNF
1959 Tulip rally	Jack Sears	1st in Class
Then converted to 3000 specification		
1959 Liège-Rome-Liège	Gerry Burgess	DNF
1959 Portuguese rally	Pat Moss	1st Ladies

REGISTRATION NUMBER	ENGINE SIZE	MODEL TYPE
TON 792	**2639CC 6-CYL OHV**	**100-SIX BN6**

Nancy Mitchell about to start the 1958 French Alpine rally in TON 792 – she would take 12th Overall.

For the 1958 French Alpine rally TON 792 (a car based in Birmingham as the registration number confirms) was commandeered at very short notice, rushed to Abingdon and made ready to compete. This was because BMC, which had originally planned to enter MGA Twin-Cams for this event, suddenly found that the MG's launch date had been delayed and that the cars could therefore not be homologated.

"As we only had three cars of our own," Marcus Chambers once told me, "in addition to the Healey company's UOC 741, we had to borrow another demonstrator from the Austin Motor Company. This car was red-and-black and was normally used by BMC's vice-chairman, George Harriman. He very sportingly released it for this event, and we allotted it to Nancy Mitchell." Nancy was at the peak of her career, having been crowned European Ladies' Champion in 1956 and 1957, but was already preparing to retire from front-line motorsport as it was clear that the youthful Pat Moss was about to overtake her as the best female driver in European rallying.

Nevertheless on this, her first experience of a 100-Six, she put up a stirring performance and, apart from the flying Miss Moss, was equal to all the men in the team. Nancy's co-driver, Gillian Wilton-Clarke, was not only rather inexperienced at this fierce level of motor sport but also definitely overawed by the 100-Six. A navigational error at one point caused Nancy to be penalised, but otherwise she kept going strongly and finished twelfth overall. The fact that she could not win her class was entirely due to three other BMC 100-Six team cars, driven by Bill Shepherd, Pat Moss and Jack Sears, all finishing narrowly ahead of her.

Undaunted, Nancy then agreed to tackle the Liège-Rome-Liège as her swansong for BMC, planning to retire at the end of the season. She renewed her on-off partnership with Anne Hall, with whom she had tackled many tough events, and once again used TON 792. Four 100-Six team cars tackled the event and three completed the Marathon, one of them being this grittily-determined team. In the end, Nancy and Anne Hall brought TON 792 back to Liège by way of the Italian Dolomites and the French Alps, taking second in a fiercely contested Ladies' category behind the sensationally fast Pat Moss, and also sharing victory in the Manufacturers' Team Prize. It was Nancy's last event and – as it happened – the last for TON 792 as well.

Nancy Mitchell and TON 792, high on the Mont Ventoux hill climb speed test of the 1958 French Alpine rally.

Competition Record

1958 French Alpine rally	Nancy Mitchell	12th Overall, 2nd Ladies
1958 Liège-Rome-Liège	Nancy Mitchell	2nd Ladies

REGISTRATION NUMBER	ENGINE SIZE	MODEL TYPE
SMO 744	**2912**CC 6-CYL **OHV**	**3000 BN7**

With the launch of the new Austin-Healey 3000 road car in mind, BMC's Competitions Department made sure that they also had a new clutch of those cars for International motorsport, which meant that three brand-new machines – SMO 744, SMO 745 and SMO 746 -were made ready for a high-profile debut on the French Alpine rally of 1959.

As can be seen from their events records, all these cars were worked harder than any previous BMC works machine – in only one-and-a-half years SMO 744 started no fewer than eight International events. Somehow or other, though, it never became anyone's 'favourite', for seven drivers tried their hand in the car in those eight events and it retired on three. Its high point came on the toughest of all -- the Liège-Rome-Liège, which it started twice and finished twice, winning its class on one of them.

For its first appearance on the rally scene, the French Alpine of 1959, PMO 744 was allocated to Bill Shepherd who, along with his co-driver John Williamson, had performed so well in 1958 in a 100-Six, so it was truly unfortunate that on this occasion the repeat performance should end in retirement caused by under-car damage. Although the team had already concluded that some of the target times for selective sections were quite impossible for the larger-engined sports cars (those times, incidentally, were different for various classes), BMC had entered three brand-new 3000s in the hope that they might win their class, or even the category, even though there was no chance of winning a coveted Coupe des Alpes.

81

Somehow or other this was not an event in which the 3000 was destined to shine, for there was torrential rain early on, particularly for the Monza speed test, but until the final long section from St Gervais-les-Bains to Cannes began, Bill Shepherd was leading his capacity class when he encountered two deep cross-track gullies on the Col d'Ornon at high speed; there was a sickening crunch as the sump hit the gulley, the casting was cracked open, all the engine oil ran out and within minutes the crankshaft bearings had failed.

Next on the agenda was the Liège-Rome-Liège Marathon, where Peter Riley got his first opportunity to grapple with the powerful car. Before the event, and with two months to carry out the work, Abingdon had worked hard at making the 3000s more rally-proof – in particular by devising a more substantial sump guard.

Peter got it right straight away, becoming faster and more assured as the event progressed, and in spite of the sheer length (92 hours) of this gruelling Marathon, he produced a near faultless performance ("I only managed to go off the road once, in Yugoslavia"), coming home a well-earned tenth overall and winning his capacity class.

That, though, was the height of SMO 744's early career (not for nothing did Pat Moss come to christen it 'The Thing') as in a matter of months it retired from the 1959 RAC rally, the 1960 Circuit of Ireland and the 1960 Acropolis, each time with a different driver at the wheel.

On the 1959 RAC rally a lucky handful of crews managed to navigate their way (with high penalties) around the snow-blocked roads in the Scottish Highlands – which caused weeks of protests to fly from those who had not even attempted the climb

– but there were few memories to cherish. John Williamson tried his best to stay on course with SMO 744, and was apparently leading the event for a time (he had started from No. 1), but in view of what was to follow he might have been relieved when his gearbox failed.

On the Circuit of Ireland of 1960, run over the Easter weekend, it was Pat Moss's turn to wrestle with this rather unpopular machine, and she had no better luck than the previous drivers had had. While waiting for her new-for-1960s 3000 to be completed (URX 727, which would make her lastingly world-famous later in the year) she had already tackled the Lyons-Charbonnières in SMO 746, an event which resulted in a massive accident that might have killed her, and the Geneva in SMO 745, so she can be excused for disliking SMO 744, calling it"The Pig' or 'The Thing'.

There was no change of luck for Pat on the Circuit either. It relied more on manoeuvring tests and the occasional speed test/hill-climb, but this was before the days of special stages, so Pat and 'The Thing' had little chance to shine. Fast up the hills, and making headlines wherever she went, Pat laboured against mechanical problems. With a car which seemed to be suffering from a slipping clutch throughout (according to her biographer, "To get up steep hills they had to keep going under the car with a fire extinguisher to spray the clutch in the hope that this would blow out the oil causing the trouble. When the gearbox packed up, they retired and weren't really sorry". That was in Co. Galway, near the west coast of Ireland, and it was a long way home.

Perhaps it was asking too much for Peter Riley to get the best out of 'The Pig' on the Acropolis rally which followed less than six weeks later. Nor did he, for the Greek roads were at their roughest, most corrosive and most dusty, and it can have been no surprise to him when one of the still-experimental Dunlop Duraband radial tyres blew a tread at high speed. In the rush, confusion and hassle which followed the car and its crew were thoroughly unsettled, and not long afterwards they crashed. In what started as a very high-speed accident, which seemed to go for a long time, the hardtop was whipped off and both crew members, who had not refastened their seat belts after the wheel-change, were ejected from the car as it plunged down a mountainside – fortunate for them, as the stricken machine carried on down the rocky hillside for some distance without them. Happily neither was seriously hurt.

Recovering the wrecked car took time and the rebuild which followed was extremely lengthy, so it was August before SMO 744 was once again rally-worthy, this time being allocated to David Seigle-Morris to tackle the Liège-Rome-Liège. He had just joined the team from the works Triumph operation, which was closing down.

Most people tend to remember Pat Moss's magnificent win on the 1960 Liège in URX 727 and know less about what happened to other team members, so this is surely the right place to emphasise how Seigle-Morris immediately slotted into the team, took to the 3000 – even SMO 744 – as to the manner born and recorded a splendid fifth place overall in the harum-scarum atmosphere of the demanding Liège-Rome-Liège, where the roads and tracks in Yugoslavia were daunting and where the time schedules were almost ludicrously hard to achieve.

Starting at No. 66, behind two of his four team mates, David settled in like the professional that he had already become and, in his own words, "The love/hate relationship which one acquired grew by the hour and on the third night of the Marathon, high in the Yugoslavian mountains, with but a few competitors left in the rally, I began to appreciate what a great car it was. But even as the love was welling up, so was the hate and the dust and the heat".

All the reports were that this car behaved magnificently (apart from punctures, which afflicted every car on the event), as did the crew, though a brake servo pipe broke soon after the start and could not be replaced in the time available, which meant that Seigle-Morris, a very fit body-builder, needed all his stamina

to keep a servo-less 3000 on the road for nearly 3,000 miles.

The post-event statistics make fascinating reading: of the 82 starters only 13 made it to the finish. Three of the four works 3000s were among them, in first, fifth and tenth places, winning their class and category and lifting all the available team prizes. Seigle-Morris had urged SM0 744 into fifth place, which was undoubtedly its finest performance, having incurred 18 minutes more penalties than the flying Miss Moss.

Were SMO 744 and its crew now going to get a good rest? Not a bit of it, for no sooner had it returned to Abingdon than it was prepared for use by Donald Morley on the German rally. He had not been able to take part in the Liège because, as a working farmer, it was harvest time in East Anglia. Seigle-Morris would take Stuart Turner with him to drive SMO 745 on the same event.

The German rally was mainly based in the French Alps, with a smattering of speed and hillclimb tests but little hard open-road motoring. It was also one of those events where there were different target times for different categories. Accordingly, although the 3000s were the fastest and most successful of the GT cars, finishing first, second and third in the category, it was Gunnar Andersson's Volvo PV544 saloon that won the event outright.

Now, surely, it was time for SMO 744 to get a rest but no. For the end of the season and its last works outing, 'The Pig' was allocated to Ronnie Adams and Johnnie Williamson for the RAC rally. Unhappily, its career ended in the same way as it started, with no result to boast about. Even on the first night, in the tight road sections in Yorkshire and south Scotland, the crew lost time in the foggy conditions and never recovered from that setback. Things did not improve as the event progressed, for although Adams was very fast on speed tests he lost time on the road sections. Then, on the very last speed test at Brands Hatch he started his race on the front row alongside Donald Morley, Peter Riley and Don Grimshaw's Triumph TR3A, but apparently span off and incurred more penalties. Was it significant, therefore, that neither Adams nor his co-driver John Williamson was ever again invited to join the BMC works team?

To the relief of those in the BMC who thought that 'The Pig' was a jinxed car it was then sold off, to be replaced by new-for-1961 works cars which were being prepared instead.

Competition Record

1959 French Alpine rally	Bill Shepherd	DNF
1959 Liège-Rome-Liège	Peter Riley	10th Overall, 1st in Class
1959 RAC rally	John Williamson	DNF
1960 Circuit of Ireland	Pat Moss	DNF
1960 Acropolis rally	Peter Riley	DNF
1960 Liège-Rome-Liège	David Seigle-Morris	5th overall
1960 German rally	Donald Morley	2nd in GT Class
1960 RAC rally	Ronnie Adams	4th in Class

REGISTRATION NUMBER	ENGINE SIZE	MODEL TYPE
SMO 745	**2912CC 6-CYL OHV**	**3000 BN7**

The second of three brand-new 3000s (SMO 744 and SMO 746 were the others) was made ready to compete in the French Alpine rally of 1959 and was entrusted to the ultra-reliable John Gott, whose co-driver was Chris Tooley. Starting well, Gott faced the Monza speed test in the wet with some trepidation but managed to beat his target time, retaining his Coupe for the time being. This test alone left four cars in the same class (but not Jack Sears in the third car) with penalties.

Later, after being penalised on narrow, twisty and steep climbs in Austria and faced with a whole series of impossible target times, Gott found himself losing points and having to battle with the 2.2-litre TR3As, though he was still leading his class. The final blow, in more senses than one, came on the Turracherhöhe in Austria, where the poorly protected underside of SMO 745 had allowed a stone to to hit the radiator drain tap and cause a steady water leak which took ages and several bodges to be stopped. Before the car could carry on, late but with Gott determined to reach the finish, much time had been lost, though in the end Gott took second in his capacity class.

There was less good fortune on the Liège-Rome-Liège Marathon, where Gott took Ken James with him as his co-driver. The two had never rallied together, and it was unfortunate that while Gott took a nap and left James to drive and find his own way he took a wrong turning and ended up about 18 miles down the wrong road in a sparsely-populated part of northern Italy. Gott takes up the story: "I got out the maps and found that we had overshot the fork by about 18 miles. I told Ken to stop and get out and that he was now going to have to pay for his error by being frightened out of his mind as I tried to make up the lost time back to the fork and to the control. We had to average 75mph, I think, to make it on time. I missed it by 1 minute 45 seconds, and we were excluded on overall lateness."

The only way this car could enjoy a change of fortune, it seemed, was to have a different driver in it for the RAC rally which followed. That duly came when the Morley Twins got their very first works drive, which they carried out with great skill. As already noted in the SMO 744 description, this event included a snow-blocked section in the Scottish Highlands. The Morleys benefitted by running at No 9, which meant that they were near the head of the field, could make an about-turn when faced with the blockage, and were then able to drive very fast on a long diversion route round the mountains north of Balmoral. They lost more than 30 minutes of a possible 60 minutes lateness allowance by this tactic but everyone else who tried it was in the same situation – the result being

that the Twins finished fourth overall, and steered the first of the large-engined Austin-Healeys to the finish. In a way this secured their place in the BMC team, where they were happily integrated for the next six years.

In April, Pat Moss took the car on the Geneva rally while her brand-new and later legendary URX 727 was still being prepared at Abingdon. Her participation was a remarkable achievement as it came only five weeks after she had been involved in a horrid Big Healey crash on the Lyons-Charbonnières rally (see SMO 746). Perhaps this is why she described this Geneva event, which was mainly held on familiar French Alpine hills and tests, as "A fast tight rally over the usual twisty and mountainous roads. I was really twitched and worried and nervous and for the first time I was a bit frightened of the big fast car. Even on the first bit I had to force myself to drive competitively, and I was much slower in corners than ever before, but I improved steadily and grew more confident as I realised how well the car handled, and how safe it was on dry roads".

The car behaved perfectly, which was a great relief to Pat and to the team, and except for one point where they hesitated before the end of another tight section, turned back to a junction before realising that they were right after all, and lost several minutes and several places. Seventh place, a class win and the Ladies' prize were only a minor consolation.

Abingdon then had about five weeks to prepare the car for the demanding Acropolis rally, where Pat once again took the wheel. For her it was not a happy event. She started well but the Big Healey took a fearful battering from the awful Greek roads and at a service point near Larissa they discovered that there were serious cracks in the chassis, while the steering was also deranged. As Pat's biographer later noted, "Some of the Volvo team people kindly welded up what they could, and they could have continued, but by then they had lost about an hour, and Pat had misgivings about the steering, so they retired."

SMO 745 was put back into good shape for the French Alpine rally and was allocated to an 'old hand', John Williamson, and a new-recruit, Ronnie Adams from Northern Ireland who had won the 1956 Monte Carlo rally in a Jaguar Mk VIIM. This duo had no luck at all as before the first day/night run had been completed the car arrived at one BMC service point with a gearbox which would only engage first and reverse, so retirement was inevitable.

By this time the BMC team had concluded that their works cars – which probably had about 170bhp instead of the 124bhp of standard showroom models – were now proving to be too much for the basically-standard gearboxes, and it was therefore something of a miracle that Pat Moss put up such a fabulous performance in URX 727 to take second place overall.

Soon SMO 745 was readied for the German rally, one of three works 3000s taking part, and with the new and sturdier gearbox the prospects for the team were good. This time it was David Seigle-Morris, with Motoring News Rallies Editor Stuart Turner alongside him, who set out to tackle the event. David's car suffered from electrical problems on the tough and demanding Col de la Cayolle, causing his headlamps to dim, but he was lucky enough to be overtaken by Pat Moss in URX 727 and thus to tag on behind her until he could reach service. Severe speed tests on Mont Ventoux and on the Col de Rousset proved just how fast and consistent the Big Healey had become, and by the time the three surviving 3000s reached the finish in Baden-Baden they were dominating their class.

A month later SMO 745 tackled its last event as a works car, allocated to Peter Riley and Tony Ambrose for the RAC rally. It started from Blackpool, trekked all the way up to the far north west of Scotland, included four specially timed stages (three on public highways closed for the occasion), and finally after several days ended with a series of sprint races on the Brands Hatch circuit.

The short story of this event is that accurate navigation had as much to do with a good performance as did the use of a very fast car, but since Tony Ambrose had already won an RAC rally (in 1956) he had no problems with this, especially as the car started from No. 9. Even so, there was enough fog, and enough difficult route finding, for Peter Riley to lose a total of seven minutes in road penalties (the outright winter, Erik Carlsson, was un-penalised throughout). Nevertheless, Riley finished second in his class to Don Morley in a 3000 sister car, was tenth overall, and helped BMC to win the Manufacturers' Team Prize.

Competition Record

1959 French Alpine rally	John Gott	2nd in Class
1959 Liège-Rome-Liège	John Gott	DNF
1959 RAC rally	Donald Morley	4th Overall, 1st in Class
1960 Geneva rally	Pat Moss	1st in Class
1960 Acropolis rally	Pat Moss	DNF
1960 French Alpine rally	John Williamson	DNF
1960 German rally	David Seigle-Morris	1st in Class
1960 RAC rally	Peter Riley	10th Overall

REGISTRATION NUMBER	ENGINE SIZE	MODEL TYPE
SMO 746	**2912CC 6-CYL OHV**	**3000 BN7**

All in all, competing in the French Alpine rally of 1959 was not a happy occasion for the 'SMO' trio of 3000s. Like the other two cars, SMO 746 suffered from an assault by the elements, and Jack Sears, who was noticeably faster than either of his team-mates on this event, was forced to retire. Having started well by comfortably achieving his target average speeds at the Monza speed test, Jack then tackled the rocky Passo Vivione in the Italian Dolomites, where his 3000 encountered a gulley at high speed, the engine jumped on its mountings and the cooling fan hit the radiator. So that was that.

Suitably refreshed for the Liège-Rome-Liège, SMO 746 had a spot of bother when it was lent to the new team recruit Peter Riley for a familiarisation run around the Berkshire lanes. In spite of Riley's doubts about a works 3000's handling all went well – until his proposed co-driver took a turn, promptly

putting the car off the road and into a pond. That co-driver was sacked and Peter instead took the Rev. Rupert Jones on the Liège. For the event itself the car was entrusted to a pair of reliable team members, Jack Sears and The Autocar 's Sports Editor Peter Garnier. Their efforts, meritorious as they were until the last set of high-speed sections in the French Alps, were described by Garnier in an Autocar feature headed 'Well – we tried'.

With Sears at his best, the pair had placed the car well into the top eight by the time the much depleted field emerged from Yugoslavia, but then the trouble started, for in Italy at one point the Healey went off the road and buckled two of its wire wheels. Finally, in France the organisers had set a seemingly impossible target average speed around the infamous 'St Jean Circuit' so that, along with a route-finding mistake, a patch of thick fog and an unwise stop for fuel, the luckless duo ran out

The lull before the storm, with Jack Sears/Peter Garnier and SMO 746 ready to tackle the toughest sections of the Liège-Rome-Liège event of 1959.

of time, though still with a healthy car.

The car was so speedily repaired that when Pat Moss was entered for the German rally just six weeks later she 'inherited' this machine and therefore drove a works 3000 for the first time. Her biographer Stuart Turner recounts that she was rather nervous about grappling with a 3000 and consulted Jack Sears for some guidance: "The discussion obviously paid off, because she put up the fastest time on every test, two seconds a lap faster than the 100-Six had been on the Monza circuit, and two minutes faster up Mont Ventoux. Very promising indeed."

It was only because the event was being run on a 'class improvement' basis, and Erik Carlsson's Saab had been outstanding among the sub-1-litre saloons, that Pat was robbed of outright victory because "The girls tied for first place with Erik Carlsson. If there was a tie the smaller car would be declared the winner, so Pat and Wiz ended up second".

In November Pat was happy to hand back the 3000 to Jack Sears so that he could tackle the RAC rally with the experienced Willy Cave alongside. This would be Jack's last rally for BMC as he was about to go on to bigger and better things on the race track.

The confusion, the post-event protests and counter-protests, and the bad feeling which followed the discovery that one of the roads over the Scottish mountains was blocked by snow has already been detailed (see SMO 744 and SMO 745), but because Sears and Cave elected to assume that the Braemar control, which they did not even attempt to reach, would be cancelled, they were docked a colossal 300 marks and thrown

right out of contention, to finish seventeenth and second in class to the Morleys. A post-event re-cap showed that if the Braemar control had been cancelled, as many competitors thought it should be, Sears and Cave would find that they had only lost one mark on the road sections making up the rest of the route, and accordingly would have been awarded tenth place overall.

Next, after a winter's lay-off, Pat Moss was sent off to tackle the Lyons-Charbonnières event, which included a high-speed sprint test at the Solitude race circuit in Germany, not far from Stuttgart. SMO 746 was described as being 'a little tired' by this stage but Pat used it for practice, being intended to use SMO 745 in the event itself. Purely by chance this car was involved in an accident just before the rally so (the reasoning is not perfectly clear) Marcus Chambers asked the service team to take the registration number, licence disc and identification plates from SMO 745 and to transfer them temporarily to SMO 746.

Part way through the event, when she was holding her own against a stiff sports/GT class which include ACs, TR3As and Porsches, she set out to tackle the Solitude test, which was a time trial on several laps of the race circuit. This, according to her biographer Stuart Turner, is what happened next: "The circuit was 7.1 miles long, with quite a few corners and kinks, and with only one practice lap allowed… They needed a fast time so Pat planned to have a go in spite of the greasy track. Cars started at five-second intervals and Pat was the last of her class to go; it was still teeming down so Wiz watched from the restaurant. Pat managed to pass all the other cars in the class, taking the last one, a Porsche, fairly close to the corners she had not driven at speed. She changed from overdrive top to overdrive third but went into the last corner, which loops round like a long hairpin, far too fast and hit the safety barrier sideways. It was made of railway sleepers. One broke loose and tore through the wheel and wheel-arch like a lance, and went through the car, drilling through the passenger seat and out again through the boot, which opened.

"The sleeper missed Pat. The 3000 sailed over the bank behind the barrier, somersaulted, then miraculously landed the right way up, on its wheels. Pat switched off, amazed to be alive… It was a horrendous crash, yet all Pat suffered was a knock on the leg and a bloody nose".

One miracle and a written-off car would have been amazing, but what followed was equally so. The wrecked 3000 had to be shipped back to Abingdon with the railway sleeper still well and truly impaled in it but it was then repaired by two first-class mechanics, Den Green and Tommy Eales. Their first job was to use brute force to cut the sleeper into pieces before it could be extracted, after which the damage (much of the left front corner, the front suspension, the front bulkhead, and the rear passenger bulkhead) had to be rectified, and new panels and body sections had to be fitted. Sounds unfeasible? Indeed it does, but as recently as 2017 the author confirmed with Den

Green that this was indeed what was done. They did such a good job that the car was restored to good health in a mere three months and made ready for John Gott to drive it on the French Alpine rally. The event led to Austin-Healey winning the Manufacturers' Team Prize and other team prizes too (Gott's car was one of them), but all this was quite overshadowed by the magnificent performance put up by Pat Moss, who took a rousing second place in URX 727, which would shortly reach immortality status in the Liège-Rome-Liège which followed.

By comparison with the Lyons-Charbonnières adventure, SMO 746's experience in the French Alpine must have felt like a routine day out, for although the timing of the event was very tough – only six cars made it to the finish in Cannes without penalties on the road section – the experienced Gott kept going steadily and finished eighth overall, second in class to the redoubtable Ms Moss. All went well for this crew until the very end, where the fearsome Sigale-Quatre Chemins section (n the mountains north of Grasse had to be tackled, and it was on this 21-mile section that Gott finally suffered a slide on loose gravel, took time on the very narrow road to turn straight again after juddering to a halt, and missed his time by a mere 23 seconds.

Just one more event, the Liège-Rome-Liège, lay ahead before SMO 746 qualified for a long rest. It was then pansioned off and replaced at Abingdon by one of a new batch of 3000s. Reports of this Liège are invariably dominated by the story of Pat Moss's amazing success in URX 727, but one should never forget the efforts of the two crews – David Seigle-Morris in SMO 744 and John Gott in SMO 746 - who backed her up.

John Gott, this time accompanied by Rupert 'The Bishop' Jones, captured tenth place and third in class behind Pat Moss and David Seigle-Morris in a 3,000 mile event which started and finished in Belgium but took in Germany, Austria, Italy, Yugoslavia, Italy (again) and France, all without an official rest halt, and totalling nearly four days of exhausting motoring.

By Liège standards – which meant having to accept a loss of time at controls due to some of the target times being practically impossible – this was almost a routine outing for Gott and Rupert Jones, although there was one frightening moment when the car's bonnet catches failed and the bonnet flew up, totally obscuring the view ahead. It took some minutes of pushing, pulling, swearing and improvising before

wire was employed to hold everything together until the car next reached a BMC service halt and received more permanent repair. This was SMO 746's final works appearance, though it was then sold to John Gott, who spent years modifying and progressively improving it to be driven as a racing sports car for British events.

Jack Sears, in SMO 746, leads Donald Morley in SMO 745 on the special speed test on the Aintree GP circuit, during the 1959 RAC rally. The Morleys went on to take fourth place overall.

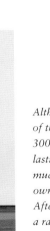

Although SMO 746 was one of the original fleet of works 3000s built in 1959, it achieved lasting fame in later years as a much-modified race car, when owned and driven by John Gott. After competing extensively as a rally car in 1959 and 1960, it was the sold to John Gott, and progressively modified – as this picture shows.

Competition Record

1959 French Alpine rally	Jack Sears	DNF
1959 Liège-Rome-Liège	Jack Sears	DNF
1959 German rally	Pat Moss	2nd Overall
1959 RAC rally	Jack Sears	2nd in Class
1960 Lyons-Charbonnières rally	Pat Moss	DNF
1960 French Alpine rally	John Gott	8th Overall
1960 Liège-Rome-Liège	John Gott	10th Overall

REGISTRATION NUMBER	ENGINE SIZE	MODEL TYPE
SJB 741	**2912CC 6-CYL OHV**	**3000 BN7**

This car did not make its first appearance for BMC as a works rally car until May 1960, one year after the 3000 was introduced, but the chassis number confirms that it was one of the very first 3000 road cars to be built in the spring of 1959, and possibly the first. The assumption – and it is only an assumption – is that this car had other non-motorsport duties at Abingdon before being handed over to the Competitions Department. As a competition car it was only used four times, all during 1960, and on three out of those four times it was entrusted to the Morley Twins. In a way it was the most consistent and least abused of the first-generation cars being used at that time, certainly leading a less eventful life than the SMO 744/745/746 series.

Its first outing was in the 1960 Tulip rally, which the Morleys

no doubt viewed with some pleasure as it was on the previous year's event that they had suddenly burst into the spotlight by winning in their own Jaguar saloon. Coincidentally, SJB 471was one of only two works 3000s entered in the 1960 rally, the other being another debutant car, URX 727, which would go on to become famous in its own right.

Success in rallying at this time often involved a mathematician's skill as much as a driver's bravery, for in 1960 there were 15 specially timed road sections and five speed hill climbs in a route which stretched all the way from Holland to the south of France and back.

As it happens, only ten cars (one of them being driven by Pat Moss) completed the tight section up to the peak of the Col du Turini without penalty, and the fact that the Morleys missed out

This peaceful scene, in a small French town, was of SJB 471 (the Morley Twins) and URX 727 (Pat Moss/Ann Wisdom) competing in the 1960 Tulip rally – an event where Pat took eighth place, and won her class. SJB 471 was the first of all the fleet of works 3000s to be built.

by a matter of seconds put them way down according to the Tulip organisers' calculators! SJB 471, however, was in good shape afterwards and the whole team was pleased with the immediate maturity of the new team members.

Only a few weeks later the car and crew all turned up at the start of the French Alpine rally which (as far as is known) the Morleys had not previously tackled; on this occasion they had one of the four works 3000s which took the start. Three of those cars would finish, the Morleys, speeding up as they learned the event, finally taking third in their capacity class behind Pat Moss's and John Gott's sister cars.

Not that it was entirely routine. The car clouted a rock at the side of the road on the Mont Ventoux speed test, which caused a tyre to deflate, though they kept going, and a gearbox fault (third gear went AWOL) meant that the resourceful mechanics had to rejig the electrical connections so that overdrive operated on all (surviving) forward gears, which was, to put it mildly, a gamble. The Morleys struggled on, eventually ending up with only top gear, and if the triple-carburettor 3000 engine had not been so amazingly flexible they would surely have had to retire. As it was, they preserved their clean sheet until the very last tight section – Sigale to Quatre Chemins – which would have been demanding with a healthy car but in their car-crippled condition cost them four minutes. No matter, for third in class was assured and the Morleys were members of the team which won every available team award too.

Peter Riley at the wheel of SJB 471 in the 1960 Liège-Rome-Liège rally. Mechanical problems meant he did not finish.

DONALD MORLEY

The affectionate nickname Pat Moss gave Donald Morley, 'The Little Devil', was incredibly apt. Outside the car, and especially when dressed in his farmer's tweeds, Donald was a small, wiry man, always courteous, but when driving a Healey he was one of the most ferociously fast of all BMC's works team. Although he was neither as successful nor seemingly as comfortable in a Mini-Cooper S, he was the absolute master of the Healey, had great success in it, and made sure that he bought one of the team cars (XJB 876, his French Alpine-winning mount) when it was finally pensioned off.

After stumbling across rallying in the 1950s to give him a change from working his large arable farm in East Anglia, he and his non-identical twin brother Erle (the larger of the twins) used unsuitable cars including an Austin A90 Atlantic successfully in British rallies. In 1959, though, he startled the rally world by winning the Tulip rally in his privately prepared Jaguar 3.4. Signed up by Marcus Chambers to join the BMC works team, he rapidly became the master of the Big Healey. Unless asked to do an event during the harvesting season (which the twins would never do), they were willing to throw the Big Healey at any challenge, on tarmac, snow and ice or gravel.

Donald was never analytical of his driving talents or methods, unlike Rauno Aaltonen, who agonised over both, and was certainly not brutal with his machinery (Timo Makinen, need I say more?) but he was always super-fast and rarely crashed his cars. The fact that a Big Healey driven to the limit could be difficult to control seems to have escaped him, probably because he had little experience of other fast sports cars before joining BMC.

He and Erle often looked as if they had come to rallying from an earlier age. They usually rallied in suits or sports jackets, with crisp shirts and ties, at a time when the thrusting young Finns were wearing racing overalls but they were always comfortable with their cars and their tasks. As well as rallying the best and fastest Healeys of all, Donald occasionally raced them too, while he and his brother also won the GT category of the Monte Carlo rally in an MGB.

Because 1960s rallies were often riddled with regulations which favoured a 'class-improvement' index rather than outright performance, Donald was robbed of several much-deserved outright victories. The records show that he officially and deservedly won the 1961 and 1962 French Alpine rallies in Big Healeys, but he also set up the best outright performance on no fewer than four Tulip rallies – in 1962, 1963, 1964 and 1965 – and also achieved a Coupe d'Argent (Silver Cup) for being unpenalised on the tough road section of three French Alpine rallies too. Only the most cruel bad luck (a broken differential in 1963) robbed him of an even more prestigious Coupe d'Or (Gold Cup) for three consecutive such runs.

The Morleys were too gentlemanly and too committed to their farming profession to let top-grade rallying take over their lives, and they retired while still at their sporting peak. Prestigious offers from Porsche were refused, and the twins became much-admired elder statesmen of rallying instead.

SJB 471 was often driven by the Morley Twins in 1960. Here, at a time control on the 1960 RAC rally, Donald Morley (dressed, as so often, in a jacket and pork pie hat) prepares to tackle a difficult Scottish section. His twin brother/co-driver, Erle, (back to the camera, close to the passenger door) prepares to clock out. The car finished third on the event. It was then sold off into private ownership.

Next came the ultra-tough Liège-Rome-Liège, which would result in Pat Moss winning outright in URX727, but the Morleys could not (or would not, more likely) compete because they both had farming commitments at harvest time in East Anglia. Peter Riley got the plum job instead and looked after SJB very carefully. Unhappily, even before the route led through Yugoslavia, Riley reported a sticking throttle linkage which (according to team boss Marcus Chambers) at one time allowed the big engine to over-rev to 7,000rpm, but it was not until the return through Italy, when the car was still extremely well placed, that one of the blades on the cooling fan broke away and punctured the radiator. There was neither the time nor the available manpower to repair or exchange this, so the car had to be retired.

Just one event remained on this car's busy 1960 schedule, the British RAC rally, where the Morleys were reunited with SJB 471, and started No.1 on the road. On an event which proved to have much tougher road sections than expected, only Erik Carlsson in his amazing Saab 96 remained unpenalised, but right behind him, both having lost two minutes at time controls, were the Morleys and John Sprinzel in his Sebring Sprite. Marks lost on the various speed and manoeuvring tests (which included an infamous well-soaped skid pan at Wolvey in Warwickshire) then had to be considered, the outcome being that the Morleys were awarded third place overall, and of course won their capacity class.

That was the end of its short works career, after which it was sold off to the privately financed driver Derrick Astle.

Competition Record

1960 Tulip rally	Donald Morley	2nd in Class
1960 French Alpine rally	Donald Morley	3rd in Class
1960 Liège-Rome-Liège	Peter Riley	DNF
1960 RAC rally	Donald Morley	3rd Overall

REGISTRATION NUMBER	ENGINE SIZE	MODEL TYPE
UJB 143	**2912CC 6-CYL OHV**	**3000 BN7**

This was one of the very rare occasions when the identity of a car originally prepared for circuit racing at Warwick was transferred to the Abingdon rallying fleet.

The original UJB 143, having raced at Sebring and Le Mans in 1960 (see Chapter 8), was then sold off and re-registered by its new owner, David Dixon, as DD300. This meant that UJB 143 became an identity looking for a car to adorn. Accordingly, BMC, looking to replenish its rallying fleet after what had been a destructive early part of the season, prepared a brand-new car which they promptly registered as UJB 143! This car then had a two-event rallying career: Midnight Sun 1961 and Tour de Corse 1961.

Because of the nature of the event, with its high-speed, loose-surface special stages, the Midnight Sun was hardly likely to be an ideal challenge for the works 3000, but in one of the last rallies he oversaw before handing over the manager's job to Stuart Turner, Marcus Chambers sent Peter Riley to do his best.

Starting and finishing in Stockholm, the route included nineteen high-speed special stages and the 3000 put up a remarkably assured performance, although, as expected, it proved difficult for Peter Riley to match the pace of the local Scandinavian drivers. Only one non-Scandinavian driver (René Trautmann, in a Citroen DS19) finished in the top ten, while the 3000 finished second in its class to Hans Walter's Porsche 356 Carrera, so its 12th place overall was seen as a considerable achievement.

Months later, in the search for extra points to urge her towards the 1961 Ladies' Championship, Stuart Turner entered

Pat Moss in the Tour de Corse in UJB 143, but conditions were not ideal. The car was somewhat big and heavy for the event and – of all things – there was unexpected snow at one point! All this and tempestuous winds which resulted in trees being blown down caused the organisers to abandon the event after only twelve hours. In the circumstances a class win was the best that could be expected – and it was duly delivered.

UJB 143 was a registration number which originally figured on a 3000 built to race at Sebring in 1960, but after that car was sold off (see Chapter 8) the number was re-used on a new rally car in 1961. This car only competed twice – in Sweden and Corsica – and is seen here on the Tour de Corse, where Pat Moss won her capacity class.

Competition Record

1961 Midnight Sun rally	Peter Riley	12th Overall
1961 Tour de Corse	Pat Moss	1st in Class

REGISTRATION NUMBER	ENGINE SIZE	MODEL TYPE
URX 727	**2912CC 6-CYL OHV**	**3000 BN7**

Is this the most famous works 3000 of them all? Very likely. What other car ever delivered such a remarkable result, not only helping a very popular driver to her most famous rally victory, but in what was agreed to be the roughest, toughest, most damaging and most gruelling rally of the period.

Like its then sister car, SJB 471, this machine had a very short career and tackled only four International events in 1960, yet it not only won one of them, the Liège-Rome-Liège, but finished second overall in another, won its class in a third and never had to retire. Pat Moss, incidentally, later bought the car and then shortly afterwards sold it. It still

URX 727 was, and is, probably the most famous works 3000 of all time, for it was in this machine that Pat Moss and Ann Wisdom won the 1960 Liège-Rome-Liège marathon outright.

Pat Moss met up with Erik Carlsson during her time at BMC. They later married and Pat later drove for Saab, and for Lancia, in a distinguished career.

exists, often seen at classic events.

Brand new in the spring of 1960 and immediately prepared for Pat Moss to use during the season, it was ready for her to contest the 1960 Tulip rally, where it started alongside the Morley Twins in SJB 471. As already noted in the description of SJB 471's career, this particular Tulip roamed all around France, but the whole event was settled by the challenge of a very tightly timed ascent of the Col du Turini from the western side, where only 11 minutes were allowed from a standing start for the twelve-kilometre climb. Of the entire 165-car entry, only eleven cars reached the summit within the time limit, with the redoubtable Ms Moss just nine seconds inside the schedule. That, though, was all that was needed to assure her of a class win and eighth overall. It also gave her an undying respect for her new car.

Next the car went back to Abingdon to enjoy a four-week rebuild before the French Alpine rally, which started from Marseilles, trekked all the way through the Alps, across to the Monza circuit near Milan in Italy, and then after a night halt in Chamonix made its way to the end in Cannes. BMC's works entry was of no fewer than seven cars, of which four were pristine 3000s. All the cars had the latest triple-SU engines, though there were now recurrent worries about the durability of the gearboxes.

This was a very demanding event in which there were several other full-strength factory-backed teams, but the result was finally dominated by an ultra-special works Zagato-bodied Alfa Romeo Giulietta SS driven by Roger de Laganeste and Henri Greder. Happily, Pat's 3000 was reliable and sympathetically driven and seemed to survive where others had mechanical problems. She even managed to beat the required time over the fearsome Quatre Chemins section, though years later she told the author that it was really quite easy if one didn't go off at any point, for the road was very narrow and a spin almost inevitably led to a crash and to difficulty turning round. The reason for this comment was that, as she said in a much earlier interview, "After another mile we came to a bend with no stones at all on the apex, just liquid tar. We spun. The road was only about two feet wider than the length of the car.... we finished up round the corner, but across the road diagonally and with my door nearest to the bend". She needed help from the next car along, Edward Harrison's works Ford Zephyr, but all was recovered in the very nick of time.

All in all this was a remarkable performance and one which should could only surpass by winning an event outright – which, in August, she duly did. Before then, however, two important changes were made to her car. One, shared with the other 3000s entered in the Liège and in subsequent events, was a stronger gearbox, which Marcus Chambers had 'begged' from Charles Griffin, Alec Issigonis's very able and enthusiastic deputy, and the other – Pat Moss's own idea – was much lower gearing. Pat had concluded that the 3000s as normally geared, were far too fast for many of the roads they would be using. To quote her biographer, "Pat got them to fit a diff from a London taxi, the lowest ratio made by BMC. It cut their top speed in direct top to about 80mph, but the acceleration was better, with 0-60mph in around six seconds." For the record, at this time the works 3000s usually ran with a 4.1:1 final drive ratio, but Pat had asked for and got a ratio of 4.875:1.

Much attention had gone into preparing the team cars and Pat and Wiz were buoyed up by their 'so-nearly' performance on the French Alpine. The prospects for success in the Liège were very encouraging. Even so, it was not until the much depleted field of cars came out of Yugoslavia – only 30 out of the 83 starters made it through the dust, the rocks and the searing temperatures (never mind the lack of a scheduled rest halt) – that Pat and URX 727 began to move towards the head of the column.

Her 3000 was beginning to wilt under the strain: in Yugoslavia the overdrive failed and the car had to be driven in direct top gear, sometimes at engine speeds perilously close to the safe limit, while the clutch began slipping intermittently. The 'bushman's solution' simply to keep the car going was to keep squirting the clutch with fire

Pat Moss in URX 727, on her way to a storming second overall in the 1960 French Alpine rally. Only weeks later, the same car/crew combination would win the Liège-Rome-Liège marathon outright.

extinguisher fluid, but there was a time schedule to be met and no prospect of service crew assistance until hours later. Pat and the 3000 were in the lead, only 15 cars were still running, but would the car last through northern Italy, the mountains of France and all the way back to Belgium?

Later, a hurried investigation showed that the gearbox drain plug had gone AWOL, much of the gearbox oil had departed, and even when that was remedied it was clear that an oil seal at the front of the 'box had fried and was persistently leaking. Efforts to find a replacement seal (including getting a French mechanic to start driving from the BMC dealer in Nice to meet the cavalcade) were fruitless, and when the team gathered at a small garage near Barcelonnette, at the foot of the Col d'Allos, there was only an hour left to bodge up another seal. As history now relates, a suitable seal from another make of car – Pat thinks it was from a Fiat – was found, a change was made, and Pat rushed off to tackle the speed test up the Col d'Allos, where the marshals were still in residence but not, frankly, expecting to do any more business that night. Local non-rally traffic, in fact, had already been released on to this narrow road, so Pat's fourth fastest time was a really stupendous performance.

The rest of the French section was almost routine by Liège standards, with the 3000 setting fast times on several other tight speed sections. It was a very proud pair of girls who somehow managed to stay awake for the next 24 hours without any competitive motoring to do, and there was time to give the car a wash before it led the two other team cars, SMO 744 and SMO 746, into the finish in Liège. Only 13 cars, of which three were 3000s and one was John Sprinzel's Sebring Sprite, made it to the end. All in all, Pat, Wiz, the 3000 and the BMC team had set a series of fantastic results which might not (and were not, in truth) ever be matched on this event.

By comparison with the fabulous Liège, the German rally,

which followed at the end of September, was something of a sideshow, and in spite of having to battle with unfavourable handicapping regulations, three works 3000s finished first, second and third in the entire GT category. In the meantime URX 727 had been rushed back from Belgium to Abingdon, where the mechanics found to their amazement that apart from needing a change of gearbox it was still in remarkable condition. On the German, therefore, Pat finished a rather relaxed third in the GT category, having blown her chances of winning the Ladies' category by taking a wrong turn on one tightly timed section, behind team-mates David-Seigle-Morris in SMO 745 and Donald Morley in SMO 744.

After the German rally, which ended on Sunday 2 October, Abingdon and their colleagues in the BMC Exhibitions Department had a couple of weeks to retrieve the car and put it back to its pristine best, though Pat had never damaged it, before putting it in pride of place on the Austin-Healey stand at the Earls Court Motor Show, complete with authentic Liège rally plates and with the number 76 on the doors. Was this the real deal or a mock-up? The real one, no question

– no exhibition department could ever have mocked up all the details that were on show. In any case, no works 3000 carrying the famous URX 727 ever again took part in an event, for before the end of the year the car was sold at a very favourable price to Pat Moss.

Pat, who always said that Big Healeys frightened her, used it very sparingly for less than a year – never at all for motorsport – and eventually decided that hard cash (useful for financing her continuing passion of horse jumping) was much to be preferred to sentiment. URX 727 was marketed through John Sprinzel's thriving little garage/workshop in Lancaster Mews, London W2. In an advert published in Autosport in November 1961 it was described as a "'fabulous motor car" and, "With the complete factory modifications and a fantastic performance, URX 727 has covered a total of less than 12,000 miles, and has NEVER had even the smallest bump or scratch on its red and cream coachwork… Built at a cost of well over £2,500 and now offered at £1,295 with a full-three-month warranty". Were ex-works cars really sold off so cheaply in those days?

Competition Record

1960 Tulip rally	Pat Moss	1st in Class
1960 French Alpine rally	Pat Moss	2nd Overall
1960 Liège-Rome-Liège	Pat Moss	1st Overall
1960 German rally	Pat Moss	3rd in GT Class

REGISTRATION NUMBER	ENGINE SIZE	MODEL TYPE
XJB 870	**2912cc 6-cyl OHV**	**3000 BN7**

For 1961 BMC clearly decided that they needed to rejuvenate their entire fleet of works 3000s, for no fewer than five brand-new cars were acquired, taking up the well-known XJB sequence of identities: XJB 870, XJB 871, XJB 872, XJB 876 and XJB 877. Immediately before this multi-car preparation began, six of the older 3000s were sold off at the end of the 1960 season, and there was then a sizeable gap, with no 3000s entered in events until May 1961, the Tulip rally.

XJB 870 might have had the earliest registration number but it was the fourth consecutive chassis-numbered car of the five newcomers to roll off the assembly lines a few yards away from 'Comps'. It was one of the last of the bunch to take its bow in International rallying, and its front-line career covered four events in seven months, after which it was retired and used for a time as a practice car to support the ARX series. In real competition it was always driven

by David Seigle-Morris and finished three times out of four starts !

As a brand-new car it first tackled the 1961 French Alpine rally, where team-mate Donald Morley won outright in XJB 876, like its sister cars using the new type of Dunlop radial-ply tyre, the herringbone-pattern SP with textile bracing, which was much to be preferred over the steel-braced Durabands which had been used earlier.

Seigle-Morris started well but it was in the 'St Jean Circuit' (north of the Col du Rousset) that he had to withdraw following a spin and a crash which saw the 3000 straddling a bank on the edge of a drop. Although he managed to retrieve the car he was delayed too long to continue, but he then used it as a high-speed 'spares-on-the-hoof' machine until the surviving 3000s reached the end in Cannes.

XJB 870's second outing was the 1961 Liège-Sofia-Liège, where it and driver David Seigle-Morris distinguished themselves by finishing sixth overall and second in the entire GT category to Hans Walter's Porsche Carrera. By the time the crew arrived at the four-hour rest halt in Sofia – four hours only, and there were no other rest halts in the four-day event – they were apparently leading.

Conditions on the return trip towards Italy were as horrifying as the practice sessions had suggested, but even so the 3000 was still well placed when Seigle-Morris entered one bend a little too fast, slid off the road and ended up with a car which was little damaged but could not be retrieved without a tow. It was more than half an hour before team-mate Don Grimshaw arrived in XJB 876 (the French Alpine-winning car) and did the honours. Somehow or other they got going again, struggled manfully with exhaustion and the conditions, suffered several punctures and a broken rear leaf spring, and yet finally made it back to Liège after completing 3,420 miles, the only Big Healey to survive this event.

The car had taken a hammering on the Liège but it was still sound enough for the team to get it back into tip-top condition for David Seigle-Morris to tackle the RAC rally, the first event to include a number of Forestry Commission special stages. BMC started with every hope of winning the event but they reckoned without the sheer genius of Erik Carlsson and his two-stroke Saab 96. Of the three 3000s which started two finished, with Seigle-Morris in fifth place.

Starting from No. 5 immediately behind Pat Moss, David was well placed to put in a good performance, and set off from Blackpool in high spirits. In a 2,000-mile route which stretched from the far north of Scotland to West Wales, finishing in Brighton, there were 24 special stages to be tackled, along with a good deal of tight navigation in Yorkshire and in Wales. David suffered an early 'off' after taking a wrong slot in one of the forest sections. Nevertheless the 3000 was always up and among the leaders, one particular high point being the setting of fastest time overall on the 11.5-mile Eppynt tarmac stage. At the end of the event, though, he had to settle for fifth overall and second in class to Pat Moss, the only other cars finishing ahead of him being Erik Carlsson, plus Peter Harper and Paddy Hopkirk in works Sunbeam Rapiers.

XJB 870 was used in one further International event in January 1962 when it was entered for the Monte Carlo rally, where on this occasion conditions were remarkably mild. Five lengthy special stages and a circuit test in Monaco at

the finish, were enough to test the professionals. Starting from Paris (the author was one car behind him, co-driving Peter Procter's Sunbeam Rapier) he had to spend day after pointless day driving around France before the hard work and special stages began in Chambéry.

There was snow, lots of it, on the first lengthy stage after Chambéry, but none at all on the ascent of Mont Ventoux. The patchy conditions did not always suit the Big Healey, which slipped back on the stages, though Seigle-Morris made up for it by being second fastest overall behind Lyndon Sims' Aston Martin DB4 on the four-lap sprint around the Monaco GP circuit which brought the event to a close. In the end Seigle-Morris not only won his GT capacity class but also won the entire GT Category.

This was the ideal time for XJB 870 to be retired and to be used for a time as a practice car, for the new set of ARX cars was now on the way.

David Seigle-Morris at the wheel of XJB 870 on a road section of the 1961 RAC rally. He would take fifth place overall.

Competition Record

1961 French Alpine rally	David Seigle-Morris	DNF
1961 Liège-Sofia-Liège	David Seigle-Morris	6th Overall
1961 RAC rally	David Seigle-Morris	5th Overall
1962 Monte Carlo rally	David Seigle-Morris	1st Class, 1st GT category

REGISTRATION NUMBER	ENGINE SIZE	MODEL TYPE
XJB 871	**2912cc 6-cyl OHV**	**3000 BN7**

This car only appeared twice in International events, both times driven by Peter Riley, who finished third overall in the 1961 Acropolis, and crashed following a brake failure on the French Alpine which followed.

BMC entered four cars for the Acropolis but three of them were 848cc Minis, with Peter Riley driving the sole works 3000. Fortunately for him and for the car he ran at No.3, which meant that the rough gravel roads had not had much of a chance to cut up before the low-slung Healey had to tackle them.

Starting in Athens under the Parthenon and ending back in Athens after a tough high-speed circuit of Greece, the rally proved to be ideal for cars and crews that were used to such conditions, which may explain why Erik Carlsson's Saab 96 won outright, with Gunnar Andersson's Volvo PV544 in second place. Peter Riley, partnered by Tony Ambrose, put

XJB 871 was new for 1961, but was only used twice by the works team. Here it is on the French Alpine rally just before it crashed and was too heavily damaged to continue.

up a magnificent performance in XJB 871 to take third place overall and won the entire GT category outright. Forty-five of the original 74 starters made it to the finish.

It was not an event without incident as at an early stage the 3000 gave electrical trouble, traced to a defective dynamo, but a change of component solved that problem. Peter Riley then fought a rally-long duel with Hans Walter's Porsche 356 Carrera, which was a sturdily built factory-prepared machine, and gradually pulled away from it in spite of suffering a high-speed tyre blow-out.

XJB 871 had had a hard time in Greece but it had not suffered any chassis or body damage, so there was time to get it back to Abingdon for a full-scale refresh before it had to be sent off to Marseilles (using the invaluable car-train ferry which existed in those days, from Boulogne to Avignon) for the start of the French Alpine rally.

All five of the new-for-1961 XJB 3000s were to start the Alpine, with Peter Riley and Tony Ambrose in the middle of the bunch. This was an ultra-tough event where target average speeds were high and the 3000s had to be driven hard throughout. Peter and Tony started well and rushed through the original French sections but on the famous Stelvio pass the car suddenly suffered a brake failure, spun viciously off the road and was severely damaged. Peter suffered broken ribs and had to take time away from rallying to recover; he did not reappear in a BMC works car until the start of 1962.

As to the car itself, there never seemed to be enough time to repair its battered hulk; during 1962 it was sold to Rauno Aaltonen and did not re-appear as a works machine.

Competition Record

1961 Acropolis rally	Peter Riley	3rd Overall, 1st GT car
1961 French Alpine rally	Peter Riley	DNF

REGISTRATION NUMBER	ENGINE SIZE	MODEL TYPE
XJB 872	**2912cc 6-cyl OHV**	**3000 BN7**

This was one of the five new cars commissioned in 1961. It was probably the least lucky and the shortest-lived of all the 3000 fleet, doing its first event in June 1961 and its second and last just eight weeks later in August. It was not used again in motorsport. John Gott drove the car on both occasions, him-

self retiring from active BMC rallying at the end of the season.

Gott, the most experienced of all the contemporary BMC driving team, always listed the French Alpine as one of his favourite events, but on this occasion he was not to enjoy it much. Although he was no longer as fast as some of his compatriots – Pat Moss and Donald Morley were truly the pace setters – he could usually be relied upon to anchor the entire effort. This time though his effort faltered on the climb out of Chamonix when he misjudged an 'open air' corner at high altitude and slid off the road, landing in a meadow about 25 feet below the road. Gott and his co-driver somehow managed to extricate themselves via the gate to the field but much time had been lost and in the end they could only finish sixteenth overall, and third in class behind the Morleys, who won the event, and Eugen Böhringer's Mercedes-Benz 300SL.

There was even less luck for the reunited car and crew on the Liège-Sofia-Liège, which delved further into the Balkans than ever before, the run-round point being Sofia in Bulgaria, and no longer took in France. The machinations of the organisers were such that the average speeds required to stay in the event were higher than ever, and a series of rough roads in Yugoslavia along the Adriatic coast between Skopje, Split, Novi and the Italian border made this event a real car breaker. In the end, of the 85 starters only eight made it to the finish.

One of those who crashed in a combination of dust, fog, and, one suspects, exhaustion was John Gott, who mangled the 3000 so much that it could not continue. The car was not used again but after being repaired it was sold off to Derek Astle, a well-known and successful rally driver from the north of England.

XJB 872, with John Gott at the wheel, in Yugoslavia on the 1961 Liège-Sofia-Liège. It was forced to retire when the rough conditions caused a broken engine sump.

Competition Record

1961 French Alpine rally	John Gott	3rd in Class
1961 Liège-Sofia-Liège rally	John Gott	DNF

REGISTRATION NUMBER	ENGINE SIZE	MODEL TYPE
XJB 876	**2912CC 6-CYL OHV**	**3000 BN7**

Purely by chance, one surmises, the first of the 1961 generation of works 3000s to appear were the two with the highest registration numbers, XJB 876 and XJB 877, which made their debut on the Tulip rally, allocated to the Morley twins and Pat Moss respectively. XJB 876 would only appear four times during the year and was then sold to Donald Morley, who kept it in private ownership for some time.

The 1961 Tulip was one of those infuriating events where the overall classification was decided on what was known as a 'class-improvement' basis, which meant that if a car was dominant in its class it would automatically be placed high up in the final results, whereas one which had merely scraped home would not. This, in fact, was an event in which 'Tiny' Lewis retired his works Triumph Herald on the very finishing line so that the privately-entered Herald in front of him driven by Geoff Mabbs could benefit.

As usual, the 'meat' of the Tulip was a series of sprints and 15 speed hillclimbs in France, where the Healeys fought hammer and tongs with Tak's Mercedes-Benz 300SL and Hans Walter's Porsche 356 Carrera. Before and after the overnight halt in Monte Carlo neither 3000 put a wheel wrong, and although Pat Moss set FTD on several tests, with the Morley Twins mere seconds adrift, neither could benefit from the odd marking system unless the other withdrew.

Neither Donald Morley nor Pat Moss – nor, for that matter, team-boss Marcus Chambers – would stoop to such low tactics, and at the end of the event (and before the 'class comparison' formula had been applied) it became clear that in 'the real rally', Walter (Porsche) would have beaten Pat

XJB 876 was new for the 1961 rally season, and leapt to fame by being the outright winner of the French Alpine rally of that year.

Sold to Donald Morley after the 1961 RAC rally, it has since been restored. It orginally ran triple SU carburettors but now has Webers.

by just eighteen seconds, while in turn was only ten seconds ahead of the Morleys. Officially, however, the Morleys finished a lowly 14th overall, their car being as fresh as a daisy at the close. Austin-Healey at least had the honour of winning the Manufacturers' Team Prize, and almost the entire rally field agreed that the 'real' rally had been a real motor race from start to finish.

For the French Alpine of 1961 BMC's 3000s were at the peak of their development, with the triple-SU carburettor engines benefitting from free-flow tubular exhaust manifolds. The Morleys soon began to set the fastest speed hillclimb times and were one of a dwindling group of teams without road penalties, but they soon lost Pat Moss (accident), David-Seigle-Morris (accident) and Peter Riley (accident), leaving only John Gott (who had also had an accident from which he recovered after much delay) to support them.

Not in the least perturbed, it seemed, the Morleys carried on, unpenalised on the road sections and very fast on the speed hillclimbs that abounded in this generation of French Alpine rallies. But it is not generally remembered that their performance nearly ended in disappointment: as team boss Marcus Chambers recalled in later years. "I did not think they were going to finish when they lost second gear before the final stage before Cannes (the infamous Sigale – Quatre Chemins section which had broken so many hearts in the previous event)... and when we got to Cannes we asked spectators if they had got in, and they told us that they had won the rally outright." Not only had the Morleys won outright but they were the only crew that had finished unpenalised for lateness on the road section – second place man Jean Rolland (Alfa Romeo GSZ) had lost a minute and third place man Paddy Hopkirk (Sunbeam Rapier) had lost two minutes. It was a quite remarkable achievement.

Three months later XJB 876 was ready to tackle the Liège-Sofia-Liège, but not with the Morleys, as the twin brothers were both staying at home dealing with the harvests on their large east Anglian farms, Instead, a 'one-off' drive was awarded to Don Grimshaw (who had recently bought SMO 745 for use in British events). This was the now notorious Liège in which only eight cars made it to the finish, and unhappily Grimshaw's steed was not among them, for on the return dash through the rough, hot and amazingly demanding Balkans, near Split, the 3000 suffered a rear suspension failure which immobilised it.

The car's next and as it transpired last works appearance was also disappointing: the Morleys were anxious to perform well on the RAC Rally of Great Britain, but were let down by events. Starting at No.2, immediately behind 1960 winner Erik Carlsson and his Saab 96, they began well, clearing the Kielder forestry section – one of only seven crews to make it unpenalised – and were leading the Healey contingent after the Rest and be Thankful speed hilllclimb test, but the car needed a new exhaust system. Next, having had to deal with what *The Autocar* called the "incredibly bumpy 2.6-mile Onich special stage", they holed their sump, but there was enough slack in the timing of the road section for BMC mechanics to change the sump in a roadside garage.

Yet still their problems were not over, for the car then suffered a sheared dowel in the rear axle, and before arrival at the Inverness night halt it needed a complete gearbox change. The fact that it was then lying second overall to Carlsson's Saab was one consolation, and 24 hours later, as the route came back from Scotland into England, the car was still securely in second place. Then came the final disappointment. On the passage of two Borders stages – Newcastleton and Kershope – the hard-worked rear axle cried enough and immobilised the team for good.

Although this was the end of its short and tempestuous career, the Morleys clearly liked the car so much that Donald arranged to buy it immediately afterwards.

Competition Record

1961 Tulip rally	Donald Morley	14th Overall, 2nd in Class
1961 French Alpine rally	Donald Morley	1st Overall
1961 Liège-Sofia-Liège	Don Grimshaw	DNF
1961 RAC rally	Donald Morley	DNF

REGISTRATION NUMBER	ENGINE SIZE	MODEL TYPE
XJB 877	**2912CC 6-CYL OHV**	**3000 BN7**

As already noted in the description of XJB 876's career, XJB 877 was brand-new for Pat Moss to drive in the 1961 Tulip rally, and it was Pat who would go on to drive it throughout the season; although she was not actually rude about it, many years later she would describe it as a 'characterless' machine. In 1962 and 1963 it was driven by no fewer than four drivers, became progressively less well loved than the 1962-generation ARX'machines which were taking all the limelight, and would be ceremonially written off after its battering in the 1963 Liège. In three years, however, no other works Healey had a harder life. It started nine International events, retiring five times, and was used as a practice car before other events.

First time out Pat Moss drove it on the 1961 Tulip rally, an event which was quite ruined by an over-complicated 'class-improvement' marking system. Although Pat was marginally outpaced by Hans Walter's four-cam Porsche 356 Carrera, she set fastest time outright on several of the speed hill climbs and would surely have merited second place overall if the marking system had allowed it.

Her experience in the French Alpine which followed was at once both more eventful and less satisfying. Although Pat was still enjoying a penalty-free run after the first high-speed tests, on an open road section on the Col de Prayet in the French mountains she was (self-admittedly) "not paying enough attention", spun on loose stones and crashed at a relatively low speed. The car rolled, the hardtop flattened, and the car was further damaged as the girls attempted (finally successfully) to get it back on its wheels. They got going again but in the accident the gearbox oil had drained away and shortly the gearbox seized.

That was the end of the event for them, but a gearbox

Pat Moss at speed in the French Alps in XJB 877, competing in the 1961 Tulip rally.

Pat Moss (XJB 877) leading Donald Morley (XJB 876) on the 1961 Tulip rally. They finished first and second in their class.

change allowed the car to be returned to the workshops at Abingdon, where it was restored to as new condition for the Liège-Sofia-Liège Marathon, which in 1961 looked likely to be even more demanding than the 1960 event which had already made Pat's name.

But things did not go well. Deep in the Yugoslavian countryside they first lost time by stopping and towing Eugen Böhringer's big Mercedes-Benz out of a roadside ditch, then their Healey suffered a broken front shock absorber, and finally they put it off the road for keeps. A bungled countryside repair (which included a helpful local 'enthusiast' driving the car and crashing it!), brought the shambles to an end. After a four-day sojourn in this tiny village there were finally rescued by Erik Carlsson. The car somehow could drag itself along, getting out of Yugoslavia into Italy, where Pat and Wiz abandoned it, and it was eventually returned to the UK.

This was not the end of XJB 877's 1961 adventures, however, as the Abingdon mechanics turned it into a viable rally car once again and Pat drove it in the 1961 RAC rally, where she started Britain's first 'special stage' event at No.4, behind only 1960 winner Erik Carlsson in his Saab 96, the Morley Twins in a works 3000 and Hans Walter in his Porsche 356 Carrera.

Right from the start Pat was on the pace, for in spite of her dislike for this 'characterless' 3000 she was holding third or fourth place overall for many hours. Once the Morleys had been forced to retire (see XJB 876 above) Pat found herself in second place not only on the road but in the standings, behind Erik Carlsson. Not that this was an easy run as the 3000 suffered badly from the ultra-rough stages, went off the road in Scotland more than once, and hit a disturbed pile of cut logs at one stage – but the result was that Pat finished second, won her class and naturally lifted the Ladies' prize too.

Pat must now have thought that she was well rid of this car, particularly as she had fallen in love with a remarkable Mini-Cooper (737 ABL, with which she won the 1962 Tulip rally outright) and knew that a brand-new 3000, 77 ARX, was being prepared for her exclusive use. Yet when an entry was made in the Acropolis, Pat discovered that 77 ARX was being reserved for the French Alpine and that she would be driving XJB 877 yet again.

This was the first rally that Pat contested with a new co-driver, Pauline Mayman; her long-time regular co-driver Ann Wisdom had just announced her immediate retirement from motorsport: Ann, recently married to Peter Riley, was now expecting her first child and wanted to become a full-time mother. Pat's new link with Pauline Mayman was destined to

A year after her famous victory in the 1960 Liège-Rome-Liège rally, Pat Moss tried to repeat the trick in XJB 877 in 1961, but had no luck.

Pat Moss drove XJB 877 into a remarkable second place overall (immediately behind future-husband Erik Carlsson's Saab 96) on the 1961 RAC rally. Here she is, accelerating hard out of the final hairpin at the top of the Rest and be Thankful hill climb in Scotland.

be brief (Pat would move out to drive for Ford in 1963) but it started well for the two of them when they finished eighth overall on the rough, hot and very demanding Greek classic event, where Pat won her capacity class too.

This time XJB 877 got a rest as the new ARX 3000s were made ready for the French Alpine rally, but it was then prepared for the 1962 Liège-Sofia-Liège Marathon, to be driven by Rauno Aaltonen, who would be rallying a 3000 for the first time, with Tony Ambrose as his co-driver.

Unhappily this all ended in farce. Running towards the front of the field, the team arrived unscathed at the Yugoslavian Belgrade control after a penalised run through Germany, Austria, Italy and northern Yugoslavia. Having left the car for a short time while they went to have a coffee before starting out again towards Sofia, they returned to find that the all-important Road Book had disappeared. It seems that some bone-headed 'enthusiast' had got into the 3000 (they could not be locked), purloined the Book, and perhaps would be waving it around as a souvenir forever after. Without a Road Book, of course, this rally entry ceased to exist and had to be disqualified from the results. The Book has never been found.

Peter Riley then used XJB 877 on the RAC rally which followed in November 1962, and started well, but when he reported to the control at Brechin in the North East of Scotland he admitted that the 3000 had already suffered an

Another view of Pat Moss on the 1961 RAC rally.

Pat and XJB 877 surrounded by a crowd of admirers at the end of the 1961 RAC rally.

electrical fire connected with the car's lighting system. Then his outing ended in disaster when the 3000 lost a wheel in the Newcastleton (near Carlisle) special stage, plunged into the forest and could not be retrieved.

By this time XJB 877 was beginning to look like the jinx car in the works fleet, but after it was recovered from the woods it was given a long rebuild back at Abingdon, used as a practice car for the next few months, and reappeared as a front-line rally car in June 1963 when Paddy Hopkirk drove it in the French Alpine rally. He was fast on the first speed test close to the outskirts of Marseilles but shortly put the car off the road. Nevertheless he got it to the finish, the only one of the four works 3000s that had started the event to do so. Not only that but (as seen in the description of Rauno Aaltonen's adventures in 77 ARX), he had lost valuable time

on the Vivione Pass trying to help haul Rauno Aaltonen's stricken 3000 77 ARX back on to the narrow mountain pass, to no avail, but Paddy and XJB 877 made it back to Liège, taking sixth place overall and being the best two-seater car in this gruelling event where there were only twenty finishers: according to the official results, if Paddy had not stopped to aid Aaltonen he would not have been penalised as much at the next control and would have taken fourth or even third place overall.

By this point XJB 877 was what could be called 'battered but unbowed',and because team boss Stuart Turner was already planning to invest in several brand-new BJ8 cars for 1964 (ARX 91B and ARX 92B being the first of four), it was ceremonially written off during the winter of 1963/64. Few 3000 watchers, it must be said, were sorry to see that happen.

Competition Record

1961 Tulip rally	Pat Moss	1st Class
1961 French Alpine rally	Pat Moss	DNF
1961 Liège-Sofia-Liège	Pat Moss	DNF
1961 RAC rally	Pat Moss	2nd Overall
1962 Acropolis rally	Pat Moss	1st class
1962 Liège-Sofia-Liège	Rauno Aaltonen	DNF
1962 RAC rally	Peter Riley	DNF
1963 French Alpine rally	Paddy Hopkirk	DNF
1963 Spa-Sofia-Liège	Paddy Hopkirk	1st in Class

REGISTRATION NUMBER	ENGINE SIZE	MODEL TYPE
37 ARX	**2968CC 6-CYL OHV**	**3000 BN7**

Here was one of the first of an all-new 1962 fleet of 3000s which would comprise 37 ARX, 47 ARX, 57 ARX, 66 ARX and 77 ARX. These not only had new platform/inner bodyshells but were also the first Abingdon-prepared works cars to be equipped with the recently developed engine combination of aluminium cylinder heads and triple twin-choke Weber carburettors. That of course was only what could be seen, for there was also a new type of exhaust manifold, a higher compression ratio, and a different camshaft profile.

The engines were not much more powerful than the last of the triple-SU types had been in 1961 – perhaps 210bhp instead of 190bhp – but they were considerably more torquey than before. As will be discussed in the next Chapter, much of the initial design and development work had been shared between Eddie Maher's development team at BMC (Morris) Engines in Coventry and Geoff Healey's team in Warwick, along with Abingdon's Doug Hamblin who had spent time on the MG testbeds at Abingdon. As far as is known, once these

The two brand new 3000s – 37 ARX and 47 ARX – on the Spa GP circuit on their way to the special test further along the road in the 1962 Tulip Rally. Donald Morley (in 37 ARX, closest to the camera) won his class and set a string of fastest times.

power units had been made reliable in their first season little further development was carried out as Abingdon's attention gradually moved towards the Mini-Cooper and Mini-Cooper S cars instead.

Like its four sister cars, preparation of 37 ARX began in the winter of 1961/62, the plan being for it and 47 ARX to be made ready for the Tulip rally in May 1962, with a full team of four examples to be available for the French Alpine which followed in June.

Compared with the 1960/61 fleet, externally 37 ARX and its sisters looked virtually unchanged but there was one important new detail: a removable panel in the left side of the front body panel which surrounded the bonnet that could be removed for adjustment of the Weber carburettors. Images exist of these cars tackling special stages with that panel absent due to lack of time at a previous service halt for refitting it.

If ever there was a case for BMC to feel smug it was on the 1962 Tulip, where 37 ARX appeared, shiny-new, with the Morley Twins in charge, dominated throughout, beat all its opposition and was First Time Out, First. Although the byzantine regulations which were applied on this event (in 1961, for instance, one Triumph Herald had been 'gifted' an outright victory by the late-stage withdrawal of another Herald to make its 'class improvement' position more

37 ARX, still smart and fresh, ready to start the French Alpine rally of 1963.

In the 1963 Tulip rally, Donald Morley drove the self-same Healey 3000, 37 ARX, as he had used to contest the 1962 event. As before, he set a string of fastest times, overall – but found his search for outright victory foiled by a complex handicap marking system.

favourable!) made it difficult to achieve outright victory, no true enthusiast really cared that officially this Healey only took a class win.

From Holland to Monte Carlo and back again nothing could match the 3000s. Neither of them gave trouble, apart from adjustments to the new-fangled carburettor set-up from time to time, and the Morleys defeated Peter Riley's 47 ARX (no team orders!) by just a few seconds. A good start for a great type of car.

37 ARX then got a rest from rallying but not from work, as it was used as a working test and development car and was also loaned to Mercedes-Benz rival Eugen Böhringer to drive in a GT race at Solitude in Germany. It was typical of the way BMC liked to work its fleet that this trip involved 37 ARX racing and then carrying on to do a Liège-Sofia-Liège recce in the hands of Rauno Aaltonen and Tony Ambrose. The record shows that Böhringer (a prisoner of war in Russia for years after the 1939-45 conflict had ended) was impressed. Fast and competent, he finished third in class behind two Ferrari 250GTs in spite of never having driven such a 3000 before.

Then nothing until May 1963, after which it was used three times in six months before being scrapped.

In the Tulip rally the Morleys faced the near-impossible task of making theirs the most class-dominant car in the event though there was little likelihood of them winning outright. The official results show them as only being second in the

GT category behind a privately-entered Porsche 356. *The Autocar*, however, printed an alternative listing showing that the 3000 had in fact being the fastest of all cars of every type on the speed tests – a repeat performance of what had been achieved in the same car a year earlier.

An outstanding performance by the same crew in the same car in the French Alpine rally was now expected, and would surely have been delivered if a new type of limited-slip differential had not failed on the start line of the Col d'Allos on the last night of this gruelling event.

Now it was Rauno Aaltonen's turn to grapple with Healey power on the wet, boggy, loose-surfaced RAC Rally, but there was no luck for 'The Professor' on this occasion. Starting from Blackpool at No.2, he was at least able to enjoy driving over well-manicured stage surfaces (before, that is, nearly 150 other competitors had churned everything up), but on the very first special stage, in the Lake District, the 3000 burst a tyre, which wrecked a wire wheel and then the hub.

Undaunted, the Finn recovered rapidly and set a whole series of fastest stage time in the next two days, beating Timo Makinen in 47 ARX on several occasions. Even so, and on the 'couldn't have happened in a worse place' principle, 37 ARX's transmission failed in the Bin forest stage, close to Inverness, the northernmost section of this far-flung event.

With a new-generation of BJ8s due to arrive at Abingdon for 1964, this car was then written off.

Competition Record

1962 Tulip rally	Donald Morley	1st in Class
1962 Solitude (race)	Eugen Böhringer	3rd in Class
1963 Tulip rally	Donald Morley	1st in Class
1963 French Alpine	Donald Morley	DNF
1963 RAC rally	Rauno Aaltonen	DNF

REGISTRATION NUMBER	ENGINE SIZE	MODEL TYPE
47 ARX	**2968CC 6-CYL OHV**	**3000 BN7**

The second of the new-generation 1962 works cars made its debut in the Tulip rally with Peter Riley at the wheel, and like 37 ARX this car featured the latest type of engine with aluminium cylinder head and three twin-choke Weber carburettors. On this event – Holland to Holland by way of the French Alps and an overnight halt in Monte Carlo, with many speed tests along the way – Riley's principal competition came from the Morley twins in 37 ARX. Finally, and by a very small margin, he finished just a few seconds adrift of the other works 3000 and therefore took second in the capacity class.

Quite fresh after this start to its career, the car was once again allocated to Peter Riley to compete in the French Alpine rally alongside three other near-identical ARX cars. All went well until the event reached the speed test around the Monza GP circuit, when Riley left the track at the entrance to the notorious Parabolica corner (brake failure or driver error were both suggested but not confirmed) and ended up stranded on top of an earth bank and forced to retire.

The car was recovered and driven back to Abingdon, there to be prepared for a very tough test – the Liège-Sofia-Liège Marathon. It was allocated to the Scottish motor trader

This shot of a bustling preparation workshop at Abingdon can be dated to September/October 1962. 47 ARX, in the centre aisle, has just completed the Liège-Sofia-Liège, when driven by Logan Morrison, 67 ARX (in the far corner) finished eighth in David Seigle-Morris's hands, while the car on the left of the picture, thought to be XJB 877, is having a complete rear axle change.

Logan Morrison (Peter Riley was driving a much-modified Morris 1100). Of the four works Healeys that started just two finished, and in an event which plumbed the awful depths of Yugoslavian tracks Logan put in a very steady performance to take fifth place overall, beating his new team-mate David Seigle-Morris.

With Abingdon's interests turning rapidly to the sparkling performance of the new BMC Mini-Coopers for events run on gravel or on snow and ice, 47 ARX then got a winter off, and was finally made ready for a return to the Tulip rally where

had it started its career a year earlier. Once again this was an event whose marking system dampened the enthusiasm of many a driver. Logan Morrison drove this car again, while Donald Morley drove 37 ARX..

As the records show, the Morleys put up the best times overall, but cruel luck saw Morrison's car expire when a core plug blew out of the cylinder block of 47 ARX. He had no better luck on the French Alpine rally which followed just weeks later, for although he was fourth fastest up the first speed hillclimb test (the Col d'Espigoullier, just to the east of the city of Marseilles), soon after this the car left the road on another high-speed section in France and was eliminated.

Having taken time out while other 3000s were pitted against the horrors of Yugoslavia in the 1963 Liège, 47 ARX was allocated to Timo Makinen, along with Mike Wood, to tackle the British RAC rally, a November event which started from Blackpool, finished in Bournemouth and took in no fewer than 43 special stages along the way. Timo had already established himself as the 'Finnish wild man' of the BMC team and had already demolished 57 ARX on the Liège, so his new co-driver could be excused for being rather apprehensive about what was to follow.

This was, by all accounts (including the author's, watching from the side-lines), a real 'crash-bang' affair in

Timo Makinen drove 47 ARX into fifth place in the RAC rally of 1963.

which Makinen seemed determined to ignore the laws of physics, particularly regarding tyres/surface friction and the practicalities of centrifugal force, so that although he was almost always phenomenally fast he also went off on several occasions, while always managing to have the long-suffering machine retrieved and to carry on.

From the very start he was scrapping for the lead with other Scandinavian heroes such as Tom Trana or Gunnar Andersson in Volvo PV544s and Erik Carlsson in his Saab 96, but on Stage 11, in the Trossachs in central Scotland, he plunged off the track just before the end of the 5.4-mile stage, spending several minutes in the undergrowth and ceding several places. Thereafter it was a matter of struggling to close the gaps again, and in the end Timo arrived in Bournemouth in fifth place yet still managed to win his capacity class.

Back at Abingdon, what was almost a rolling wreck was cold-bloodedly examined, stripped of everything valuable and scrapped.

Competition Record

1962 Tulip rally	Peter Riley	2nd in Class
1962 French Alpine rally	Peter Riley	DNF
1962 Liège-Sofia-Liège	Logan Morrison	5th Overall
1963 Tulip rally	Logan Morrison	DNF
1963 French Alpine rally	Logan Morrison	DNF
1963 RAC rally	Timo Makinen	5th Overall

REGISTRATION NUMBER	ENGINE SIZE	MODEL TYPE
57 ARX	**2968CC 6-CYL OHV**	**3000 BN7**

The third of the five-car fleet of 1962 works 3000s in the ARX sequence was prepared in time for the Morley twins to drive it to a near-unblemished victory in the French Alpine rally, but thereafter it did not even finish any of the events it tackled. As we will see, it came to a completely ignominious end in the 1963 Liège when Timo Makinen lost a battle with a large truck.

Starting from Marseilles in June 1962, with Competition Number 5, the Morleys set the pace throughout, made no mistakes, and led the event at the start, in the middle and at the finish in Cannes. Except for early competition from Henri Oreiller's Ferrari 250GT, which eventually failed to complete the course, they were unchallenged, not even by Pat Moss or David Seigle-Morris in sister cars. Their only heart-stopping moment came at a late stage on the Col d'Allos speed hillclimb in the French Alps, where the crew started the test without fixing the bonnet strap. It then flew up, obliging co-driver Erle Morley to dismount rapidly, refasten the item and carry on!

This was the Morleys' second successive victory on the Alpine, a marvellous achievement by any reckoning as this was undoubtedly a tough event. Only five cars reached the finish unpenalised on the tight road sections, one of them being the Morleys', the other being Pat Moss in 77 ARX. David Seigle-Morris, incidentally, finished eighth in 67 ARX, which meant that BMC not only achieved 1-2-3 in their capacity class but also won every available team prize. This was a highlight for the car, which would tackle four more events in the next fifteen months and not complete any of them.

On the Liège-Sofia-Liège, for instance, Paddy Hopkirk was introduced to the team (having just 'transferred' himself from the fading Sunbeam team), but in the roughest part of Yugoslavia he was forced to retire the car when one of the rear leaf springs broke and began to make its way into the floor of the car near Paddy's driving seat. Then (and how rarely does a historian have to write this?) Donald Morley crashed the car on the RAC rally, seriously crumpling the coachwork and wiping off the newly-installed inner-headlamps which had just been adopted. Donald was hurt, dislocating a joint in his arm, and had to be hospitalised for a time for this to be rectified – which fortunately it soon was.

The car did not appear again, after something of a marathon rebuild, until the French Alpine of June 1963, where it was entrusted to Timo Makinen to grapple with the Mediterranean mountains. Timo apparently set out as if his very life depended on it and began to match the Morleys in what was their favourite territory, but this was not an event which BMC will remember with total joy as all four of the works 3000s retired. After only six speed hillclimb tests Timo had already recorded one fastest, three second fastest, a third fastest and a fourth fastest time, but his car was already wearing its rear Dunlop tyres at an alarming rate, and in the end a stub axle and front suspension bearing broke up, and that was that. Co-driver

The full team of works 3000s lined up in the village square at Bedoin, before tackling the Mont Ventoux hill climb on the 1962 French Alpine rally. Number 5 (57 ARX) was driven by the Morleys and would be the outright winner.

Mike Wood, they say, was rather relieved.

To close its often traumatic career – victory on its debut, then a string of retirements – 57 ARX was retrieved from the 1963 French Alpine rally after repair and prepared for Timo to use on the 1963 Spa-Sofia-Liège Marathon. On this occasion team boss Stuart Turner had arranged for Timo to be co-driven by Geoff Mabbs, who was not only new to the team but had never before accompanied Timo in a rally car.

He never would, again… Terrified by the great man's antics in Yugoslavia in a practice car, Mabbs was already reconciled to a major incident on the event itself, which duly transpired. They were running with competition No. 2 and had already passed the lead car, on roads which were open to the public. As Geoff Mabbs later commented, "He set off at the start of that stage as though he was trying to set a new world record for the standing quarter mile… It was about 20km further

Timo Makinen was flat out in the mountains of Yugoslavia, in the Spa-Sofia-Liege event of 1963, when he crashed 57 ARX head-on into a large truck…

…and wrote off the car. Not even Makinen could make it move again under its own power after this incident.

on that we went slap into the back of this lorry. We were screaming through this corner in a full-bore drift, the Healey sideways as usual... Not even Timo could miss it".

No one was hurt but the car was effectively written off. Bill Price took pictures of the wreck which showed that the entire front end was stove in, the engine wrecked, the chassis crumpled – and when it was finally retrieved to the UK it was indeed written off.

Competition Record

1962 French Alpine rally	Donald Morley	1st Overall
1962 Liège-Sofia-Liège	Paddy Hopkirk	DNF
1962 RAC rally	Donald Morley	DNF
1963 French Alpine rally	Timo Makinen	DNF
1963 Spa-Sofia-Liège	Timo Makinen	DNF

PADDY HOPKIRK

Behind the Irish blarney and the readiness to share a quip or give quotable quotes to any motoring writer, Paddy Hopkirk's genial facade hid a rally driver with steely determination, yet he was someone who never quite achieved as much as he thought he deserved. Amazingly enough, his most prestigious of several victories – in the 1964 Monte in a Mini-Cooper S - was achieved without making any fastest stage times in the event, and in three years he only recorded one outright victory in a Big Healey (Austrian Alpine 1964). For all that, he became Fleet Street's favourite rallying personality and kept that fame for more than 30 years after he retired.

Having begun his rallying career as a driving test specialist in Northern Ireland, Paddy started his works career with Standard-Triumph in 1956. After falling out with Triumph team manager Ken Richardson in 1958 (that was not difficult) he left the team to join the Rootes Group team of Sunbeam Alpines and Rapiers. It was only in 1962, and with the Rapiers apparently at their peak, that he approached Stuart Turner at BMC, proposing himself to join the team and (in his own words) "to get his hands on the Healey 3000". In a letter to Turner at this time he wrote, "I want to drive cars which are capable of winning rallies outright – even if I'm not!"

He soon came to terms with the high performance and rather brutal character of the car, taking second place overall in the 1962 RAC rally behind Erik Carlsson's all-conquering Saab 96, and finishing sixth in the 1963 RAC, yet Paddy always admitted that he never quite mastered the Healey and that he became much more relaxed driving the works Mini-Cooper S instead. Even so, he went on to win the 1964 Austrian Alpine rally in ARX 91B, the second of the newly-prepared wind-up window BJ8s, and was impressive in Healeys on the race track. In some cases, however, He was an unlucky 'nearly man' – as shown by his second place (in a BMC 1800) in the London-Sydney Marathon of 1968, and fourth in the London-Mexico World Cup rally (in a big Triumph 2.5PI saloon).

In his very successful BMC/British Leyland years, which lasted until the entire department closed down in 1970, Paddy was a good and supportive team player, which, to those who knew him in his Triumph and Rootes Group days, came as a real surprise. The big difference was that there was a huge and constantly growing sense of team spirit at Abingdon which had never existed in other teams. Not only that, but Paddy studiously developed his good relations with the press and became a very valuable front-man for the rally team.

REGISTRATION NUMBER	ENGINE SIZE	MODEL TYPE
67 ARX	**2968CC 6-CYL OHV**	**3000 BN7**

67 ARX was one of the least successful or least spectacular examples of the 1962 fleet – no outright wins and no headline-making crashes – yet it was also the only one of the five cars to survive its works career and be sold off. Not that it was a total jewel: BMC co-driver Paul Easter recalls competing in it in later years in classic events without much enthusiasm as he did not think it had aged very well..

Its first outing was as one of a formidable four-car effort in the 1962 French Alpine, which was won by the Morley Twins in 57. David Seigle-Morris in 67 ARX was allocated Competition No.1 and led the entire field up the series of speed hillclimbs in the Alpes Maritimes. This led to one fortunately hilarious moment on the spine-chillingly fast Mont Ventoux climb, as David once recalled: "The lower reaches consist of short straights and sweeping curves... in a 3000 you're in

overdrive top with your foot hard down. I came through one of these sweeping curves, fully committed in a well-controlled (I think) power drift when I saw this Renault Dauphine coming towards me The roads were supposed to be closed, of course, but this was France... at a combined [meeting] speed of around 140mph, it took me barely three seconds to reach her... I missed her. That is surely one French lady who will never forget the sight of a Healey in full cry".

Later in the event the car hit a trackside rock on the rough and narrow Vivione pass in the Dolomites which resulted in a tyre deflating and the need to stop and change the wheel as soon as space could be found to stop – but the jacking point had been damaged and this was not possible. By the time the car reached the next time control some time had been lost and a two minute delay proved to be enough to drop them to

eighth place overall.

Although the three-wheeled passage of this Italian section did little for the cosmetic appearance of the 3000, once it got back to Abingdon the technicians soon made it near-perfect again, this time for Seigle-Morris to tackle the Liège-Sofia-Liège Marathon. The ultra-rough roads of the Balkans damaged the rear suspension of the car and its underside, and David, who was leading at the time, had to drop back when a rear spring mounting failed. This meant limping along to find a BMC service point; it also meant a lengthy welding repair to the chassis frame. And although the crew eventually got going again it meant that they had slipped to eighth place, where they finished with a total penalty of 2hr 25min.

Two months later 67 ARX was allocated to Paddy Hopkirk to drive in the RAC rally (David Seigle-Morris had a different challenge – to try to make sense of the newly-launched front-wheel-drive MG1100 saloon, which let him down). Paddy soon discovered that the 3000was as impressively fast as he had hoped but was also difficult to drive truly flat out as he had expected.

He put up a remarkable performance, especially as he had been allocated the starting number 19, which meant that the forestry tracks were already being cut up by the time he arrived. Even so, and with 38 special stages to be tackled in

Fully committed, and in a four-wheel-drift on the Oulton Park special test of the 1962 RAC rally. Paddy Hopkirk and 67 ARX were on their way to second overall. And yet Paddy always said that he preferred to drive the Mini-Cooper S...

67 ARX was the only one of the fleet of five new BJ7s built as works rally cars in 1962 that survived a hard career; the other cars were all withdrawn from service at the end of 1963. Driven by Paddy Hopkirk, it finished second in the 1962 RAC rally.

67 ARX was one of the fleet of new 3000s which team boss Stuart Turner commissioned in 1962. These were the first Abington cars to use the Weber-carburetted engines...

...which fitted so neatly into the engine bay of these cars, albeit with an extra hatch to allow decent access to those Webers.

67 ARX had a long and distinguished career, but even in later life, when cherished by a private owner, it still retained the special steering wheel and comfortable competition seats of the original type.

a route which stretched from Blackpool to Bournemouth by way of Peebles, Inverness, the Lake District, and what looked like every special stage in Wales, Paddy beat all his team-mates and everyone in the event except the hot favourite, Erik Carlsson in his little Saab 96.

67 ARX then got a truly leisurely lay-off and rebuild – from November 1962 to June 1963 – before team recruit Timo Makinen took it to Scandinavia to tackle the Midnight Sun rally, where his bravery was to be pitted against the loose-surfaced stages of Sweden. All of which was to no avail as the car was disqualified from the event for running without bumpers. Road cars were invariably fitted with bumpers whereas the works cars usually ran without.

Logan Morrison later took the car on the Spa-Sofia-Liège but unfortunately crashed it. This left the Morley twins to try to rescue its reputation on the season's final event, the British RAC rally, but although they drove with their usual aplomb and reliability they were delayed at one point in Scotland by water finding its way into the engine's electrics, causing them

In later life, works 3000s have often seen use in more modern classic rallies, which explains the array of new-type instruments in the background – but the overdrive actuation, by a switch on the gearlever knob, was historically correct.

to drop from a fight for the lead to ninth overall and second in their capacity class behind Timo's sister car.

This was the end of 67 ARX's works career It was later sold to one of the team's co-drivers, Tony Ambrose, and would enjoy a varied career in the hands of many 'classic' enthusiasts.

Competition Record

1962 French Alpine rally	David Seigle-Morris	8th Overall
1962 Liège-Sofia-Liège	David Seigle-Morris	3rd in Class
1962 RAC rally	Paddy Hopkirk	2nd Overall
1963 Midnight Sun	Timo Makinen	DNF
1963 Spa-Sofia-Liège	Logan Morrison	DNF
1963 RAC rally	Donald Morley	2nd in Class

REGISTRATION NUMBER	ENGINE SIZE	MODEL TYPE
77 ARX	**2968cc 6-cyl OHV**	**3000 BN7**

This atmospheric shot shows why every British professional rally driver loved to compete in the French Alpine rally. The year is 1962, the location is the 'Karussel' on the Mont Ventoux hill climb, where 77 ARX is being driven by Pat Moss on her way to 3rd place overall. Mont Ventoux, incidentally, is still used, but the deep cut out in the road has now been filled in.

This was the last of the five brand-new Weber-equipped 3000s to be completed in 1962. To all intents and purposes, except for modifying the driving position and the pedal layout, it was to be used only by Pat Moss during that first season.

Like other cars in this modern fleet it was painted red with a white roof but it had one amusing individual quirk. First shown on USA TV in 1958, a slick and sometimes humorous detective series titled 77 Sunset Strip was soon seen regularly on British TV too and became very popular. So it was almost inevitable that when 77 ARX was first seen in mid-1962 it was rapidly christened 'Sunset Strip' by the mechanics and press which regularly accompanied the team. In fact, when the car was taken to the team hotel in La Ciotat, close to the start of the French Alpine rally, its rear number plate was still 'naked', and on the day before the start the author was present when a nimble BMC mechanic procured a suitable set of small stick-

This close-up study of the nose of 77 ARX shows the detail of the extra-headlamp installation, the holding down strap for the bonnet, and the protective grille ahead of the radiator.

113

Pat Moss and Pauline Mayman about to start the 1962 RAC rally in 77 ARX.

Pat in 77 ARX, on the 1962 RAC, her last outing in these cars before she left the team.

on plastic letters, adding the words 'Sunset Strip' close to the '77' part of the plate.

This event was finally dominated by the Morley Twins in 57 ARX but Pat Moss and her new partner Pauline Mayman also finished the incredibly tight road sections unpenalised, and were just seconds slower than the Morleys on the speed hillclimbs, the result being that they recorded a remarkable third place overall behind the Morleys and the redoubtable Hans Walter in his Porsche 356 Carrera.

Pat then went off to tackle the Polish rally as a 'one-off'. Her's was the only works entry from BMC, and she had very limited service support. She once commented that their rally almost came to an end at one stage because they ran out of petrol. Roadside supplies were scarce and they only survived by finding a local man with a moped, persuading him to allow them to drain off a small amount. This got them it to a nearby farm, where they scrounged some more fuel, but of such awful quality that Pat was convinced that it was paraffin.

Yet again, this was a Big Healey which objected to the super-rough roads by breaking a rear leaf spring, which then tried to force is way into the underside of the car directly under co-driver Pauline Mayman's seat. The BMC mechanics, when found, eventually used tyre levers to jam the spring back into place, and the ever-resourceful Pat carried on.

Fun and games came at the end of the event, when the final test was a 10-lap circuit race whose rules meant that Pat had to do her own pre-event preparation and where there was a running Le Mans start involving drivers and co-drivers, both of whom had to scramble aboard before firing up the engine! In spite of the bodged repairs that had been necessary and the almost Fred Karnos atmosphere around this final test, Pat stormed through the field, winning the race outright, and finished up in second place overall to Eugen Böhringer's big Mercedes-Benz saloon, which had been competing in another class.

The third event of this car's busy season came just three months later in the RAC Rally of Great Britain. As firm favourite, Pat's new husband Erik Carlsson dominated from the start and went on to win. Pat, for her part, battled with her other Big Healey team-mates, rarely seemed to put a foot wrong and ended up third overall immediately behind Paddy Hopkirk in 67 ARX.

Now it was time for the team's new recruit, Timo Makinen, to be unleashed in a works 3000. Stuart Turner chose to enter him in the 1963 Monte Carlo rally and pair him with the racing driver turned rally co-driver Christabel Carlisle. In theory this was a marriage made in hell, but one which turned out to be 'publicity gold', for not only did this unlikely pairing keep the car on the road but did so in the worst possible ice and snow conditions. Timo battled through to win his capacity class. Some years later Christabel was persuaded to give her impressions to that distinguished team manager and author Peter Browning, and I hope he will not object to me collecting one or two snatches of her memories. The pairing was not made until the last moment, so Christabel had not even met Timo Makinen before they joined up for a four-day recce of the Monte route south of Chambéry. Frightened by Timo's exuberant pace in a 3000 which was still strange to him, Christabel was all for flying home immediately and abandoning the venture but soon came to terms, resigned herself to fate, and set off on the big adventure. Starting at No.81, they were immediately faced by blizzard-like conditions throughout the event which Timo seemed to relish but stretched the 3000's abilities to its limits.

Christabel conquered all her earlier fears, not only putting in a great performance as a first-time navigator but somehow

TIMO MAKINEN

When questioned about his illustrious past, BMC rally team boss Stuart Turner has no doubts that Timo, the second of the 'Flying Finns', was the fastest rally driver in the world. For more than a decade – 1962 until the mid-1970s – Timo probably started every rally as the favourite, and led most of them. Although he rarely crashed he was hard on his cars, expecting his team to build machinery which would withstand his methods.

Originally something of a wild-man in his native Finland (among his exploits was racing a Jaguar D-Type on ice on spiked tyres!), Timo got a trial in the BMC works team after the Finnish importer called Stuart Turner to plead his case. Within a year he had mastered Mini-Coopers and Austin-Healey 3000s and no-one else could match him.

Although Timo never actually won an event in a Healey 3000 he was certainly the bravest, the fastest and probably the most exciting driver of the big red sports cars. It was his amazing class and category performances in Healeys which endeared him to so many fans – a class win in the wintriest of all Monte Carlo rally with Christabel Carlisle alongside him in 1963, and second overall in back-to-back RAC rallies (1964 and 1965) being just two such bravura displays.

He seemed to lead almost every rally he ever started but his machinery often let him down. Observers reckon that his 1965 Monte victory in a Mini was the best rally drive of all time, but others remember the 1965 RAC rally in a Healey (EJB 806C, brand new for the occasion) where he was demonstrably the fastest of all on snow, ice, deep mud and sometimes hard gravel, and was only deprived of victory by Rauno Aaltonen's Mini-Cooper S, which could get more grip more often.

In a word, as a rally driver Timo was spectacular and, let us be honest, almost impossible to control by his co-drivers. When the situation demanded it (and at other times too when he felt like it) Timo was a more flamboyant driver than any of his team mates, more sideways, more energetic, and behind the wheel was demonstrably putting more effort into his driving than they were. A co-driver had to be brave to control such a massive personality, and it was the mild-mannered Paul Easter who managed this best of all.

When Timo and his car were on song, no-one – not even Rauno Aaltonen, certainly not Paddy Hopkirk – could match his pace in similar machines. To see Timo in full flow, particularly from the terrifying vantage point of the passenger seat, was an awe-inspiring experience. Certainly he drove his cars harder than anyone else of the period, expecting them to put up with his brutal methods and to withstand assault from the rough special stage tracks. Big Healeys were better than Minis at withstanding this, though he was not often given the chance to prove it.

Like Rauno Aaltonen, Timo left the BMC team in 1968 after Lord Stokes culled the department. Since both the Healey and the Mini were past their peak he was in any case falling out with the team and despised the BMC 1800 'Landcrabs' that were replacing them.

Later, ex-BMC team boss Stuart Turner persuaded him to join the Ford team in 1970 and he then enjoyed seven seasons at Boreham. Three RAC rally wins were a highlight of this time but there were other individual highlights. Ford management did not enjoy his meddling with specifications, though, and he was released at the end of 1976.

overcoming the language barrier between the two. She was even brave enough at times to yell 'Faster' at the world's most aggressively talented Finn and must hold a Guinness Book of Records note for that very mention alone !

Makinen did everything that was expected of him and 77 ARX performed magnificently. Even so, not even Timo's bravery and genius could help him match the front-wheel-drive cars, which were more suited to the wintry conditions, yet he still won his capacity class, dominated the GT category, and on the Monaco GP circuit test which brought the event to a close he was second fastest overall behind Hans Walter's Carrera-engined Porsche 356.

All in all, an amazing performance by a fast and durable car when driven by such a talented driver. But there was more to come. Within days of the end of the Monte BBC TV organised a near-impromptu set of time trials for the teams whose cars had survived the rally around an improvised three-quarter-mile course at the snow-bound Brands Hatch circuit in the UK. This involved parts of the circuit, some of the access roads and the car parks linking everything. This event was never serious nor intended to be, but BMC sent 77 ARX along, with Makinen to drive in what was soon christened the 'Autobog' but was really the forerunner of rallycross, which came somewhat

later. Makinen, as widely expected, was fastest (and bravest!) in this charade and won outright in what was the first and only time that 77 ARX was undisputed winner of anything.

The car was not then used again until August 1963, when it was lined up for Rauno Aaltonen to drive in the Spa-Sofia-Liège Marathon. After more than two days of flat-out rallying, which included battering their way through the worst of the Yugoslavian roads and tracks, Rauno and his co-driver Tony Ambrose were tackling the serpentine and loose surfaced Vivione pass in the Italian Dolomites when suddenly Rauno slightly miscalculated a corner, the 3000 spun, hit a rock face on the outside, and speared off towards oblivion on the other side of the track, where it crashed through the railings and looked likely to plunge into an abyss. Miraculously, the car then stuck on the edge before making the final dive, though Rauno and Tony both admitted afterwards that they were lucky to avoid death. And, as Tony later said, "It took two Jeeps with chains to get that car back on the road the next day, and then I got an even bigger shock when I saw just how far we would have fallen had we lost our balance the night before".

It was no surprise, therefore, to learn that by the time the battered remains of 77 ARX were returned to Abingdon, it was written off.

RAUNO AALTONEN

One of the original 'Flying Finns in the works rally team of the 1960s, Rauno became the single most successful Mini rally driver at BMC and also the man who delivered the most prestigious Healey victory of all time, in the 1964 Spa-Sofia-Liège Marathon rally. As an analytical and compulsive re-designer of all his rally cars, Rauno did as much as anyone to keep the Healey 3000 improving in the 1960s, and was desperately unhappy when his entry in the 1967 RAC rally in the last and most special of all Healeys was aborted because the event was cancelled at the last moment.

First as a private owner in Finland, then in vast works Mercedes-Benz saloons, he caught team boss Stuart Turner's eye in those cars on the 1961 Polish and RAC rallies and was rapidly signed up for 1962. After starting in a privately-supported Cooper in the 1962 Monte, where he was nearly killed in a fiery crash, he rapidly became a fully-fledged BMC works team member in mid-1962.

Some of his most noteworthy victories were in Mini-Cooper S types – he notched up his first outright win in the 1963 French Alpine – and Rauno won no fewer than nine Internationals in Minis, including five in 1965 alone when he became European Rally Champion. Among his famous victories were the 1965 RAC rally and the 1967 Monte, and of course the 1964 Spa-Sofia-Liège in a Healey 3000.

Apart from that startling Spa-Sofia-Liège success, when he virtually obliterated all his rivals, his career in Healeys was not as glitteringly successful, and occasionally the big beasts got away from him. Even so, Rauno was super-smooth as a driver and only rarely a crasher. He was always the team's great thinker, the one with the most good ideas, and had the tendency to sketch those ideas on the backs of envelopes, on service schedules and even on restaurant tablecloths. Some found his compulsion to fiddle with specifications rather irritating but others found his mild, good-mannered character very appealing. Yet when super-fast times were needed no-one delivered more consistently than Rauno.

When the Healey's front-line life as a rally car came to an end Rauno was still reaching his personal peak, and he went on to achieve great things for BMC driving Mini-Cooper Ss. In 1968, after the formation of British Leyland, he didn't really leave the team, rather the team left him. When Lord Stokes demanded big changes at Abingdon, Rauno's (and Timo Makinen's) contracts were torn up. Having dabbled with Lancia and, in later years, with Nissan, Rauno became a much-sought-after ambassador for European manufacturers like BMW. To his great sorrow he never won the Safari, though he finished second on four occasions.

Unlike other stars of the 1960s Rauno never got involved in the growing and glamorous world of Historic rallying, preferring to make his living as a teacher and as a representative of various manufacturers.

This impromptu 'rallycross', held in February 1963 on the snow-bound wasteland of Brands Hatch was nicknamed 'Autobog' – though Timo Makinen in 77 ARX revelled in the conditions and won outright.

Competition Record

1962 French Alpine rally	Pat Moss	3rd Overall
1962 Polish rally	Pat Moss	2nd Overall
1962 RAC rally	Pat Moss	3rd Overall
1963 Monte Carlo rally	Timo Makinen	1st in GT Category and Class
1963 'Autobog', Brands Hatch	Timo Makinen	1st
1963 Spa-Sofia-Liège	Rauno Aaltonen	DNF

REGISTRATION NUMBER	ENGINE SIZE	MODEL TYPE
ARX 91B	**2968cc 6-cyl OHV**	**3000 BJ8**

Having built no new 3000s during 1963, Abingdon made amends in 1964 by preparing four new BJ8s – the first of the rally team to have the wind-up door windows, curved windscreens and modernised facia layout of the latest road cars. These machines were registered ARX 91B, ARX 92B, BMO 93B and BRX 852B and would immediately take over from the older-type 'side-screen' BN7s which had served Abingdon so well in previous seasons. Incidentally, because

of a recent change made to FIA Appendix J regulations, these cars also had to carry their road-car front and rear bumpers at all times (except on the 'run what you brung' Spa-Sofia-Liège Marathon).

Built on the road-car assembly lines at Abingdon early in 1964, ARX 91B was the first of this quartet to be completely rally prepared in the Competitions Department, with ARX 92B, which carried a consecutive chassis number and had been

Just for fun, it seems, BMC entered a works rally car – ARX 91B – for the Targa Florio race in 1965, where Timo Makinen provided most of the fireworks.

manufactured on the same day taking shape alongside it. It was immediately allocated to Paddy Hopkirk to use in the Austrian Alpine rally.

Paddy had recently been elevated to Superstar status by winning the 1964 Monte Carlo rally in a works Mini-Cooper S, and had recently competed (unsuccessfully) in the Acropolis rally. He needed a quieter life for a while but got no rest as immediately after the Acropolis he and co-driver Henry Liddon flew off to Austria to compete in the Austrian Alpine, a full-blown European Championship event with some of its route mileage in Yugoslavia.

Paddy had not rallied a Big Healey since Spa-Sofia-Liège in August 1963 (although he had, of course, raced 767 KNX in the Sebring 12 Hour race in March) but he immediately settled in to his brand-new mount and finally won quite comfortably. As he wrote in his autobiography, "With all its power, the Healey was particularly suitable on the steep, hilly, Austrian roads. But I remember Henry being told 'Ein Bus kommt' by a German at the start of a stage. I said 'What does that mean?' and Henry said he didn't know. Imagine my surprise when we met this enormous bus coming the other way, nearly causing a serious head-on. I now know what that piece of German means".

Although the car was quite unscathed after this 1,200-mile event it would not be used again for almost a year, when BMC rebuilt it as a race car for Timo Makinen and Paul Hawkins to drive in the 1965 Targa Florio sports car race in Sicily in May.

It has always been something of a mystery why this outing was chosen, for although the Warwick-based development team

had always been keen on motor racing and had made regular entries in the Targa Florio to race their increasingly specialised Sprites (see Chapter 10), Abingdon had usually kept well clear. It was almost as if ARX 91B, sulking in a corner for so long after Paddy's win in Austria, piped up and pleaded to be given something – anything – to do. We now know, however, that BMC's major oil sponsor, Castrol, had decided to make a film of the event, so BMC/Healey produced not only ARX 91B but also a 'Dick Jacobs' MG Midget and a Sprite.

For the 3000 entry, and in something of a whimsical but inspired decision, BMC and Healey chose to pair Timo Makinen with the Australian race driver Paul Hawkins, both of whom looked forward to grappling with this altogether unique type of motor race on the roads of Sicily, where the lap was no less than 44.7 miles long, taking in narrow, twisting and sometimes appallingly surfaced public roads. The longest straight fast stretch was along the northern coast of the island, the remainder being in the mountains.

The 3000 had to compete in the same class as out-and-out race cars such as the Ferrari 250GTO and it proved to be remarkably fast, lapping only about one minute slower than the fastest of those cars, but it was only credited with finishing second in its class behind the leading Ferrari. The rest of the story, which took more than seven hours to unfold, is much more interesting.

The cars were sent off at 30-second intervals – small-capacity machines first of all, the largest and fastest last – ensuring that there would be much passing and re-passing as the event progressed. The Healey's principal problem was that it wore out tyres at a phenomenal rate, which meant that a wheel change was needed every two laps, or 90 miles. As this long race progressed the car climbed to lead its capacity class – until suddenly the engine stopped because the distributor had broken its rotor arm.

This occurred soon after the car had started a lap and Paul Hawkins ran back to the pits to get a spare and fit it himself. It was only later that, in Geoff Healey's own written words, "Paul had an ignition failure and ran back to the pits for a rotor arm, only to be told that the spare was in the car's door pocket. Using some typical Australian expressions, Paul toiled up the hill, fitted the new rotor arm, and continued".

This apart, the car survived remarkably well, though its lack of suitable tyres was a real handicap. It was in such good (and un-crashed!) condition that no sooner did it get back to the UK than it was pressed into racing service again. This time it was to take part in the 1,000 mile 'production sports car race' at Brands Hatch, from which works entries were banned, so with the connivance of the BARC, which was organising this two-day marathon on the full GP circuit, it was 'loaned' to race-engine specialist Don Moore and driven by Paddy Hopkirk and a young race driver from Coventry, Roger Mac. More than fifty years after this event it is no longer possible to dig down to the details of the work done in preparation for this entry, but let us just say that Don Moore was an engine specialist, and not necessarily familiar with the Big Healey or its preparation for a long race, so much work was certainly done at Abingdon beforehand. One tiny visual quirk is that when it raced in Sicily it had a white hardtop, but at Brands Hatch another hardtop, painted red, was used instead.

Starting at 13.00HR on the Saturday, the cars had to compete over 500 miles in the first day, could then be worked on overnight, and then had to tackle the final 500 miles on the next day. The weather was fine, warm and sunny throughout. All in all this was a challenge of the greatest severity, and in fact the winning car took more than 13 hours to complete the task.

Thirty-four cars, headed by E-Type Jaguars and similar race-prepared 'production' cars, started the race. The Healey, at first driven by Roger Mac, was immediately competitive, sometimes being in the lead, though the ever-unfolding drama of refuelling pitstops sometimes made it difficult to see where the advantages really were.

With Hopkirk at the wheel the big car threw the tread of a rear tyre at one point, but this was speedily rectified at the pits.

Mac hit a spinning Sprite at another point, which required a brief hammer-wielding repair in the pits, and after five hours the car had to make an emergency stop to have its front discs changed – not the pads but the discs themselves. This put the car down the listings, and it meant that a really determined attempt would have to be made on the Sunday run to get back on terms.

Immediately after Sunday's rolling start the Healey took up second and sometimes third place and before long it was leading outright 'on the day', so began to creep back up the leader boards, but finally it was overhauled by Chris Lawrence's SLR-bodied Plus Four and finished second 'on the day'. When all the calculations had been made the Healey finished fourth overall, the race being won by John Rhodes and Warwick Banks in a 'loaned' MGB. It had completed the event in 13hr 12min 44sec and had completed 366 Brands Hatch laps in the process. As the TV advert says, You Do the Maths.

This was the end of the car's works career and it was sold to David Hiam, who at that time was the much respected Racing Manager of the Dunlop tyre company.

Competition Record

1964 Austrian Alpine rally	Paddy Hopkirk	1st Overall
1965 Targa Florio (race)	Timo Makinen/Paul Hawkins	2nd Class
1965 Guards 1000 (race)	Paddy Hopkirk/ Roger Mac	4th Overall

REGISTRATION NUMBER	ENGINE SIZE	MODEL TYPE
ARX 92B	**2968CC 6-CYL OHV**	**3000 BJ8**

The second of four new works BJ8s was completed in the spring of 1964 and was basically the same as ARX 91B though it appeared before it. Using this car, in May the Morley twins set what was now their habitual fastest scratch performance in the Tulip, and as usual they were cheated of outright victory by that event's handicap marking system. Only weeks later they took the same car out on the French Alpine rally, where they had better luck than in 1963, finishing up with a fine class win.

The car was then scheduled to compete in the Spa-Sofia-Liège rally, which as usual would not be tackled by the Morleys because this was harvest time for working farmers, so it was allocated to Timo Makinen instead. Matching the Liège with Timo, as the records show, was almost a kiss of

Here seen in its afterlife as a much-loved privately-owned car, ARX 92B was the first of the BJ8s to be prepared at Abingdon in 1964, and was driven successfully by the Morley Twins on the Tulip and French Alpine rallies of that year.

death for a rally car, as he demonstrably did not seem to enjoy the event and spent the early hours driving ultra-fast, seemingly trying to wear out the car. True to form, on the 1964 Liège, where the distance between scheduled service points was often immense, he duly did this by wearing out all his tyres (the Big Healey, of course, could only carry two spares), so when the inevitable punctures had taken their toll and the surviving rear tyres were down to the canvas he promptly retired.

Even though the car had retired before the worst of the notorious Balkan roads were encountered, it was apparently in a somewhat battered state by the time Abingdon retrieved it, and the ruthlessly logical Stuart Turner decided not to have it re-prepared but to have new cars built for 1965 instead. Accordingly it was not used again by the works team, not even as a recce machine, and it was soon sold to Peter Browning. However, in a strange but potentially exciting way, it might have enjoyed a re-registered afterlife, if plans to use it (then known as PWB 57) on the 1967 RAC rally had come to fruition.

Competition Record

1964 Tulip rally	Donald Morley	1st GT Category
1964 French Alpine rally	Donald Morley	2nd Overall GT Category
1964 Spa-Sofia-Liège	Timo Makinen	DNF

REGISTRATION NUMBER	ENGINE SIZE	MODEL TYPE
BMO 93B	**2968CC 6-CYL OHV**	**3000 BJ8**

Of the four new BJ8s which Abingdon prepared in 1964, BMO 93B was by far the most famous – for it not only won an event first time out but did so in the ultra-tough, and insanely tightly scheduled, Spa-Sofia-Liège Marathon. This was the first and last time that Rauno Aaltonen rallied a BJ8.

It was widely rumoured that there would be no more traditional-type Lièges after 1964. The local authorities in France and Italy had become increasingly nervous about the high target average speeds asked of the drivers, while the traditionally rough roads of Yugoslavia and Bulgaria were being improved with every year which passed and were also attracting more and more non-rally traffic. Seeing that this

BMO 93B, with Rauno Aaltonen at the wheel, on his way to winning the Spa-Sofia-Liège rally of 1964.

Cleaned and garlanded, Aaltonen's victorious 3000 at the end of the 1964 Spa-Sofia-Liège rally.

BMO 93B was then completely re-prepared for the Morley twins to use on the 1964 RAC rally. Here they are seen on the downhill hairpin of the Porlock Hill special stage.

Showing signs of a nodding acquaintance with a forestry ditch, Donald Morley and BMO 93B leave the Barnby Moor control towards the end of the 1964 RAC rally.

might be the last Liège, BMC put a great deal of effort into their preparations. Not only were three BJ8s entered, but they were also accompanied by three MGBs and a Mini-Cooper S.

Aaltonen and his co-driver Tony Ambrose had practiced diligently and, allocated the Competition No.3, were confident of jumping into the lead almost at once and determined to hold it for the next 96 hours. In fact, although they did just that, won the event outright, and lost a mere 57 minutes (in what was an insanely fast and impossible schedule), that put them no less than 28 minutes ahead of Erik Carlsson's Saab 96 and also of Eugen Bohringer's works Mercedes-Benz 230SL.

The works 3000s were now so well developed that it was usually only driver maltreatment or over-exuberant use of the 200bhp-plus power which caused problems – and on this event it was tyre wear and consequent punctures. Awful road conditions, route diversions which added to the total distance to be covered (without any extra time being allowed – so typical of the Liège organisers!) were all factors,

This was so much of an out-and-out race that co-driver Tony Ambrose's recollections tell their own story: "We existed almost entirely on lemon glucose drinks, the odd sandwich, some fruit that we were able to pick up at the service points, and we also carried tins of Shippam's tinned food. I found that I did not really want any solid food; I certainly had no longing for a hot meal as the temperature was so high. Just lot and lots to drink". Along with Timo Makinen's virtuoso

effort in a Mini-Cooper S in the 1965 Monte Carlo rally, this probably rates as one of the most remarkable drives in BMC motorsport history.

After the car's magnificent performance one might even have expected it to be proudly placed on a plinth, but BMC had other ideas. With Liège-winner Rauno Aaltonen choosing to drive a Mini-Cooper S on the RAC rally, BMO 93B was allocated to the Morley twins, who started from London at Competition No.11.

This, though, was not to be a repeat performance by the car, for on the first night in Wales it not only suffered a spin on one stage but hit a rock on a later Welsh section, causing enough to trouble for the crew to elect to miss the Dovey stage (the regulations allowed for this, though there was a time penalty for doing so). This, and later dramas including the need to change the front brake calipers and to rectify rear suspension maladies, meant that they struggled to get back on terms, so although theirs was the first rally car to cross the finishing line in London they could only record 21st overall.

The car was then sold to Pauline Mayman.

Competition Record

1964 Spa-Sofia-Liège	Rauno Aaltonen	1st Overall
1964 RAC rally	Donald Morley	21st Overall

REGISTRATION NUMBER	ENGINE SIZE	MODEL TYPE
BRX 852B	**2968CC 6-CYL OHV**	**3000 BJ8**

Having won the Austrian Alpine rally a few months earlier, Paddy Hopkirk must have felt reasonably happy to take charge of another brand-new BJ8 for the Spa-Sofia-Liège in August, and his aim was at least to improve on the sixth place he had taken in XJB 877 a year earlier. It was his third (and, as it transpired, his last) Big Healey drive of 1964, for he was rapidly becoming BMC's 'go-to' driver in Mini Cooper S types.

Unhappily Paddy and co-driver Henry Liddon started at No.29, which meant that they would have to struggle to overtake slower competitors on the first rough and dusty stages in Italy and Yugoslavia before hopefully being able to match Rauno Aaltonen's pace at the head of the field.

Once againt hey ran out of luck at an early stage when the engine suffered an oil leak after an external pipe had come adrift. Somehow or other they managed to make their own repairs without any service crew knowing how, when and where to meet them. This was on the road section near the Yugoslavian border at Kranjska Gora and cost them 30 minutes, which meant that a stream of other rally traffic passed them and they had to start the chase yet again.

Nothing daunted, they carried on, but when passing through Paracin, near the border with Bulgaria, to his dismay Paddy found that after changing down into second gear the lever stuck in that ratio and would not budge. Getting home took a long time...

Perhaps it was only fair to the car that it was carefully rebuilt before being handed over to Timo Makinen to make his assault on the RAC rally which took place in November 1964. On this event, accompanied by Mike Wood, he had previously finished fifth, but now, with Don Barrow alongside him, the Finn was quite determined to win.

From London to London by way of apparently very worthwhile special stages in England, Wales and Scotland, and with just one overnight halt (in Perth, Scotland), this was the sort of 2,500-mile marathon (with 55 special stages) which was ideal for a sturdy driver like Makinen, but not for a Big Healey which he was sure to break if it could not be persuaded to win for him. This time he started from No.14, so most of the stage surfaces would still be quite fresh when he tackled them.

By the middle of the first night Timo was indeed winning but he then went off on one particularly foggy stage for such a long time that he dropped off the leader board and was not even in the top six by the time the cars reached Perth. It was then that the magnificent Makinen 'Attack, Attack' phenomenon began to take effect. The cars came back through familiar Scottish

Timo Makinen was always determined to win the RAC rally in a works 3000 but never quite made it. In 1964 he used BRX 852B, brand new at the time, but had to settle for second overall just behind Tom Trana's winning Volvo.

Stuart Turner and Timo Makinen were close colleagues in the heyday of the Healey 3000.

rally stages, then through Kielder and finally into Northen Yorkshire. Then they tackled special stages on 'Dad's Army' territory near Thetford and a circuit sprint at Snetterton before making their way back to London . Unnoticed by some reporters, but not by the mass of spectators, Timo had fought his way back to second overall, beaten only by the remarkable

Tom Trana's Volvo PV444.

Remarkably, after only two events, both of them in 1964, that brought the works career of BRX 852B to a close. It was used as a test and recce car in 1965 but there were no more glamorous public appearances in store for it, and it was eventually sold to Tony Ambrose.

Competition Record

1964 Spa-Sofia-Liège	Paddy Hopkirk	DNF
1964 RAC rally	Timo Makinen	2nd Overall

REGISTRATION NUMBER	ENGINE SIZE	MODEL TYPE
DRX 257C	**2968CC 6-CYL OHV**	**3000 BJ8**

By 1965 the Abingdon fleet of works 3000s had contracted a little. All but one of the 1962 generation of ARX cars had been written off, which left just 67 ARX and the four BJ8 types of 1964 available. To redress the balance Stuart Turner then authorised the building of just three new 3000s in 1965 – these being DRX 257C (which first competed in May 1965), DRX 258C (Geneva 1965) and, right at the end of the year, EJB 806C (RAC Rally).

Some technical improvements to these works cars were still possible but almost all of them, except the raised exhaust system were never carried out. DRX 257C was therefore almost a clone of the successful 1964 fleet that had enjoyed two outright wins and a category win during the season. When the Morley twins arrived at Abingdon to pick up their new car in which to contest the Tulip rally it must all have looked very familiar to them.

On the Tulip rally the sparkling new car ran with seven forward-facing lights and with front and rear bumpers in place as demanded by the regulations. The Morleys put up their usual dominant performance on an event which featured 19 hillclimb and circuit sprint tests dotted all over the higher passes of France and Switzerland. On this occasion late-season snow was also a problem on some hills (which meant that six of the proposed tests were not actually used), but as BMC had thoughtfully brought along a supply of studded tyres the Morleys kept going steadily until the end.

Even so, on one hill near St Claude in France the burly figure of Erle Morley spent much of the climb sitting rather precariously in the boot of the Austin-Healey, though the car never actually got stuck. Later, while still setting a string of fastest times overall, they were one of only six crews who managed to beat the target time of the Col de Fouchy.

The Tulip organisers' addiction to a 'class improvement' formula that few people could understand meant that

Time for service on the Tulip rally of 1965, where the Morley Twins, who were giving DRX 257C its very first outing, put up their usual stunning performance. The author of this book is leaning into the car, talking to driver Donald Morley.

DRX 257C was one of three new works 3000s built in 1965. Here seen on a speed test during the Tulip rally, crewed by the Morley Twins, it was on its way to setting the fastest times, overall, in the rally. BMC, however, realised that an unfavourable 'class improvement' handicapping system would probably foil their plans – the event finally being 'won' by a works Hillman Rally Imp!

By 1965 the works 3000 was almost at the peak of its performance (but there would be more development to follow at the end of that season). Timo Makinen put up an absolutely startling performance in the Scottish rally of that year, but the Finn's brutal driving caused damage to the engine and transmission, and forced the car to retire.

although the Morleys had set fastest times overall for the fourth successive year they officially finished only eighth, and fifth in the GT category. When one considers that they were 'beaten' by a rag-bag of class leaders which included two works Hillman Imps and two 841cc Saabs, this makes

a nonsense of the system; a class win (over 2000cc GT Category) was little consolation.

The car seemed so fresh when it returned from Holland that it was then prepared for Timo Makinen and Paul Easter to use in the Scottish rally, where the accent was on high-speeds, clouds of dust, and rough special stages. Paul Easter later described this event as a "Liège with thistles," and Makinen seemed to treat it as a demolition derby. The long and short of it was that in the end Makinen succeeded in battering the car into submission, first by damaging the sump guard so comprehensively that a new one had to be rushed up from Abingdon, and finally by persuading a usually strong differential to fail. Along the way a distributor lead fell off and Timo went off the road for a time, so a lead which he had at the first night halt in Grantown-on-Spey deterioriated to third place at the second halt and to an abrupt but final retirement during the third day's loop.

After this event the pragmatic decision was that the structure was so badly knocked about that it was not worth rebuilding the car for more rallying It was henceforth used only for testing and was written off before the end of the year.

Competition Record

1965 Tulip rally	Donald Morley	1st in Class
1965 Scottish rally	Timo Makinen	DNF

REGISTRATION NUMBER	ENGINE SIZE	MODEL TYPE
DRX 258C	**2968cc 6-cyl OHV**	**3000 BJ8**

This, the second of the trio of 1965 works cars, was prepared in the spring of the year alongside DRX 257C and was ready for the Morley twins to use in the Geneva rally, held in June. The event was a watered down version of a French Alpine, for it used many of the same roads and speed hillclimbs as the Alpine. Apart from a handicapping system which penalised large-engined sports cars this was an ideal rally for the Big Healey, which started looking immaculate, ended up looking just the same, if slightly dusty, and was rewarded by a class win, third place in the GT category (which was won by Jean Rolland in his excellently built and driven Alfa Romeo Giulia TZ) and seventh place overall.

Only a few weeks later DRX 258C was ready to be driven by the Morleys on the French Alpine rally. This was a faster-

The author (in the passenger seat) was privileged to sit alongside Donald Morley when he was 'shaking down' the brand-new DRX258C before taking it out to compete in the 1965 French Alpine rally.

scheduled event than ever before but was ideal for the 3000, which was accompanied by a fleet of four works Mini-Cooper 1275 S types.

As far as BMC and the Morleys were concerned, to win this rally was 'Mission Impossible', not only because of the major competition from Consten's Alfa Romeo but also because – somehow – the Morleys no longer seemed to be 'lucky' on this event. In 1965 the other wild-card opposition came from Peter Harper driving a 4.2-litre works Sunbeam Tiger that amazed everyone with its pace and reliability, and from two near-race-cars, the works- backed Porsche 904s of René Buchet and Pauli Toivonen.

As it happened the 3000 put up a dead reliable and very fast performance, while the 904s disappeared. As the surviving cars crossed the line in Monte Carlo the Morleys were expected to take third place in the GT category behind Harper's Tiger and Consten's Alfa Romeo, but within hours the scrutineers had stripped the Harper's Tiger's V8 engine, found discrepancies with the homologation form, and disqualified it from victory. Thus it was that the Morleys took second place in the GT Category and easily won their capacity class.

Well in advance of the RAC rally of 1965 (its last scheduled appearance as a works car, DRX 258C became one of only four works 3000s to be treated to the fitment of the high-mounted exhaust system which has already been described. The first trial installation was assessed in the autumn on the badly bruised car (DRX 257C) which Timo Makinen had treated so brutally in Scotland. Then came the conversion of DRX 258C from normal to raised exhaust.

Thus equipped, DRX 258C was allocated to the Morley Twins for their last drive in a Big Healey. Starting at No.14, with Zasada's tiny Steyr-Puch just ahead of them and Pat Moss-Carlsson's Saab Sport and Bengt Soderstrom's Lotus-Cortina right behind, they were certainly among friends as the event led off from London towards special stages in the West Country, then Wales, North Yorkshire and the Kielder complex before the only scheduled rest halt at Perth in Scotland. They had to deal with increasing amounts of deep snow (and a strictly-policed ban on studded tyres), which

DRX 258C was new for use by the Morley Twins in the French Alpine rally, and is seen here at various points on the route.

DRX 258C at the Oulton Park speed test on the 1965 RAC rally, where it was driven by the Morley Twins.

they certainly did not enjoy, even though team-mate Timo Makinen (in EJB 806C) made light of the conditions and led the event convincingly until the very late stages.

Although first on the road after a while, and having been given the wrong (slow) stage times at one point – soon corrected – their troubles began at the Oulton Park sprint test when the crownwheel-and-pinion failed. They had to accept a maximum penalty on that test, though the team mechanics then took only 25 minutes to change the unit before sending them off towards the snows of North Yorkshire.

Well and truly out of the running after that, the Morleys soldiered on for hours until the slippery conditions got the better of them on the Loch Achray stage (near Callander in Scotland), which left the car well off the track, out of the range of spectators or any other means of retrieval. It was a sad end to the careers of this car and of the Morleys, who retired from the sport at the end of the year.

Competition Record

1965 Geneva rally	Donald Morley	1st in Class
1965 French Alpine	Donald Morley	2nd Overall GT Category/1st in Class
1965 RAC rally	Donald Morley	DNF

DRX 258C AS TESTED BY AUTOCAR

To our delight, Abingdon's Press Officer Wilson McComb lent DRX 258C to us at *Autocar* magazine immediately after its return from the 1965 French Alpine rally. This meant that technical editor Geoffrey Howard and I enjoyed a week of pure undiluted joy, not only at our usual test track (MIRA near Nuneaton in Warwickshire) but on the public highway, where its bright red and white colour scheme (plus, of course, the seven forward-facing lights and the big white competition number squares on the doors) made it rather arresting.

Our opening remarks in the illustrated test published on 3 September 1965 summarised our feelings about this icon: "Watching a works Healey carve its way up the side of an Alp on a timed special stage in an international rally makes it obvious that this is a very different car from the production Mk III [BJ8] convertible...".

No work had been done on this car since it returned to the UK (the bent near-side rear wing was still in evidence), but it was clear to us that it was still in tip-top condition. McComb supplied rolling-road power curves which showed that there was a peak of 173bhp at 5600rpm at the rear wheels, which certainly confirmed that the test bed claims of 200-210bhp at the flywheel were fact and not fiction.

Geoff Howard's first problem was that he found it difficult to get comfortable in the seat which was tailored round the dapper Donald Morley's frame, so when I (then a lofty 6ft 2in) had a go it was, shall we say, a rather cosy fit. No matter, for nothing was going to keep me away from this remarkable machine.

Howard was initially quite overcome with the raw nature of the beast but later could summarise as follows: "There is an overall taut feel to the suspension and steering that we have never experienced on other Austin-Healeys... whatever the cause, it gives immediate confidence and makes one want to go straight out on to a circuit and get the car drifting. As it was, we had to make do with some pseudo rally routes around the home counties, but even so we found ourselves driving on well into the night just for the sheer exhilaration of it all.

"With a flood of light boring a tunnel for miles ahead there is no need to reduce speed after dark. Thundering between hedges and grass banks one is forever at work: up through the gears, lift off for a curve, back on the throttle, into overdrive then out again, hard on the brakes for a sudden hazard, back on the throttle – that's the way it goes".

There was more of this but I had to add a 'good housekeeping' caution: "Living for days in the car on an international event must be exhausting, although there are a few home comforts. Intercom sets take the strain out of conversation and help kill the noise, and there's a row of vacuum flask pockets in the passenger's door. Up in the roof a big floppy bag is the only stowage space for maps and Kleenex and glucose and cigarettes."

Along the way, of course, we managed to take some performance figures. Using an accurately calibrated fifth wheel, these confirmed just how formidably fast a works 3000 actually was. It was on the return trip to Abingdon, however, that I really managed to appreciate the car's formidable character, for its very presence in the rear view mirror of most vehicles encountered along the way seemed to be enough to encourage them to leap for the nearside verge. The most satisfying detail of all, though, was that there

In many ways this is a poignant picture, for it was taken at Abingdon in November 1965, just before the Big Healey tackled its last-ever works RAC International rally. Carrying No. 14, in the far corner of the workshop, is the Morley Twins's DRX 258C, while the second Healey, on the left of the shop, is thought to be DRX 257C, which was the 'mule' for development of the high-exhaust silencer layout, but which did not compete in the event itself. Mini Cooper S No. 36, by the way, was for Tony Fall, and No. 37 (which would mysteriously changed its registration number in the next few days) was for Harry Kallstrom.

was childish delight in changing up a gear as one passed them, for the barely-silenced exhaust system protruded on the nearside of the body shell!

An extract of the performance figures which we took on that memorable day at MIRA is quoted below – and who cares that in nearly 1500 miles of use (yes, everyone seemed to want to try out the car during its stay with the magazine) it recorded a mere 13.7mpg.

All in all, an unforgettable experience.

Performance Figures	DRX 258C	Standard BJ8 (Autocar test 1964)
Final drive ratio :	4.30	3.91
Maximum speed (mph) in top	120	121
Acceleration (secs)		
0-30mph	2.7	3.4
0-60mph	8.2	9.8
0-80mph	12.9	16.2
0-100mph	23.5	35.3
Acceleration in direct top gear:		
30-50mph	6.3	6.8
50-70mph	5.4	7.9
60-80mph	5.0	8.1
80-100mph	6.4	9.9
Standing start ¼-mile (secs)	15.6	17.2

Photographed at rest in the Autocar *car park in Waterloo, West London, in August 1965, DRX 258C had just returned from competing in the 1965 French Alpine rally.*

Note: The top speed of DRX 258C was limited by the gearing employed. In direct top gear the road car achieved 111mph, while DRX 258C could only reach 100mph because of the gearing and the 6000rpm limit that was applied.

REGISTRATION NUMBER	ENGINE SIZE	MODEL TYPE
EJB 806C	**2968CC 6-CYL OHV**	**3000 BJ8**

During the 1965 RAC rally, it snowed very heavily in the Yorkshire and Kielder special stage sections. At one point, Timo Makinen (in EJB 806C) and Rauno Aaltonen (in a works Mini-Cooper S) called in for BMC service near Pickering. Because the Healey's starter motor had packed up a push-start was needed at this moment – and that is the author (in spectacles and duffel coat) helping.

Timo Makinen was at his flamboyant best on the 1965 RAC, finishing second overall (to Aaltonen's works Mini-Cooper S).

Those who know enough about BMC team manager Stuart Turner will probably agree that he was always ruthlessly logical in the way he organised, ran, planned and schemed the future programme of his teams. The fact that a brand-new, state-of-the-art BJ8 was built as a 'one-event wonder' to compete in the 1965 RAC rally blew all those assumptions out of the water. It was not ready to roll until a few days before

the rally and, as already noted, the Big Healey team was to be disbanded immediately after it. In fact, it may only have been commissioned because Turner, who came close to hero-worshipping Timo Makinen, wanted to give the Finn the chance of winning a major event while there was still a chance.

Looking back, this seemed to be ambitious, for in three seasons Makinen had started eight rallies in 3000s, failed to finish in five of them, had one second place overall (RAC rally 1964), but otherwise had never looked likely to succeed. Turner, deciding that studying the odds was for bookmakers and gamblers, thought otherwise – and EJB 806C was born.

Technically it was like all the other works BJ8s and was fitted with the same high-mounted exhaust as had been adopted by DRX 258C for the RAC rally. Timo loved it, though his co-driver, Paul Easter, complained about the extra heat which permeated the cabin.

The looks and the sound of these two special machines were exciting enough, but once the event got under way it was Makinen's driving of EJB 806C which caught the media's attention. While the Morleys lost 30 minutes when their rear axle failed, Timo overcame awfully slippery conditions, occasional off-road excursions, a flat battery and a full-blooded blizzard in the Yorkshire stages to lead the event until the closing hours. At one point team manager Stuart Turner had mechanics scouring pet shops in Yorkshire towns in search of dog leads to turn into impromptu tyre chains!

The Morleys retired when they crashed in Loch Achray forest but Timo thundered on in spite of getting stuck in the snow on more than one occasion. Before the end of the event neither of the car's doors fitted properly any more, almost every panel had been creased against snow banks, trees or even other competitors, and on a slippery stage in Wales his car ground to a halt, to be passed (on the road and in penalties) by his team-mate and rival Rauno Aaltonen in a Mini-Cooper 1275S.

Although Rauno finally beat Timo by 3min 8sec, it tells us everything about Timo's (and the Healey's) performance that he set 28 fastest stage times, 11 second fastests and three third fastests, but that he also suffered from two maximum penalties. Rally winner Aaltonen, in the Mini-Cooper was only fastest on 10 occasions but had no maximum penalties.

Although the car was in a somewhat battered state it was sold immediately after the event and survives to this day.

Competition Record
1965 RAC rally

Timo Makinen

2nd Overall

REGISTRATION NUMBER	ENGINE SIZE	MODEL TYPE
PWB 57 (RE-REGISTERED FROM ARX 92B)	**2968CC 6-CYL OHV**	**3000 PROTOTYPE**

Two years after Big Healeys had last tackled an international rally one final attempt to win the RAC rally was proposed. In 1967 for the first time the organisers decided to include a category for nonhomologated prototypes – FIA Group 6 machines – which meant that a Big Healey could once again compete.

A single very special works 3000 was prepared for Rauno Aaltonen and Henry Liddon to drive, but by then Abingdon no longer had any 3000s on its fleet. An ageing 1964 Mk III team car (ARX 92B), which had been sold at the end of 1965 to Peter Browning, then became available. Peter had re-registered it PWB 57 for his own road use, and was 'persuaded' (his description) to loan it back to the company for this event.

As re-prepared, this car was probably the most powerful road-going 3000 ever built. An all-aluminium engine (basically the same as planned for use in the MG MGC GTS race cars) was fitted, bored out to 2968cc and fitted with three 45 DCOE Weber carburettors, giving a power output of nearly 200bhp at the rear wheels! The additional load of rally gear, sump and underside guards, etc, brought the weight up to just 24cwt (2688lb/1219kg), which was carried on four sturdy Minilite magnesium alloy wheels shod with Dunlop 185-15 SP44 radial Weathermaster tyres.

Naturally the car had a developed version of the high side-exit exhaust system, this time with the silencer hidden behind louvres in the door skin panel. This was also the first and only works Healey rally car to be equipped with dual circuit brakes and twin vacuum servo units, and because the engine was much lighter than the standard unit (about 100lb/45kg, some say) the car was found to handle much better than any of its predecessors.

The result was magnificent and according to the form book it should have been a winning car, but on the evening before the start of the event, when the car had already gone through pre-event scrutineering, the rally was cancelled. A very serious outbreak of foot-and-mouth disease (which affects animals with cloven hoofs) was sweeping through the British countryside, and since this disease was easily transmitted by the tyres and undersides of cars there was no way the event could be allowed to go ahead. Therefore the world's finest Austin-Healey 3000 rally car, never even started an event. It was returned to Peter Browning in 'as-prepared' condition

(naturally he was delighted to receive it in such a fresh state!) and was eventually sold to Arthur Carter, a collector in East Anglia. Perhaps it was fitting that production of Austin-Healey 3000s came to an end just weeks after the RAC rally of 1967 was cancelled.

For the 1967 RAC rally, which was unfortunately cancelled at the last moment, BMC proposed to use the all-alloy engine of one of the MGC Sebring race cars (like this example) in the much-modified 3000 PWB 57.

Peter Browning, who had been running the works race car efforts for some time at Abingdon, became BMC's Competitions Manager in January 1967.

Competition Record

1967 RAC rally	Rauno Aaltonen	Non-starter (event cancelled at less than 24 hours' notice)

CHAPTER 8:
100-SIX AND 3000
IN MOTOR RACING

After savouring the excitement generated by the four-cylinder 100S's racing career, which carried on in private owners' hands into the late 1950s, Healey took their time in developing race-car versions of the six-cylinder 100-Six model, but they never went as far as they had with the ultra-special 100S.

There were several reasons for this. One of the two most important was the fact that the 100-Six was considerably heavier than the 100S had been. Official figures suggested that an unladen 100S weighed 1924lb, while the first of the 100-Sixes weighed in at 2435lb, an increase of no less than 26 per cent. The second reason was that the company already had a hearty dislike of the C-series six-cylinder power unit which had been wished on them by BMC management.

The story of the arrival of this new engine is detailed in the panel C-Series Engine – a difficult birth (see page 67).

Once Healey at Warwick had come to terms with commercial reality – namely that if they wanted to continue with a credible and hopefully successful motorsport programme it would have to be with progressively developed and more powerful versions of the engine – they settled down to work.

The story really started with the building of special cars for record-setting purposes on the Bonneville Salt Flats (described in Chapter 6), diverted into the initial development of a single ex-press car (UOC 741) for rallying and for use in the Mille Miglia, and then settled on the occasional build and preparation of race cars based on the 100-Six and 3000 road cars.

Healey did not have enough space, time or budget to tackle a serious motor racing as opposed to rallying programme with the Big Healey, so tended to confine their attention to the Sebring 12 hour race, where the pre-race and post-race publicity benefits would certainly help boost the brand's image in the USA. Yet there might be little to gain at Sebring, where the Healey-prepared cars had to compete with world-class racing sports cars from Ferrari, Maserati and others.

However, at the very end of the works Big Healey's motorsport career, in 1965, BMC used one car, ARX 91B, to contest two long-distance sports car races – the Targa Florio and the Guards 1,000 mile race at Brands Hatch, these two exploits having been detailed in the previous Chapter.

REGISTRATION NUMBER	ENGINE SIZE	MODEL TYPE
UOC 741	**2639cc 6-cyl OHV**	**100-Six BN4**

This two-tone hard-top BN4 started life in the summer of 1956 as a press, publicity and photography car for BMC, was then taken into the care of Healey at Warwick, and as already noted in Chapter 7 competed in the Sestriere rally of February 1957 in the capable hands of Tommy Wisdom and his co-driving daughter Ann.

It was then returned to Warwick where in a matter of weeks it was made more suitable for Wisdom and his non-driving partner Cecil Winby (of the Brico Piston group in Coventry) to take on the Mille Miglia. Even at this stage it still looked surprisingly standard, for it ran with front and rear bumpers and with the standard fold-flat windscreen still in place, though locked into the flattened position to help the aerodynamics. The engine had a gas-flowed six-port cylinder head and was carefully balanced but was virtually standard. One of the obvious modifications made for what was after all an endurance event was the fitment of a larger-capacity fuel tank.

Because the car was due to leave the start at Brescia at 04.14, after daylight had broken, extra driving lamps were not fitted (though these would figure on the car when running in rallies). It had centre-lock spoked wheels with Dunlop racing tyres. Hidden from view and fortunately not noticed by the scrutineers was a strengthened chassis frame which incorporated all the stiffening and sturdier bracketry of the 100S, including provision for larger-than-standard DAS10 Armstrong rear shock absorbers to be installed.

Neither Tommy Wisdom nor his co-driver Cecil Winby were young any more, both of them being experienced competitors from as early as the 1930s, so no fireworks were expected from this car's appearance in the Mille Miglia, but it nevertheless finished the 1,000-mile race with honour. The car completed the long public-highway course in 13hr 4min 10 sec and was classified 37th overall.

This effectively brought UOC 741's racing career to an end,

for Healey then prepared it for rallying and saw it compete in the 1958 Monte Carlo. Then, to quote Geoff Healey, "Marcus Chambers, then heading BMC Competitions, had been persevering with the more mundane BMC vehicles in competition, and quickly saw the potential of the car. He rang me and persuaded me to lend him the car for some rallies. We were also able to let him have drawings and specifications of all the special parts and equipment used... With the departure of UOC 741 to Abingdon, our involvement in rallies was greatly reduced".

UOC 741's career as a works rally car is covered in detail in Chapter 7.

Competition Record

1957 Mille Miglia	Tommy Wisdom/Cecil Winby	37th Overall

REGISTRATION NUMBER	ENGINE SIZE	MODEL TYPE
NOT REGISTERED	**2639CC 6-CYL OHV**	**100-SIX BN4**

Early in 1957 Healey prepared three new BN4s to compete in the Sebring 12 Hour race (in Florida, USA), these being the first of a series of lightweight (relatively speaking) Big Healeys for competition in long-distance motor races. To ensure that they were as specialised as possible for this well-publicised race they ran as non-homologated prototypes.

The cars, which seem not to have carried any UK registrations, were significant as they were the first of the progressively more special race cars developed at Warwick in the next few years, and in their styling were based on the long-nose/long-tail shape of the latest 'six-hour' record cars.

The special development department at Morris Engines in Coventry worked hard to produce these new and powerful 2.6-litre power units. They used the very first of the separate inlet-manifold cylinder heads (which would be fitted to all BN4 road cars from the late autumn of 1957, nearly a year hence), along with triple twin-choke Weber carburettors, nitrided crankshafts and special camshaft profiles. No less than 150bhp was developed at 5500rpm – this being a dramatic improvement on the mere 102bhp developed by the standard BN4 road cars of the day.

The Sebring entry was masterminded for Healey by Hambro

Automotive of the USA, who were Morris importers, and at their recommendation all the drivers were American nationals. Team management was by Ken Gregory, who also functioned as Stirling Moss's racing manager. One of the drivers was John Bentley, a respected US motoring writer, who reported on the event in detail for *The Autocar*.

Fortunes during the race were mixed, for although all three cars circulated strongly for a time, two were eliminated by catastrophic failure and breakage of connecting rods, which blew holes in the crankcases. Here, however, was a case of racing improving the breed, for the cause of the breakage, a quirk of the series-production machining process, was soon ascertained, changes were made, and no such failures every again occurred.

The Geitner/Cuomo car was lucky to survive: it was forced off the road on only the eighth lap by an unaware competitor, leapt in the air over a kerb and then nosed into the ground at high speed, damaging the chassis and bodywork, but somehow it was coaxed back to the pits, checked out, repaired, and continued at reduced speed until the end.

None of these cars was ever used again as works machines and all seem to have been sold off in the USA.

Competition Record

1957 Sebring 12 Hour race	Major Gil Geitner/Ray Cuomo/	26th overall, 2nd In Class
	John Bentley/Phil Stiles	DNF
	Roy Jackson-Moore/Forbes Robinson	DNF

REGISTRATION NUMBER	ENGINE SIZE	MODEL TYPE
NOT REGISTERED	**2639CC 6-CYL OHV**	**100-SIX BN4**

For the 1958 Sebring 12 Hour race Healey entered three 100-Sixes which were significantly different from those which had taken part the previous year. On this occasion it was decided that they should run in the homologated Grand Touring category. Accordingly the cars were taken direct from the production lines at Abingdon, and although the 2639cc engines were carefully-prepared by Morris Engines of Coventry, they were fitted with visually near-standard carburation, which included twin SU HD6 carburettors.

Along with these slightly enhanced engines they had front-wheel disc brakes and wore low-profile Perspex windscreens, but these 'screens were turned down by the scrutineers in Florida, meaning that the cars had to be hastily re-equipped with standard folding windscreens and factory-type hardtops.

The cars enjoyed trouble-free runs in contrast to the varied traumas of the 1957 expedition. All finished in good shape and came home triumphantly to win the prestigious Manufacturers' Team Prize. The USA importers naturally were delighted.

None of these cars was used again as a works competition machine.

Competition Record

1957 Sebring 12 Hour race	Phil Stiles/Gus Ehrmann	17th overall
	Fred Moore/Col. Bill Kincheloe	23rd Overall
	Major Gil Geitner/Ray Cuomo/Dr Harold Kunz	14th Overall and the team prize

REGISTRATION NUMBER	ENGINE SIZE	MODEL TYPE
UJB 141/142/143	**2912CC 6-CYL OHV**	**3000 BN7**

Jack Sears and Peter Riley drove UJB 143 at Le Mans in 1960, but unhappily it failed to complete the course.

Healey produced yet another variation on a Sebring theme for 1960, this time by using the newly-launched two-seater type BN7 3000s, which complied with the latest Grand Touring GT specification. In fact five near-identical cars were prepared, three of them for use as works cars at Sebring, one for Austin's own domestic campaign in Canada, the fifth being a practice or spare car.

The three Sebring race cars were prepared to Healey's then-ultimate homologated condition complete with hardtops and with aluminium skin panels for their bodywork. They had the latest chassis specification, which was evolving fast as a result of the intensive rally programme being carried out. This included different road spring and damper settings along with 14-leaf rear springs and DAS10 Armstrong rear dampers. There were Girling disc brakes at front and rear, a homologated extra which more and more owners ordered when building up their own cars for motorsport use. In addition the cars had more robust centre-lock wire wheels (Geoff Healey quoted a 54-spoke variety) and a vast 25-gallon fuel tank to give a long racing range. Power was by courtesy of special Morris Engines-built 2.9-litre power units with special camshafts, flowed cylinder heads, a pair of 2in SU HD8 carburettors and a competition-type exhaust system, along with an AP competition clutch, a non-overdrive gearbox and a 3.54:1 final drive ratio.

All three cars started well in the 1960 Sebring 12 Hour race, circulating at an agreed, not-flat-out pace, until Fred Stross strayed off course on one corner in UJB 142, hit built-

UJB 143 vies for position with a works Triumph TRS in the 1960 Le Mans 24 Hour race.

in obstacles at the edge and rolled the car, which damaged it significantly and caused its retirement. The British duo, Peter Riley and Jack Sears, then took up the lead in the team but were then forced to make two lengthy pit stops, once for a complete gearbox change, the second to investigate a potential failure of the replacement 'box. Eventually the car was reduced to circulating slowly with only top gear available, allowing the Geitner/Breskovitch car to pull out a very satisfying lead. In its class it was only beaten by a 3-litre Ferrari 250GT.

Following this race two cars, UJB 141 and UJB 142, stayed behind in the USA, whereas UJB 143 was shipped back to the UK to be prepared for Peter Riley and Jack Sears to compete in the Le Mans 24 Hour race.

Entered in the 2.5-litre to 3.0-litre category, where it had to compete against no fewer than nine Ferrari 250GT coupés, there was little prospect of a class win, so Healey set out merely to demonstrate the sheer reliability of this brave car. Looking very

standard in hardtop form, and running with two extra driving lamps, rally-style, it started strongly and must have given Riley and Sears a satisfactorily snug ride in the rain which attacked the race from time to time. Unhappily, after completing only 89 laps in a little more than seven hours the engine expired with a failed big end bearing. Official figures showed that its fastest race lap was in 5min 2sec (99.7mph) and that it was timed at 130mph on the Mulsanne Straight.

This was the end of the car's official works career. It was sold to David Dixon, re-registered DD 300, and competed with honour as a private entry in British and European motor racing events.

Number plate identity collectors and historians should note, however, that after the car had been sold off the registration number UJB 143 was resurrected and a new car began a short-lived works rally career based at Abingdon; this second career has been detailed in Chapter 7.

Competition Record

1960 Sebring 12 Hour race	UJB141 (Maj. G.Gietner/Jack Breskovich)`	15th Overall, 2nd in Class
	UJB 142 (Fred Spross/Lou Spencer)	DNF
	UJB 143 (Jack Sears/Peter Riley)	3rd in Class
1960 Le Mans 24 Hour race	Jack Sears/Peter Riley	DNF

REGISTRATION NUMBER	ENGINE SIZE	MODEL TYPE
54/56/57 FAC	**2912cc 6-cyl OHV**	**3000 BJ7**

Having concentrated on Sprites (occasionally badged as Midgets) in the 1961 and 1962 Sebring races, Healey returned to Sebring in 1963 with the latest iteration of the 3000, complete with triple-Weber-carburettor engines,

A team of new lightweight, 3000s were built to compete at Sebring in 1963, 57 FAC being one of them. The specification, including all-alloy skin panels, and a triple-Weber carburetted engine, was familiar.

aluminium cylinder heads, and as many aluminium panels as possible. Although apparently three near-identical cars were built, just two of them raced in the 12-Hour event; 57 FAC was what might be described as the 'travelling spare' but was never intended to be raced in Florida. In fact it was later sold in North America without turning a wheel in anger.

Although both the other cars started well in the race, the Abingdon pairing of Paddy Hopkirk and Donald Morley experienced misfortune when their engine began to suffer from oil surge, the oil pressure sometimes dropping to nearly zero. The only remedy would have involved dropping the sump pan, thus a lengthy pit stop, so this was not attempted and the car continued to circulate slowly and eventually ended up 21 whole laps behind the other team car.

In 56 FAC Bob Olthoff, a South African who had worked on the production lines at Abingdon, and Ronnie Bucknum, a respected American race driver, circulated much faster, taking a rousing twelfth overall and fourth in their 'prototype' class. This twelfth was achieved in the face of formidable opposition from Ferrari, Jaguar, Porsche and Cobra opposition, with Ferrari race cars taking the top six places overall. In the Prototype category the car was beaten only by the 3-litre Ferraris, which also took 1-2-3 in the race.

Competition Record
1963 Sebring 12 Hour Race	56 FAC	(Bob Olthoff/Ronnie Buckman)	12th Overall
	54 FAC	(Paddy Hopkirk/Donald Morley)	26th Overall

REGISTRATION NUMBER	ENGINE SIZE	MODEL TYPE
767 KNX	**2912cc 6-cyl OHV**	**3000 BJ8**

This ice blue//white hardtop 3000 was the only BJ8 Healey Warwick prepared for long-distance motor racing. It appeared at Sebring in March 1964, just weeks after the new model with wind-up windows and a modernised fascia had been revealed to the public.

There were high hopes of a good performance by this car as it included every bit of development that had gone into the chassis since Bob Olthoff and Ronnie Buckman had taken a magnificent twelfth place at Sebring just a year earlier. Although no more powerful and certainly no lighter than the BJ7 of 1963, the car benefited from the dropped

chassis side rail which allowed the rear axle more bump and rebound movement (as described in Chapter 7).

Unhappily the race at Sebring in 1964 proved to be an unmitigated disaster for the team. On the very first lap, with Paddy Hopkirk at the wheel, the new car picked up a puncture and had to crawl round the circuit before the wheel could be changed. Paddy then drove like a hero and passed at least 30 cars in three hours before handing over as planned to his driving partner the Canadian Grant Clark. This is where it all went wrong, as Geoff Healey summarised so well: "Clark managed four laps before he overturned the

This immaculately maintained BJ7 was built by Healey in Warwick to compete in the Sebring 12 Hour race. In all major respects it was running to the same basic specification as the current works rally cars – though of course it was even lighter than they were.

3000, seriously damaging it. Clark had been selected by the Canadian operation, and was not an appropriate pairing. He lacked Paddy's skill and had no hope of keeping up the scorching pace set by his co-driver".

Some sort of recovery was then made in 1965. For 1966, because the FIA announced that there would be major changes to Appendix J, which governed the eligibility of production cars, including the banning of alternative cylinder heads and of light-alloy body panels, BMC management decided that the magnificent 3000 should be retired from International competition at the end of the 1965 season. Thus the entry of a 3000 BJ8 at Sebring in March 1965 was the last occasion in which a works 3000 appeared in Florida and, to save time and money, the damaged car from Sebring 1964 was rebuilt.

For the 1965 event BMC and Healey combined to enter no fewer than seven cars including two works Sprites (described in Chapter 10) but only one of the cars was a works 3000 from Warwick. In the face of considerable challenges, Abingdon's Peter Browning team-managed an impressive operation, particularly as this was a race where a monumental cloudburst flooded the track at one stage and,

There was nothing fancy about the driving compartment of a Warwick-built works 3000 race car

135

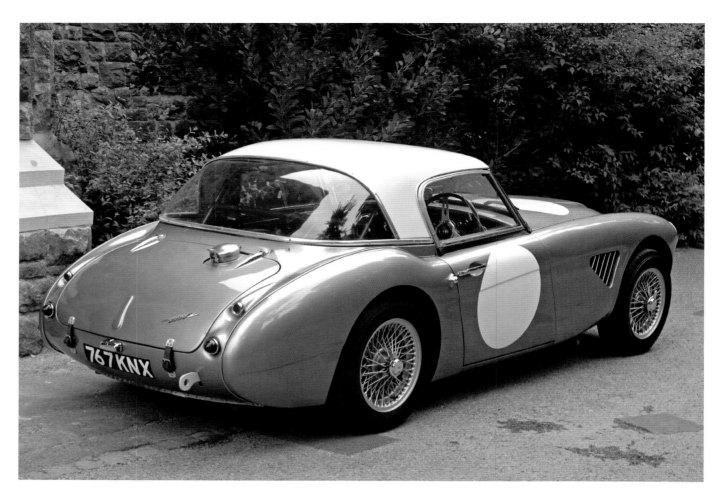

The standard-looking rear end of 767 KNX hid an extremely large fuel tank, and a nicely-detailed installation of the race-type filler cap.

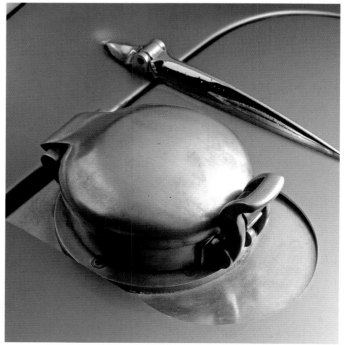

Competition Record

1964 Sebring 12-Hour race	Paddy Hopkirk/Grant Clark	DNF
1965 Sebring 12-Hour race	Paul Hawkins/Warwick Banks	1st in Class

as Geoff Healey later wrote, "The pit lane was eight inches deep in water with spare tyres and wheels floating away".

Throughout this biblical downpour the BMC team kept going, the result being that all the cars made it to the finish. As far as the 3000 was concerned, there was almost a personal disaster when what was diplomatically described as a 'stomach upset' afflicted Warwick Banks, who felt quite incapable of driving and proposed to leave it to team-mate Paul Hawkins to complete the event.

Geoff Healey, however, spotted a race regulation which specified that no driver could drive for more than four consecutive hours without taking a break and had to insist that at one point Banks should complete just three four-minute laps, which he did while in personal distress. The result was that the gallant crew brought the car home to win its capacity class.

With a triple 45DCOE Weber carburettor setup and hotter cams in a six-port aluminum head, 767 KNX produced about 180bhp

CHAPTER 9:
SPRITES IN RALLYING

The Austin-Healey Sprite was an extremely successful little sports car and soon inspired the rebirth of the MG Midget name, but the Sprite of 1958 found very little favour as a works rally car, though it would become both active and successful in motor racing (see Chapter 10). Perhaps one credible factor in this was the 'right car, wrong moment' syndrome, because when the Sprite became available the Austin-Healey 100-Six/3000 models were becoming increasingly effective in International events and would soon set all standards by which other rally cars were measured. No sooner had this situation stabilised at BMC, where most funds were being directed at the Big Healey, than the front-wheel-drive Mini-Cooper also came on to the scene, so thereafter there were rarely enough funds – or facilities – to take the Sprite to its limits.

Eventually, therefore, Marcus Chambers's works competition department elected to treat the Sprite as a 'family pet' rather than as a serious machine, though they were happy to see it evolve as

This was the running gear of the 948cc-engined Austin A40, most of which (except for the steering) was 'donated' to the design of the new Austin-Healey Sprite.

a race car, with all the work involved in its development being concentrated at the Healey company in Warwick. This process, steady but ultimately truncated by political and marketing issues within British Leyland, and by the limits of the 1.3-litre A-Series engine, is described in detail in Chapter 10.

Soon after the Sprite had gone on sale Abingdon and Warwick jointly built and prepared three different cars – PMO 200, XOH 276 and XOH 277 – it surely being significant that only PMO 200 had a local-to-Abingdon identity, the other cars having Birmingham/Warwickshire-based registrations, which emphasises that most of the effort would be located at the Healey workshops in Warwick. To make an initial splash for publicity reasons it was decided that three cars should be entered in the French Alpine rally of 1958 which, being held in summer and on all-tarmac roads, was thought to suit the Sprite as a potential class-winning car. The PMO 200 number tells us how close that car was to Abingdon's heart at first, as its 100-Six 'big sister' cars (PMO 201/202/203) were being prepared at the same time.

In their first event the cars were still nearly standard as it was only weeks since the Sprite had met its public for the first time, and the XOH cars remained in that basic state of tune through their short works careers. PMO 200, on the other hand, which soon became John Sprinzel's favourite rally car, began a process of progressive modification, first to the engine (where Speedwell, John Sprinzel's North London-based tuning firm was much involved), then to the bodywork, which gradually changed from the standard steel body to one which had light-alloy skin panels, a permanent fixed-head coupé top and eventually a Frank Costin-designed front end in which the headlamps were moved to the front corners of the smoother shape; this was a characteristic of the cars which Sprinzel himself later developed into the non-factory 'Sebring' model.

The Sprite's life as a works rally car was brief. Apart from supporting Sprinzel's PMO 200 in various events (British and International) in 1959, there was no factory involvement, for at that time the major efforts were going into the Austin-Healey 3000s, the MGA Twin-Cams, and (if only tentatively at first) into the Minis.

Quite suddenly, though, the prospect of Pat Moss once again becoming European Ladies' Champion in 1960 inspired the team to enter her in a number of different cars in different rallies. In the case of the Sprite, two brand-new cars, WJB 707 and WJB 727, both of which looked more standard than PMO 200 had been when seen in its last works appearances, were built at Abingdon and prepared by Sprinzel's company in London.

That, however, was that. At the end of 1960 the career of the Sprite as a works rally car was brought to an end, though work continued at Warwick on the race cars. A year later, when Stuart Turner took over from Marcus Chambers as BMC Competitions manager, he immediately commissioned a new series of Sprite-based machines (registered YRX 727/737/747). In theory, and

according to the log books, these were originally identified as MG Midgets, but at least one of these cars was rebadged (and. therefore, given a different grille) to become a Sprite on later events! This practice, incidentally, was also carried out of various works Mini-Coopers at times, for sometimes they were seen as 'Austin' and sometimes as 'Morris' machines.

Even so, and no matter what badges were finally being carried, from 1963 there were no more works Sprites or MG Midgets used in rallying, though these cars carried on strongly and successfully as race cars (see Chapter 10) until British Leyland put a stop to everything.

This was the standard A-Series engine/transmission assembly as fitted to Sprites (and MG Midgets too) in the early 1960s. Race tuning could produce at least 100 per cent more power and torque.

REGISTRATION NUMBER	ENGINE SIZE	MODEL TYPE
YAC 740	**948CC 4-CYL OHV**	**MK1**

Manufactured in April 1958, YAC 740 was one of the very earliest production-line Sprites to leave the gates of the Abingdon factory. This light-yellow-coloured car was immediately delivered to Healey in Warwick (which is why it qualifies as a works machine in this context), where it was to be used as a promotional vehicle for the first few months of its life.

It was used on a route survey for the 1958 Mille Miglia and then was pressed into service as a works rally car. Prepared at Warwick for competition in the French Alpine rally of mid-1958 (and, at the time, running in the same mechanical condition as PMO 200), it was entrusted to two well-respected motoring writers, Tommy Wisdom and *Birmingham Post* motoring editor Jack Hay.

In that event, the official BMC team comprised no fewer than five of the larger 100-Six BN4s (see Chapter 4), while John Sprinzel's later-famous PMO 200 was also in the supporting cast from Abingdon.

On the Alpine, held in the hot high-summer of the South of France, Wisdom and Hay valiantly kept their near-standard new car going well and finished strongly. In the end, they finished second in the 1-litre GT class, beaten only by John Sprinzel's PMO 200. That, however, was the one and only occasion in which the car appeared in motorsport with quasi-factory backing.

Following the 1958 French Alpine rally, Tommy Wisdom's Sprite was paraded in front of the crowd at the British GP race at Silverstone.

Competition Record

1958 French Alpine Rally	Tommy Wisdom	2nd in Class

REGISTRATION NUMBER	ENGINE SIZE	MODEL TYPE
PMO 200	**948CC 4-CYL OHV**	**MK1, LATER SEBRING**

PMO 200 is one of those vehicle identities whose works significance fell with every successive vehicle which it adorned. The original PMO 200, as covered here, was a very important works car, but once it passed into John Sprinzel's personal ownership, not only was the identity eventually applied to different Sprites, but the evolution continued quite independently of the works team, and the same number plate later appeared on completely different makes and models of car; in recent years, it has even been seen on a 'Frogeye' Sprite which John Sprinzel keeps in his home on a Hawaiian island!

The original car was a very early example, delivered to Abingdon in the spring of 1958 (it was registered in the same sequence as the forthcoming 100-Six team cars) before being prepared under John Sprinzel's supervision in London. The first iteration had a standard-looking blue-painted body complete with the white factory hard top. Its first event was the French Alpine rally of July 1958, where Sprinzel was accompanied by Willy Cave as his co-driver and led a team of three Sprites, the others being Tommy Wisdom in a Warwick-prepared car (YAC 740) and Ray Brookes in a privately-prepared example.

Apart from Sprinzel's car overheating (Sprinzel got round this problem by hacking an unsightly hole in the top of the bonnet), all the cars performed with great honour, and PMO 200 started as it meant to go on by winning its capacity class.

Its next outing came only six weeks later when Sprinzel and *The Motor* journalist Richard Bensted-Smith competed in the Liège-Rome-Liège Marathon, the first rough rally tackled by a Sprite. Unhappily, in the depths of Yugoslavia the Sprite lost its left front wheel complete with stub axle, which plunged into the nearby river and beginning to float away. The rescue of the wheel involved the help of a local who dived in to retrieve it, followed by the services of a local blacksmith to bodge everything up so that the car could limp back to Belgium!

After a thorough refresh PMO 200 then tackled the 1959 Monte Carlo rally, where Willy Cave was once again to be the co-driver. Although this was a winter event with snow in abundance it turned out to be a rally requiring split-second time-keeping on the final sections (and, perhaps, the help of a bit of French local knowledge) so the fact that the little car finished 14th overall and third in its capacity class was a real achievement. Starting from Paris, PMO ran under competition number 201 (of 361 starters) in a team in which Raymond Baxter (No. 2) and Tommy Wisdom (No. 185) were fellow entrants. Sprinzel and the Sprite were only beaten by the organisers obsession with time-keeping, and not on the grounds of performance.

PMO 200 next spent some of its time tackling minor British and European national road events before John Sprinzel took it in hand once again, still under the benevolent umbrella of the works, and began turning it into what was effectively the prototype of the non-factory 'Sebring Sprite' model. Not only did this particular car become progressively lighter and more starkly equipped, but it was provided with a new lower design of nose with headlamps outboard.

It was in this form that it tackled the 1959 Liège-Rome-Liège, where Sprinzel was utterly determined to reach the finish in a rally which was to cause all but 14 of the 97 starters to retire. Sprinzel's co-driver was Stuart Turner, who was approaching his peak as a co-driver/navigator, and the miracle was that they kept going against all the odds of mileage, high temperatures and physical exhaustion, eventually to take twelfth overall. If there had been the usual capacity classes (not provided on this event) they would have won the 1.0-litre GT class too.

Described as the most devastating Liège so far held, it followed the usual 96-hours-without-a-break formula, taking in two passages through all the highest roads in the Italian Dolomites, a rough and tumble 24 hours on Yugoslavian dirt roads and a tough final night in the French Maritime Alps, where fog and extra-mileage diversions all added to the problems.

Yet the gallant little car made it to the finish back in Belgium, though its works career was now at an end. After

First time out in PMO 200, John Sprinzel dominated his class in the 1958 French Alpine rally, later showing off the car to the British GP spectators at Silverstone.

By September 1959, PMO had become a fully-fledged 'Sprinzel-special'. Along with co-driver Stuart Turner, John put up a magnificent show in the Liège-Rome-Liège of that year.

Using PMO 200, John Sprinzel took a fine second place in the 1960 RAC rally. The scene is the top hairpin of the Rest and be Thankful hill climb in Scotland.

By 1961, PMO 200 was John Sprinzel's personal car – and for the 1961 RAC rally he loaned it to Paul Hawkins/Vic Elford. Incidentally, on a personal note, the author was co-driving the works Sunbeam Rapier which is lined up immediately behind the Sprite at this control.

this, according to John Sprinzel, PMO 200 was gifted to him by MG's General Manager John Thornley, and it became his regular International and national car for private entry in the next several seasons.

There is therefore an 'after-story'. Following the Liège, in which the car had taken something of a battering, Sprinzel used it for one or two British outings before being given it by BMC. He then converted it to full 'Sebring' specification and it was raced and rallied, sometimes with support from Healey and the BMC Competitions Department, in 1960 and 1961. Sprinzel then kept it for a number of years. The car became a full-blown Sebring Sprite later in 1960, and the registration number was in time attached to other cars in his hands (Sprites, Midgets, Triumph TR3As and other models) for some years.

Competition Record

1958 French Alpine rally	John Sprinzel	Class win
1958 Liège-Rome-Liège rally	John Sprinzel	DNF
1959 Monte Carlo rally	John Sprinzel	3rd in Class
1959 Lyons-Charbonnières rally	John Sprinzel	DNF
1959 Liège-Rome-Liège rally	John Sprinzel	12th

By the time PMO 200 was fully developed it sported this neat front end style, which later was a feature of all 'Sebring' Sprites produced by John Sprinzel's BMC-backed business.

A little badge (not a factory fitting, but as devised by John Sprinzel) tells its own story.

The fully-developed version of the Sebring Sprite featured this sleek nose, complete with extra driving lamps mounted close to the main headlamps.

143

In the author's personal experience – he co-drove this and other Sebring Sprites several times in the 1960s – to live in the fixed-head coupé environment was an invigorating and very noisy experience. But what a pretty little car it was!

The restored PMO 200 carries this rather exclusive badge, denoting that it took part in the ultra-gruelling Liège-Sofia-Liège event of 1961.

The extremely busy dashboard.

144

Like other Sebring Sprites, when new in the 1959-1961 period PMO 200 was usually powered by a highly-tuned 948cc power unit, but in later years ultra-powerful A-Series engines of up to 1275cc were fitted instead.

Doors and doorshuts were drilled for lightness.

REGISTRATION NUMBER	ENGINE SIZE	MODEL TYPE
XOH 276	**948CC 4-CYL OHV**	**MK1**

There has been some confusion about the heritage and works history of this car, but conclusive pictorial evidence confirms that in January 1959 it was prepared by the works to compete in the Monte Carlo rally and loaned to Raymond Baxter, who was motoring correspondent of the BBC. Accompanied by the experienced co-driver Jack Reece, Baxter started the event from Lisbon and this team was progressing well until, three days into the long run from Portugal and with close to 600 miles to go, they encountered a French truck, injuring Reece enough for him to be a barely functioning passenger for the rest of the event. Baxter then coped valiantly as driver and co-driver combined but ran out of time before the final arrival control.

Some stories suggest that this car was used instead of XOH 277 (see below) on some events, carrying that car's registration plates, but the Monte Carlo rally of 1959 definitely seems to have been the first event that XOH 276 tackled as a works car.

It competed twice more as a 'semi-works' machine in the French Alpine rallies of 1959 and 1960. The term 'semi-works' is used because for neither event is it listed in Bill Price's chronicle of the works cars of the period. It was driven on both occasions by Tommy Wisdom with Jack Hay as his co-driver. In 1959 Wisdom took second place in his capacity class, while in 1960 he was eliminated after running out of time towards the end of the rally. But under which guise did which car compete in 1959? This is why its exploits are listed here and below.

Competition Record

1959 Monte Carlo rally	Raymond Baxter	DNF
1959 French Alpine rally	Tommy Wisdom	2nd in Class
1960 French Alpine rally	Tommy Wisdom	DNF

REGISTRATION NUMBER	ENGINE SIZE	MODEL TYPE
XOH 277	**948CC 4-CYL OHV**	**MK1**

As in the case of XOH 276, 60 years have allowed myths and legends to develop, particularly regarding this car's use behind different registration plates – but both it and XOH 276, whether appearing as themselves or wearing the other's plates, seem to have had short and rather undistinguished lives as a works cars.

By this time in his fascinatingly varied career Tommy Wisdom was a well-liked, versatile but no longer front-running driver. In both of the snow-ridden events which this car contested on behalf of BMC, and the French Alpine rally which was held in high summer, he brought the car home to a steady class placing.

By this time in BMC's works department's development, however, management had rather lost interest in the Sprite, although encouraging the Healey company to carry on evolving the car for motor racing purposes, so the car was sold.

Competition Record

1959 Monte Carlo rally	Tommy Wisdom	5th in Class
1959 Sestriere rally	Tommy Wisdom	5th in Class
1959 French Alpine	Tommy Wisdom	2nd in Class

REGISTRATION NUMBER	ENGINE SIZE	MODEL TYPE
WJB 707	**948CC 4-CYL OHV**	**MK1**

Abingdon was delighted with John Sprinzel's rallying efforts in PMO 200, a car which (as John told the author) was gifted to him after the 1959 season, but it showed no further interest in rallying the Sprite for some time. It was only in October 1960, when the team suddenly realised that Pat Moss might once again become European Ladies' Rally Champion, that it commissioned John Sprinzel's London-based tuning business to prepare a new Sprite for her to drive in the Tour de Corse. A 3000 was not considered for this outing, not only because the team rightly considered that it would be uncompetitive in its class, but also because the entire Abingdon fleet was being prepared for the RAC rally, which would take place very soon after the Tour de Corse.

As far as one can see WJB 707 had no previous motor sport existence before it was made ready to rally in Corsica, In Harnessing Horsepower (his biography of Pat Moss), Stuart Turner commented: "The 24 hour Tour was very fast on twisty roads. All the roads were closed, and only competitors and service vehicles were allowed down them, and there were police at every junction. In effect it was a road race, flat out all the way. The Sprite was not nearly as quick as other small sports cars entered, like the Alpine-Renaults, and only made about

two controls on time before the gearbox broke, perhaps not surprising considering the strain of a couple of gear changes every five seconds or so." Prompted by Pat's reminiscences he went on to say: "Also, Pat probably contributed to the failure herself by refusing to have a front roll-bar fitted to the car, which meant the inside wheel lifted up and down on almost every corner; a roll-bar tends to stop this happening, and saves the gearbox from continual shocks." This cannot be true, for the gearbox shocks would be caused by the rear axle (not a front wheel) frequently breaking traction – and in any case available action pictures clearly show that WJB 707 was indeed fitted with a front anti-roll bar.

The car ran with standard bodywork and a hardtop, with four extra driving lamps, wire spoke wheels and a tuned-up engine (though no details seem to have been published); because the regulations allowed it the front bumper was removed. The gearbox broke after about ten hours rallying, stranding the girls near the top of a mountain road in the Corsican hinterland.

This was the car's one and only appearance as a works rally machine, and it was soon sold to Ian Walker, later being converted into a full Sebring Sprite.

Competition Record

1960 Tour de Corse	Pat Moss	DNF

REGISTRATION NUMBER	ENGINE SIZE	MODEL TYPE
WJB 727	**948CC 4-CYL OHV**	**MK1**

Even though the Sprite outing in the 1960 Tour de Corse had not been a success, if Pat finished above Volvo's Ewy Rosqvist in the 1960 RAC rally she could still be European Ladies Champion for that year. A 3000 could certainly have been made available to her for the RAC but it was decided to enter her in a Sprite – not the car which had let her down on the Tour de Corse but in a new one registered WJB 727.

Preparation involved John Sprinzel's business and the car was more highly tuned than before, apparently using some components which would become familiar to Sebring Sprite owners in the next two or three years. As readied for Pat and Ann Wisdom to tackle the RAC rally it had wire spoke wheels, a highly tuned engine, a different auxiliary lamp layout than

that seen in Corsica, and a non-standard lightweight front-end moulding (reputedly by Williams & Pritchard) which featured the headlamps in a conventional position rather than let into the central bonnet region. Incidentally, Bill Price's book about the history of Abingdon states that for this rally there were two works Sprites. The other one, taken back under the factory's wing for the occasion, was undoubtedly PMO 200, which by then belonged to John Sprinzel.

Here was a long rally that started from Blackpool, trekked all the way to Inverness for an overnight halt, took in four special stages in Scotland, and finished in London. Pat started well and was particularly fast up the Rest and be Thankful hill-climb, but a mix-up over control positions, time cards and checking out procedure saw her stranded for a time when trying to leave Inverness, where she incurred penalties. She was later to learn that her principal rival Ewy Rosqvist had lost time on a road section further into the event, as a result of which Pat beat Ewy to the finish and won the Championship after all. In fact she took second in her capacity class behind John Sprinzel's privately-prepared PMO 200, so BMC's team management was delighted.

As with WJB 707 (see above) this was the only time that WJB 727 appeared as a works rally car, and it was soon sold to David Seigle Morris, who had it converted to full Sebring Sprite specification.

Thereafter, future 'Spridgets' prepared at or blessed by Abingdon would usually be badged as MG Midgets.

Competition Record

1960 RAC rally	Pat Moss	2nd in Class

REGISTRATION NUMBER	ENGINE SIZE	MODEL TYPE
YRX 727	**995CC 4-CYL OHV**	**MIDGET MK1**

For the 1961 RAC rally Abingdon produced two brand new 'MG Midgets', which were effectively Austin-Healey Sprite Mk IIs. Derek Astle drove YRX 727, to win his capacity class.

No sooner had Stuart Turner taken over as BMC Competitions Manager in September 1961 than he gained approval for the building of three new works MG Midget rally cars complete with hardtops. They were of course the same as Sprite Mk IIs with minor cosmetic differences but with totally identically structural, mechanical and homologated specifications. These were registered YRX 727, YRX 737 and YRX 747.

The first of these cars, YRX 727, was one of two entered in the 1961 RAC rally, which was the first to feature the use of Forestry Commission special stages, and it was driven by Derick Astle/Peter Roberts.

With only two months to go before the rally there was no time for a lengthy and thoughtful development programme, so the specification of the cars was a mixture of race car experience from Warwick and the rally experience built up by cars which had already featured strongly in British rallying. The specification included a slightly-enlarged 995cc A-Series engine to near-Formula Junior tune and the liberal use of light-alloy body panels, though the standard steel wheels and drum brakes were retained.

In spite of the rough conditions on special stage and of the handicap of competing against much larger and more powerful opposition, this Midget was urged into eighth place overall and a well-merited class victory.

The car however was a 'one-event' wonder, for apart from being used in pre-Monte Carlo reconnaissance it was not seen again as a works car and was soon sold.

Competition Record		
1961 RAC rally	Derick Astle	1st in Class

REGISTRATION NUMBER	ENGINE SIZE	MODEL TYPE
YRX 737	**995CC 4-CYL OHV**	**MIDGET MK1/SPRITE MKII**

John Williamson drove YRX 737 in the French Alpine rally of 1962, where he took second place in his capacity class.

The second of the three new Midgets (see YRX 727, above) was also made ready for the 1961 RAC rally and was in the same mechanical tune as that car. Driven by a very experienced northern crew – Mike Sutcliffe and Roy Fidler – it shadowed YRX 727 for much of the event and took second in its class.

YRX 737 was then significantly modified and – just to cause confusion to historians – was also rebadged as an Austin-Healey Sprite, which involved no more than fitting a new front grille and other bits of trim, all of which the mechanics could obtain by strolling across the yard to raid the Sprite/Midget assembly lines.

For the 1962 Tulip rally the 'new' Austin-Healey was treated to wire-spoke wheels and front disc brakes and was driven by Tom Gold and Mike Hughes. The team fought valiantly against this rally's much-disliked 'class improvement' system which has already been described in an earlier Chapter, and brought the car home third in its capacity classs. Pat Moss won in a works Mini-Cooper, and the first of the Weber-carburetted Austin-Healey 3000s made an impressive first appearance.

Only a few weeks later, the car was made ready for the French Alpine rally, where BMC's main works interest was in four Weber-carburetted 3000s. Almost as an afterthought, it seems, YRX 737 (still badged as a Sprite) was allocated to John Williamson and David Hiam. Williamson, once a regular driver in the Marcus Chambers era, was no longer in the regular works team. In this, his swansong appearance, he drove steadily and finished ninth overall in the GT category, second only to an Alpine-Renault in his capacity class.

The car was then entered in the 1962 RAC rally (there were nine works cars – four Big Healeys, three Mini-Coopers, an MG1100, and this Sprite). Once again Tom Gold got the drive, this time with co-driver Tony Dyke. He started well and ran consistently until on Stage 26 (well over half-way through the event) when he put the car off the track on the Coed Y Brenin stage, leaving it on its nose down a steep bank, and was obliged to retire.

Thereafter it was retrieved, patched up and sold

Competition Record

1961 RAC rally	Mike Sutcliffe	2nd in Class
1962 Tulip rally	Tom Gold	3rd in Class
1962 French Alpine rally	John Williamson	9th GT Category/2nd Class
1962 RAC rally	Tom Gold	DNF

REGISTRATION NUMBER	ENGINE SIZE	MODEL TYPE
YRX 747	**995CC 4-CYL OHV**	**MIDGET MK1/SPRITE MKII**

The third car of the new MG Midget trio was not completed until the winter of 1961/62 and was allocated to Peter Riley and Mike Hughes for the 1962 Monte Carlo rally, where there were five long special stages and (as it transpired) not much snow. The objective was not to win the event outright (that would have fallen into the 'vain hope' category) but to look for a class win, which Peter Riley duly delivered. At this point the car was still in the same mechanical condition as the sister cars, and it still ran on steel wheels.

For the rest of 1962 it remained parked at Abingdon until it was brought out of store, re-prepared, given wire-spoke wheels and the latest power train modifications and entered for the 1963 Monte Carlo rally.

On this occasion, starting at No 158 from Glasgow, it was allocated to 'the two vicars' – the Rev. Rupert Jones and the Rev. Philip Morgan. Jones was already a seasoned BMC team member, but for Philip Morgan this was his first and only works drive.

The weather on this Monte was foul and blizzard-like but the pair kept the Midget on the road, losing a little time due to the conditions, and came home with a much-merited Class win. This was the car's final outing in works colours and it was soon sold off into private ownership, bringing the 1960s use of works Midgets/Sprites to a neat close.

Competition Record

1962 Monte Carlo rally	Peter Riley	1st in Class
1963 Monte Carlo rally	Rev. Rupert Jones	1st in Class

CHAPTER 10:
SPRITES IN MOTOR RACING

Almost from launch in 1958 works Sprites began to be raced all around the world, not only at Le Mans and in the Targa Florio but also at Sebring in Florida. BMC had elected to concentrate on rallying activities, based at Abingdon, and not to involve itself much in motor racing, leaving the Healey company to build and develop works or works-backed Sprite race cars. Eddie Maher of BMC (Morris Engines) at Courthouse Green, Coventry, would advise on and supervise much of the development work on the engines. Over the years Eddie's team worked repeated miracles, providing tuned production-type engines which would survive high revs for improbable distances. Between 1958 (when badged as Austin-Healeys) and 1968, when company policy had turned them into MG Midgets, the plucky little A-series engine grew from 948cc to 1293cc, with power boosted from the 948's 40-odd bhp to a race-reliable 110bhp from the 1293cc unit.

From time to time in the 1960s, at Geoffrey Healey's invitation, the author used to call in at the Healey workshops in Warwick, to see how the latest of his works-backed competition cars – Sprites and 3000s – were progressing. It was amazing that such a simply equipped and sparsely financed operation could continue to produce such remarkable results.

Over a decade until Lord Stokes's new British Leyland organisation cancelled what they decided were 'frivolous' programmes, almost all works race cars emanated from Warwick. Abingdon only occasionally got involved in producing racing machinery, invariably MGB, MGC or Austin Healey 3000 types.

Because I refuse to be too pedantic about the badging of the cars in this family, I crave the indulgence of the reader by suggesting that almost all of the works race cars in this programme were really Austin-Healey based and are therefore covered in some detail whether they were theoretically MGs or not.

This is how the racing A-Series-engined cars evolved in the early years, and in particular it shows how the Healey/BMC effort at Le Mans progressed as far as it did. Incidentally, and as I have previously noted in other books in this 'In Detail' series, race cars sometimes did not carry registration numbers, sometimes carried false plates, were not homologated, and sometimes underwent very major changes from year to year. Accordingly, while I have quoted registration numbers where they are known, I have tended to treat this section chronologically – i.e. race-by-race – rather than on a car-by-car basis.

Apart from their regular visits to Le Mans, Healey somehow found time to send race cars (100s, 100Ss, Sprites and Healey 3000s) to other classic events, notably the Targa Florio and the endurance races on the airfield at Sebring in Florida. They also indulged themselves and their drivers by sending cars to take part in events in the annual Nassau Speed week in the Bahamas, but these were little more than frivolous 'party pieces' (the Speed Week was noted more for its social life than for its motor sport) and have not been detailed in this Chapter.

The first Sprite entry in the Targa Florio came in 1959, when

By the mid-1960s, and with advice from Weslake, BMC had finally produced an eight port version of the 1.3-litre A-Series engine, which released more power than ever before. This was issued simultaneously to works Minis and Austin-Healey racing teams. Images are very rare – this being of a Mini-Cooper S installation of 1967.

Tommy Wisdom and the French photographer Bernard Cahier took a Warwick-prepared car to the legendary Piccolo Circuito delle Madonie. In spite of a promising start, the unlucky duo's car suffered from a fuel spillage (from a spare can carried in the car) and a broken throttle cable, but still managed to finish sixth in class; one development tweak to come out of this was that Healey never again used a standard cable, but a modified motorcycle clutch cable, to do the same job.

Five years later in 1964, Healey went back to Sicily with a much more highly developed Sprite, with a smoothly-shaped lightweight body which would eventually form the basis of the Le Mans cars. Unhappily it broke a half shaft part way through the first session. A year later a similar though further developed car with a 1.3-litre A-Series engine and a twin-choke Weber carburettor went to Sicily, where it was allocated to Rauno Aaltonen and Clive Baker. This time there was a problem with a sticking front brake caliper, but the little Sprite still managed 15th and second in class.

In 1965 the same car became a coupé (registered EAC 90C), looking rather like the Le Mans machines, but it faltered after Rauno hit a rock and deranged the rear suspension; third in class was no reward for a sterling effort. Then came 1967, when a brand-new 1293cc-engined car was prepared, but Clive Baker crashed it when trying to avoid a spectator who was running across the inadequately policed public road.

Two more Targa Florio entries followed, the 1968 event being

WORKS SPRITE RACERS – CARS AND EVENTS

In ten years the tiny Warwick factory produced no fewer than 27 Sprite race cars that started events, plus others which were reserve or unraced ones. This is the line-up of individual cars which actually took part in events and the races that they tackled. In cases where the cars were road-registered, this identity is used.

Car	Events	Car	Events
Unregistered (one of three)	1959 Sebring 12 Hours	770 KNX	1964 Sebring 12-Hour race
Unregistered (second of three)	1959 Sebring 12 Hours		1964 Le Mans 24 Hours
Unregistered (third of three)	1959 Sebring 12 Hours		1965 Sebring12-Hour race
7080 AC	1959 Targa Florio	776 KNX	1964 Sebring 12-Hour race
	1960 Sebring 4-Hour race	693 LAC	1964 Targa Florio
5983 AC	1960 Sebring 12-Hour race		1964 Nurburgring 1000km
	1960 Le Mans 24-Hours	DAC 952C	1965 Sebring 12-Hour race
8423 UE	1961 Sebring 4-Hour race	EAC 90C	1965 Targa Florio
8424 UE	1961 Sebring 4-Hour race		1966 Targa Florio
8425 UE	1961 Sebring 4-Hour race	ENX 415C	1965 Le Mans 24 Hours
8426 UE	1961 Sebring 12-Hour race	ENX 416C	1965 Le Mans 24 Hours
8427 UE	1961 Sebring 4-Hour race	HNX 455D	1966 Sebring 12-Hour race
	1961 Sebring 12-Hour race		1966 Le Mans 24 Hours
1411 WD	1961 Le Mans 24 Hours	HNX 456C	1966 Sebring 12-Hour race
	1962 Sebring 12-Hour race		1966 Le Mans 24 Hours
9251 WD	1962 Sebring 3-Hour race		1967 Sebring 12-Hour race
9252 WD	1962 Sebring 3-Hour race		1967 Le Mans 24 Hours
	1963 Sebring 3-Hour race		1968 Le Mans 24-Hours (running de-registered)
9253 WD	1962 Sebring 3-Hour race	LWD 959E	1967 Targa Florio
9254 WD	1962 Sebring 3-Hour race		1968 Sebring 12-Hour race
	1963 Sebring 3-Hour race		1968 Nurburgring 1,000km
	1963 Nurburgring 1,000km	LNX 629E	1967 Sebring 12-Hour race
58 FAC	1963 Sebring 12-Hour race		1968 Sebring 12-Hour race (badged as MG Midget)
	1963 Le Mans 24 Hours		1968 Targa Florio
			1968 Circuit of Mugello (Italy)

Note: According to Geoff Healey, speaking of the car which raced at Le Mans in mid-1968, "This was the last time we ran a Sprite in a serious competition. From now on, it was up to the private owners."

contested in yet another brand-new car complete with Le Mans-type dry-sump 1293cc engine and five-speed gearbox. Although this car was fast it eventually had to retire when it boiled.

The 1969 race was to have been contested by another new car which looked effectively like a Le Mans example but had been rebuilt as an open car. It was equipped with the very last of the 1293cc Le Mans-type A-Series race engines with a cast iron eight-port cross-flow cylinder head, a dry sump and Lucas fuel injection, and was ready to race in 1969 but did not actually make the start because Lord Stokes's hierarchy slashed the British Leyland motorsport effort to ribbons

In the meantime, Healey also enjoyed regular trips to Florida for the races on the bumpy ex-airfield racetrack at Sebring, in March every year, though the team's fortunes were mixed. The first attempt in 1959 for the 12-Hour race was with three lightly tuned (57bhp) 948cc-engined cars, which carried basically standard bodywork and had front-wheel disc brakes. To everyone's delight they took first, second and third in their class.

For 1960 there was a 4-Hour race for smaller-engined cars which Geoff Healey was convinced the Sprite could win, so Stirling Moss (who was about to compete in the 12-hour race in any case) was duly hired to drive a much-modified version of the 1959 Targa Florio machine. Without the need to change tyres and to refuel Stirling might indeed have won, but he actually finished a very close second to a very special Abarth. In the Twelve Hour race, a special Sprite with Falcon fibreglass body won its class in spite of blowing a cylinder head gasket, which had to be replaced in front of the pits.

An even bigger effort was mounted for 1961. Two Sprites were entered in the 12-Hour race. Three Warwick-built cars were enterd in the 4-Hour race and they, along with three privately prepared cars including two from John Sprinzel, took third to eighth places inclusive inclusive. In the 12-Hour one car managed fifteenth. It was a similar story in 1962, when four 998cc-engined cars contested the 4-Hour and one started the 12-Hour, with Walt Hansgen's car second in the 4-Hour, and an engine failure (main bearing cap broken) in the 12-Hour.

For the rest of the 1960s Healey made regular visits to Sebring, always having to face more specialised, low-production, opposition. In 1963 and 1964, 1098cc engined cars won their class, in 1966 and 1967 Le Mans-style 1293cc cars also won their class, as did standard-style cars in 1968 and 1969. This was the point at which British Leyland's financial support dried up and the Sprite's works racing career came to an end.

SEBRING RACES 1959

Healey Code	Engine size	Model type
ST200	948cc	Mk1

After the Sprite had been launched, sales in the USA began in earnest in mid-1958, and it was not long before it was agreed to enter a team of near-standard cars in the prestigious Sebring 12-hour race of March 1959.

With little time, little background knowledge and – most important – a limited budget, Healey built up four new Sprites with Speedwell Blue paintwork and white Jensen-type hardtops. The ever-resourceful Morris Engines development staff produced modified A-Series engines for which 57bhp was quoted, the newly-homologated Dunlop disc brakes were added to keep the performance in check, and although Dunlop centre-lock wire wheels were fitted, the tyres were Dunlop Road Speed. The measured top speed of these cars was approximately 98mph.

All four cars were shipped to Florida for the model's very first Sebring entry, but although all of them qualified for the event only three took the start. Since none were road-registered at this time, one can only identify them by their driver line-ups and their results. Healey were looking to win the up-to-1.0-litre capacity class, and were delighted to do so, taking 1-2-3. The only reported failure on any of the cars was that second gear 'disappeared' from the gearbox of the third-placed car, for which Geoff Healey resolutely refused to place any blame.

After the event the Austin-Healey importers, Hambros, took over all four cars and sold them to private owners in North America.

Competition Record

1959 Sebring Races	Hugh Sutherland/Phil Styles	1st in Class
	Ed Leavens/Dr Harold Kunz	2nd in Class
	Fred Hayes/John Cristy/John Colgate	3rd in Class

Targa Florio 1959

Healey Code	Registration	Engine size	Model type
TFR1	7080 AC	948cc	Mk1

This was the first of several occasions when Healey developed a special Sprite to compete in the Sicilian road race, and by comparison with the cars which would appear in Sicily in later years it was much more nearly standard than any of them.

The car had virtually standard 'frog-eye' styling except that the bumpers were removed and the standard windscreen was replaced by a smaller Perspex one. Thanks to Morris Engines in Coventry, the 948cc engine was equipped with twin 1½in SU carburettors, a gas-flowed cylinder head and a special camshaft,

Healey's first outing in the Sicilian Targa Florio road race came in 1959, when Tommy Wisdom and Bernard Cahier took this near-standard-looking Sprite to a creditable seventeenth overall.

while larger-than-standard drum brakes (lifted from an Austin A40) were fitted to the front – an easy substitution to make as the two models' front suspension was virtually the same. Dunlop racing tyres were used on standard steel disc wheels.

Incidentally, how times and motor racing have changed. The new car was driven (not trucked or trailered) all the way from Warwick, across Europe and down the entire length of Italy to be shipped over to Sicily, by Tommy Wisdom and Bernard Cahier, who were to be the race car pilots.

Because the circuit measured 44¾ miles, and this was to be a 14-lap event, the fact that the little Sprite only had a standard six-gallon fuel tank was going to be a constant worry, so an extra five-litre plastic petrol can was put behind the seats. This proved to be a nightmare, for after only one lap the can burst and spilt its petrol all round the car's interior!

Then the throttle cable broke on the last lap. Wisdom, who was driving, managed to cobble up a temporary repair and then used the ignition switch to cut off the engine when he needed to slow for a corner, and after a 20-minute delay on the roadside in mid-lap to make the repair the Sprite finished the event in 13hr 22min 05sec, which was more than two hours behind the winning Porsche but was still good enough to deliver seventeenth overall. According to the results belatedly published by the organisers, the car was second in the 1100c capacity class.

Once refurbished, the car was driven by Stirling Moss in the Sebring 4-hour race of 1960 and later still by Tommy Wisdom and Jack Hay in the 1960 Alpine rally before being sold off.

Competition Record

1959 Targa Florio	Tommy Wisdom/Bernard Cahier	17th Overall

Sebring 4-Hour race 1960

Healey Code	Registration	Engine size	Model type
Ex-TFR1	7080 AC	948cc	Mk1

For this race, which was limited to homologated Grand Touring Cars, Healey entered the much-rebuilt TFR1 car (which had raced in Sicily in 1959), and persuaded Stirling Moss to drive it. Healey would be competing against the latest twin-cam Fiat-based Abarth cars, but with Moss behind the wheel an outright win was hoped for.

Compared with its mechanical specification on the Targa Florio, the 948cc engine had more power (how much more was not stated), but it let the side down in pre-race testing

when the cylinder head casting developed a water leak. Basic welding repairs had to be made in a local workshop to make the car mobile again as Healey did not carry major spares with them on such expeditions.

The outcome of the race was in doubt up to the finish, for although Moss was held at bay at first by the leading Abarths, he overtook them both when they made routine stops for fuel and tyre changing, but then relinquished that lead after two-and-three-quarter hours when the Sprite, too, had to visit its pit. A second splash-and-dash fuel stop served to push him further back, and in the end of he

finished just one lap down, close to outright victory but not quite close enough.

Competition Record

1960 Sebring 4-Hour Race	Stirling Moss	2nd Overall

SEBRING 12-HOUR RACE 1960

Registration
5983 AC

Engine size
948cc

Model type
Mk1

This car first featured at the Nassau Speed Week in December 1959 but its serious motor sporting career began at Sebring in March 1960.

Here was a real oddity. Healey's paymasters – BMC in the UK and Hambros, the Austin-Healey importers in the USA – would have liked the team to race cars which looked like those on the showroom floor, but the car which turned up to contest the 12-Hour race in 1960 was anything but that.

It had a standard Sprite platform and inner structure but was clad in a strange, rather sketchily detailed but simple glass-fibre shell – as available to any private owner at the

time – by Falcon of the UK, topped by a large Perspex windscreen which had not been fitted in the Nassau Speed Week.

Mechanically, the car was virtually the same as had appeared during 1959, and any attempt by the drivers to set competitive times was thwarted when the car suffered cylinder head gasket problems which, although the gasket never failed catastrophically and lost all the cooling water, made it a struggle to get keep going – so it was something of a miracle that the car reached the finish, though way down in 41st place.

Competition Record

1960 Sebring 12-Hour Race	John Sprinzel/John Lumkin	41st place, 1st in Class

---

LE MANS 24 HOUR RACE 1960

Registration
5983 AC

Engine size
996cc

Model type
Mk1

The first works entry in the Le Mans 24 Hour race came in 1960. Healey wanted to run two cars but the French organisers would only accept one. Driven by John Colgate and John Dalton, this was a modified version of the Falcon-bodied car that had raced in the Sebring 12-Hour event in Florida in March. It weighed a mere 1090lb. To meet the Le Mans rules the windscreen, in glass, was much larger than Healey would have wished. A Jaguar D-Type style hump was fitted behind the driver's head to improve the aerodynamics, though apparently no aerodynamic testing either on the track or in a wind tunnel was ever carried out to confirm that it worked! In addition, a soft cover was fitted over the passenger seat which, though always empty, had to be fitted.

The engine, one of the early competition types, was of

996cc (with 64.5mm bore and 76.2mm stroke) and came from the development department of the BMC (ex-Morris Engines) factory in Coventry. It produced 67bhp at 6,300rpm. By comparison with what was to follow that doesn't sound much, but knowledge of the engine's capabilities was still building up – and the team recognised that 24 hours of racing was a very long time.

As for the running gear the car had Dunlop disc brakes at all four corners, centre-lock wire wheels and 5.25 x13 Dunlop Racing tyres. Experience showed that it could run in stints of 2hr 50 minutes before having to stop to refuel and change drivers. There was a late panic when an oil leak from the engine's oil filter developed, alleviated by the age-old ploy of squirting fire extinguisher fluid into the clutch housing to reduce the possibility of slipping. The car eventually finished the full 24 hours.

This effort was rewarded initially by twentieth place, at 85.64mph, and a well-earned class win, but this was raised to sixteenth place following the disqualification of four cars which had finished higher than the Sprite. In spite of the modest power output of the engine, the best lap had been at a rousing 90.98mph. The fact that the Sprite had won the 1.0-litre class ahead of a phalanx of French DB-Panhards went down well with the Brits but rankled with the French !

The car was later allowed to enjoy itself in the 1960 Nassau Speed week and was then sold to an American private owner.

Competition Record		
1960 Le Mans 24 Hour Race	John Colgate/John Dalton	16th Overall

SEBRING 4-HOUR RACE 1961

REGISTRATION	DRIVER	ENGINE SIZE
8423 UE	Ed Leavens	998cc
8424 UE	Briggs Cuningham	998cc
8425 UE	Bruce McLaren	998cc
8427 UE	Walt Hansgen	998cc

This was the layout of the Sprite race car engine, at Sebring in 1961 complete with twin SU carburettors and a tubular exhaust system. There was a lot more to come in future years.

A lot of time, effort and budget was sunk into a mass works entry for the 1961 Sebring races, where Healey produced a total of five new Sprites – four of them for the 4-Hour race (one of which would also take part in the 12-Hour). Once again they were aiming for outright victory, and once again it was the works Abarths that would provide most of the opposition. In addition, John Sprinzel brought along two of his own cars, to be driven by Stirling Moss in PMO 200 in Sebring-bodied state, and Pat Moss in another Sebring-styled machine.

The Healey-built cars all looked deceptively standard, but were much lighter than usual because they had glass-fibre shells whose panels had all been produced by the simple process of using a standard 'frog eye' as the styling buck. 8427 UE differed from the other cars by having an alloy hardtop.

As in 1960 the Sprites' performance in the 4-Hour race was sparkling, and without the two Abarths that won all six of the competing Sprites would have been scrabbling for outright victory. In the end Walt Hansgen in 8427 UE finished third, very close behind the Abarths, and Bruce McLaren fourth.

Hansgen's car was clearly in such a good state after the race that it was freshened up overnight for the 12-Hour race which followed.

Car numbers 1 and 2 were entered by John Sprinzel and driven by Stirling Moss and Pat Moss. You can just see the frogeye nose of one of the works-entered cars to the very left of the picture.

Competition Record
1961 Sebring 4-Hour Race

	Walt Hansgen	3rd
	Bruce McLaren	4th
	Ed Leavens	6th
	Briggs Cunningham	8th

Sebring 12-Hour race 1961

Registration	Driver	Engine size
8426 UE	Ed Leavens/John Colgate	998cc
8427 UE	Joe Buzetta/Glenn Carlson	998cc

By Austin-Healey standards this seems to have been an uneventful race, for there is scant mention of the car's performance in the contemporary race reports. That may be because the event was a highly-charged World Sports Car Championship qualifier, in which a team of 3-litre Ferraris were matched against Maseratis, with Porsches heading up a very competitive mid-engine-size field, and where works MGAs battled head to head with works Sunbeam Alpines.

In summary, although the two Warwick cars took second and third in their 1.15-litre class (and were only beaten by a tiny Lola-Climax racing sportscar) in overall terms they took fifteenth and twenty-fifth positions.

Competition Record

1961 Sebring 12-Hour Race	Joe Buzetta/Glenn Carlson	2nd in Class
	Ed Leavens/John Colgate	3rd in Class

Le Mans 24 Hour race 1961

Registration	Driver	Engine size
1411 WD	John Holgate/Paul Hawkins	1098cc

In 1961 two different Sprites were entered for the Le Mans 24 Hour – one prepared and run by the Healey company, the other loaned to the once-famous Edinburgh-based team of Ecurie Ecosse, whose glory days with Jaguar D-Types were now well behind them. The Healey car looked like a brand-new and very smart fastback coupé (but was anything but), whereas the non-works Ecurie Ecosse example was a 1961 Sebring 4-Hour race car with modified bodywork; at Sebring it had been registered 8427 UE and for Le Mans it was apparently re-registered 1413 WD.

1411 WD was the special-bodied Sprite, first seen at Sebring earlier in the year, which competed at Le Mans in 1961.

The official works entry was a much-modified derivative of the 1960 Le Mans car (5983 AC) in which the Falcon glassfibre shell had been discarded and replaced by a very smart, if unflamboyant coupé body panelled entirely in light alloy. This version of the XQHS 'Super Sprite' style had been drafted by Healey's Les Ireland for a proposed (and rejected) road car Sprite a few months earlier.

Further development work at Morris Engines had worked wonders on the engine, which according to power curves later published by Geoff Healey showed that it had been enlarged to 1098cc and now produced 73bhp at 6,500rpm, but although this very smart car lapped Le Mans at 93.70mph, after six hours the engine holed a piston crown, causing retirement.

As to the Ecurie Ecosse entry (1413 WD), this was crashed at an early stage at the notorious White House corner and immediately disappeared from the scene.

Competition Record

1961 Le Mans 24 Hour Race	John Colgate/Paul Hawkins	DNF

SEBRING 3-HOUR RACE 1962

REGISTRATION	DRIVER	ENGINE SIZE
9251 WD	Steve McQueen	998cc
9252 WD	Innes Ireland	998cc
9253 WD	Pedro Rodriguez	998cc
9254 WD	Stirling Moss	998cc

Although the race for the 'minnows' was reduced by an hour for 1962, Healey sent no fewer than four brand-new Sprite Mk IIs to compete in it, with a star-studded line-up of drivers including Hollywood superstar Steve McQueen and F1 drivers Innes Ireland and Stirling Moss. Painted in Healey Ice Blue, one of DMH's favourite colours, and wearing smart Healey hardtops in white, the cars looked extremely smart. As authorised by Appendix J regulations all the outer body panels were in light alloy.

All cars had the very latest in homologated 998cc engines, plus Girling front-wheel disc brakes and centre-lock wire-spoke wheels, and because the engine capacity limit was 1litre they were expected to fight the Abarths for outright victory.

In wet conditions, and almost as forecast, Stirling Moss gradually pulled out a nine-second lead over the best of the Abarths, but then the track dried, and because Moss had to make a hurried pit stop for more fuel with only 15 minutes to go, costing him 56 seconds, he was overtaken by Bruce McLaren and Walt Hansgen in the formidably rapid Abarths. All four cars finished and finished well. There had been 29 starters.

Following the race, the cars were returned to the UK and seemingly went into what we would now call 'dry storage', for there were no other events that Healey considered suitable for in the rest of 1962. Two cars, however (9252 WD and 9254 WD), would return to Sebring in 1963.

Hollywood superstar Steve McQueen was persuaded to drive 9251 WD in the 3-Hour race at Sebring in 1962, finishing ninth overall.

Competition Record

1962 Sebring 3-Hour Race		
	Stirling Moss	3rd
	Pedro Rodriguez	6th
	Innes Ireland	7th
	Steve McQueen	9th

Sebring 12-Hour race 1962

Registration	Driver	Engine size
1411 WD	John Colgate/Steve McQueen	1098cc

The much-travelled Sprite that had started its career at the end of 1959 once again took up its duties in March 1962, and was entered for the Sebring 12-Hour race, where it was to be driven by John Colgate and Steve McQueen. Running as 1411 WD, it had been raced at Le Mans with a very smart fastback coupé body and re-appeared looking just the same in Florida in March 1962.

In the run up to Sebring *The Autocar* carried a photograph issued by Healey of 1411 WD being readied for dispatch to the USA, and described it as a '1,411cc coupé', which must surely have been wrong as such a capacity was way beyond the capability of the current A-Series cylinder block. Geoff Healey, for his part, refers to the car as having a 1098cc engine, and it was to be several months before that engine size became standard on the current Sprite road cars.

The race covered 206 laps, a total distance of 1071 miles, and the Sprite was not expected to do other than fight hard for its own class position. It did that for nearly five hours, by which time it was leading the class. Unfortunately, at that point, with McQueen at the wheel, a crankshaft main bearing cap broke and brought the car to an abrupt halt.

Competition Record

1962 Sebring 12-Hour Race	John Colgate/Steve McQueen	DNF

Le Mans 24 Hour race 1962

Healey did not contest the French classic race in 1962, the reason thought to be financial rather than lack of desire to compete, but they would back in strength in 1963

Sebring 3-Hour race 1963

Registration	Driver	Engine size
9252 WD	Graham Hill	1098cc
9254 WD	Pedro Rodriguez	1098cc

During the winter of 1962/63, three of the four ex-Sebring race cars were liberated from store and prepared for the 1963 3-Hour event. One of the cars was 9253 WD, which would make the journey to Florida but would only be used a reserve/practice machine and was not used in the race.

Apart from a specially developed plate-type limited-slip differential, the cars were mechanically the same as in 1962.

Visually, however, 9252 WD had become an 'MG Midget' by the simple process of changing the radiator grille and adding the authentic Midget chrome strips along the flanks – and because the BMC publicists said that it was!

Unfortunately, the new limited slip differentials both broke in the opening laps of the race, so the cars, which were otherwise fresh and fast, had to be retired.

Competition Record

1962 Sebring 3-Hour Race	Graham Hill	DNF
	Pedro Rodriguez	DNF

Sebring 12-Hour race 1963

REGISTRATION	DRIVER	ENGINE SIZE
58 FAC	John Colgate/Clive Baker	1098cc

Effectively the second of the 'streamlined Sprite coupés' built at Warwick was 58 FAC, for in 1963 it took over from 1411 WD, whose inner structure/chassis was well over three years old. The new car had the latest 1098cc engine that Morris Engines could provide (95bhp was claimed) and was a lineal visual development of the final 1411 WD. It would also influence the form and function of the Targa Florio car (TFR2) which followed in 1964. The difference, in this case, was that it was a very smart fast back coupé complete with a sharply cut-off Kamm tail.

In a World Championship race which was naturally dominated by massively powerful Ferraris, Jaguars, AC Cobras and 2-litre Porsches, this 1.1-litre car could do no more than try to win its capacity class. Although Geoff Healey's book tells us that it won its class ('ahead of the Abarths') in spite of the engine suffering a cracked cylinder block, other sources state quite categorically that it failed to finish, while magazine reports placed the Abarths in the lead of the class results.

Even so, the initial impressions were good, and the same car would appear at the 1963 Le Mans race in June.

Competition Record		
1963 Sebring 12-Hour Race	John Colgate/Clive Baker	DNF

Nurburgring 1000km race 1963

REGISTRATION	DRIVER	ENGINE SIZE
9254 WD	Clive Baker/Christabel Carlisle	1098cc

It was at BMC Abingdon's request that Healey agreed to send a Sprite to Germany to compete in the Nurburgring 1000km race of May 1963. Clive Baker was teamed up with Abingdon's rising star, Christabel Carlisle, while the car was the one which had recently been driven by Pedro Rodriguez in the 3-Hour race at Sebring in March. We may assume, I

am sure correctly, that the limited slip differential which had given trouble to both Sebring Three-Hour cars was not included in the specification.

In a steady performance, where both drivers proved to be fast and safe, the Sprite was urged into second place in class, behind a full-blown works Alpine Renault.

Competition Record		
1963 Nurburgring 1000km	Clive Baker/Christabel Carlisle	2nd in Class, 17th Overall

Le Mans 24 Hour 1963

REGISTRATION	DRIVER	ENGINE SIZE
58 FAC	Sir John Whitmore/Bob Olthoff	1100cc

Although there had been no official works entry for the 1962 race, in 1963 the team returned with a modified iteration of the theme of the smart coupé of 1961 (as first raced at Sebring in March 1963), which used a very special 1.1-litre engine. As already noted, this car featured what Healey called a Kamm tail (the name refers to the scientist who originally postulated the use of a sharply-cut-off tail on some race cars of the period, which proved to cut down on both drag and high-speed lift).

As originally built, and seen at pre-race scrutineering, this style featured a transverse stabilising spoiler above the Kamm tail, but after discussing this with the drivers it was removed for the race itself. The chassis now featured Lockheed brakes, discs at the front and drums at the rear. The drivers, were 'loaned' from BMC by Stuart Turner at Abingdon for this occasion.

As for the engine, it was an extremely advanced 'Maher-special' with a 71.63mm bore and a 68.248mm stroke giving

1100cc precisely. It used a single Weber dual-choke carburettor and was actually based on the first of the Mini-Cooper 1071S cylinder blocks and heads, though Healey did not detail this relationship at the time.

To quote Geoffrey Healey: "These engines would run to high speeds with reliability, producing nearly 100bhp. They were both strong and amenable to tuning.... In his attempts to get more power from the racing engines, Eddie Maher produced a variety of heads, including one very effective casting that had two separate exhaust ports for the middle two cylinders. We were able to fabricate exhaust manifolds with this feature and as a result gained 3bhp."

The car was quick, lapping Le Mans 30 seconds faster than the 1961 car, and its fastest was at 102.66mph, with a top speed on the Mulsanne Straight of 117mph. Unfortunately driver Bob Olthoff crashed it during the night at White House corner while dazzled by photographers' flashes. He was in hospital for a short time but soon recovered.

Competition Record		
1963 Le Mans 24 Hours	Sir John Whitmore/Bob Olthoff	DNF

SEBRING 12-HOUR RACE 1964

REGISTRATION	DRIVER	ENGINE SIZE
770 KNX	Clive Baker/John Colgate	1098cc
776 KNX	Al Pease/Donna Mae Mims	1098cc

Two new cars were built for the 1964 Sebring race whichwere similar in engineering, style and engine tune to 58 FAC. In later years much controversy was caused among Sprite enthusiasts by the emerging facts, not only because 776 KNX was the only Sprite so far to have been painted red (works Austin-Healeys had habitually raced in Ice Blue), but because the drivers of that car were (a) Canadian and (b) a woman. It now appears that this was very much an 'arm's length' entry from Warwick, which concentrated most of its efforts on the blue-painted 770 KNX of Clive Baker and John Colgate.

The red car soon left the scene at Sebring when it suffered a rear axle failure, while the Baker/Colgate car soldiered on valiantly in spite of suffering an oil pump failure after eleven hours. However, as Geoff Healey later wrote, "We filled the sump way up so that the crankshaft was submerged, and they managed to run under their own power to qualify at the end."

Competition Record		
1964 Sebring 12-Hour Race	Clive Baker/John Colgate	24th Overall
	Al Pease/ Donna Mae Mims	DNF

TARGA FLORIO 1964

HEALEY CODE	REGISTRATION	ENGINE SIZE	MODEL TYPE
TFR2	693 LAC	1098cc	Special coachwork on '64 floorpan

This was the first truly special car that Healey developed specifically for the Targa Florio race. Under the skin, the platform was basically standard Sprite except that it was the first works race car to be built around the latest Mk III (HAN8) rear suspension, which featured half-elliptic instead of cantilever quarter-elliptic leaf springs. The Mk III had only just been unveiled in March 1964, with a standard 1098cc 59bhp engine.

TFR2 was powered by the latest engine developed by Morris Engines in Coventry, a 1098cc version of the familiar A-Series. In sprint form such engines were capable of producing 96bhp at 7,000rpm, but for long-distance events such as the Targa Florio they were slightly de-tuned to give about 90bhp.

The new car ran on light-alloy road wheels with a strikingly styled open-top lightweight aluminium bodyshell, a roll-bar behind the seats and a high boot lid culminating in a Kamm tail rear end incorporating a transverse rear spoiler. Although it was not immediately obvious, the windscreen was that of a BMC road car. An enlarged fuel tank with a snap-action filler cap behind the driver's head was also installed.

Registered 693 LAC, the car was driven from Warwick to Dover, treated to a ferry passage to Ostend, then shipped to Milan by an overnight car-carrying train before being driven to Naples for trans-shipment to Palermo in Sicily – all in all, a race just to get to the start of the race itself.

As for the drivers, the pairing of one of Healey's long-time favourites, the veteran Tommy Wisdom, with the famous 'superstar', Paddy Hopkirk, recent winner of the Monte Carlo rally, was thought to be controversial, but there was little chance for this to be proven, as the car broke a driveshaft during Paddy's first stint behind the wheel, which immobilised the car in the mountains and obliged it to be retired.

It was to be used again only once as a works race car. Later in 1964, after the Nurburgring 1000km race, Healey fitted and tested a smart light-alloy hard top, then sold the car to Richard Groves.

Competition Record

| 1964 Targa Florio | Tommy Wisdom/Paddy Hopkirk | DNF |

Nurburgring 1000km race 1964

REGISTRATION	DRIVER	ENGINE SIZE
693 LAC	Clive Baker/Bill Bradley	1098cc

Healey were apparently so annoyed that their carefully built car had let them down at an early stage in the Targa Florio that, once retrieved, it was speedily refreshed and entered for the equally arduous Nurburgring 1000km race at the end of the month. Clive Baker, a regular with the team by that time, was the lead driver, while Bill Bradley joined for this particular event.

This was one of the rare occasions when a Warwick-built works Sprite came up against the Abingdon-blessed (though not Abingdon-prepared) Jacobs MG Midgets. All three cars circulated tidily on the lengthy and demanding Nurburgring track for more than seven hours, averaging more than 75mph, after which 693 LAC took third place in the 1.0 – 1.3-litre capacity class.

Competition Record

| 1964 Nurburgring 1000km | Clive Baker/Bill Bradley | 3rd in Class |

Le Mans 24 Hour race 1964

REGISTRATION	DRIVER	ENGINE SIZE
770 KNX	Clive Baker/Bill Bradley	1098cc

For Le Mans there was pressure to put up a better show in 1964, not only because the team wanted to avenge their disappointment after the crash of 1963, but also because Triumph – Austin-Healey's biggest commercial rivals – had entered for the first time Spitfires, which were known to have 98bhp from their 1147cc engines and were reputed to be capable of 130mph. At this time Triumph had no long-distance racing experience with these cars (it was their first race of any type with them) but they seemed to be efficient, seemed to be learning fast, were already on a performance par with the Sprites, and were situated in the same capacity class.

The 1964 works Sprite was a new one whose engineering was developed from the 1963 car. Its body was a straightforward evolution of the 1964 Targa Florio car but was a closed notchback coupé derivative of what had been an open-top machine. In fact the aerodynamic performance of this car was disappointing to Healey as subsequent post-race testing in the Austin wind tunnels proved.

The same type of ultra-special 1100cc engine as had been used in 1963 was retained, and on this occasion there was a new driver pairing. Happily, on this occasion, it made it to the finish, ending in 24th position. Official figures showed that it could lap consistently in less than five minutes (it

Le Mans in 1964, when Clive Baker and Bill Bradley took part in 770 KNX.

recorded a best of 101.21mph), and that it had a top speed of 135.5mph. The result was gratifying. Driven smoothly and sensibly by Clive Baker and Bill Bradley, the A-Series engined Sprite finished well, and in good condition, though it was something of a surprise to find that it was just outstripped – just – by the surviving Triumph Spitfire.

Competition Record

1964 Le Mans 24 Hour Race	Clive Baker/Bill Bradley	24th Overall

---

SEBRING 12-HOUR RACE 1965

REGISTRATION	DRIVER	ENGINE SIZE
770 KNX	Paddy Hopkirk/Timo Makinen	1293cc
DAC 952C	Rauno Aaltonen/Clive Baker	1293cc

Work carried out on behalf of Healey in the BMC wind tunnel at the Austin factory in the autumn of 1964 led to wholesale changes to the coupé (770 KNX) which had first raced at Le Mans in that year, where the top speeds achieved had been disappointing. Without lengthening the tail or destroying the Kamm-tail feature Longbridge recommended that the notchback coupé shape should be superseded by a more elegant fastback design, together with a longer and more shovel-like nose. The overall height was trimmed a little, the radiator intake was made smaller, and a movable flap was built into the nose to make the intake smaller or larger depending on the ambient conditions. It was also recommended that a full undertray be added.

This car, and a new machine which latterly became known as the first of the true 'wind-tunnel' race cars, were then taken to contest Sebring in March 1965, where they were using the very latest in 1293cc A-Series engines. The published results, which survive in motorsport's archive, baldly show that the older car took third in its class and the new car second in class, but they do not commemorate the rainstorm of almost biblical proportions which fell in mid-race, reducing the race leading Ferraris, Ford GT40s and US Chaparrals to a crawl, such that at one point the Sprites were lapping faster than almost every other car in the event. At one point there was so much water coursing along the pit lane that at least one inflated wheel/tyre was seen to be floating serenely away.

Because of confusions created in the announcement of the results by the organisers after the race the Sprites were originally robbed of one of their best performances ever at Sebring. At one stage it looked as if the Sprites had taken a 1-2 in the 1.3-litre Prototype GT class, but an amalgamation then demoted then to second and third in a larger-capacity class instead. Confused? Yes – so were we at the time. t

One of the works Sprites racing at Sebring in 1965, this showing the way that a panel in the front could be raised to allow more cooling air into the radiator.

Competition Record		
1965 Sebring 12-Hour Race	Hopkirk/Timo Makinen	3rd in Class
	Rauno Aaltonen/Clive Baker	2nd in Class

TARGA FLORIO 1965

HEALEY CODE	REGISTRATION	DRIVER	ENGINE SIZE
TFR3	EAC 90C	**Rauno Aaltonen/Clive Baker**	1293cc

Building on the experience of TFR2 (which had raced in the 1964 Targa Florio), the new TFR3 was a similar-looking open-top car, though it did not feature the transverse rear spoiler, and the roll-cage had been extended to have tubular struts leading forward to the top corners of the windscreen frame. Changes had been made to the suspension set up so as to limit the understeer from which TFR2 had been found to suffer, while the fuel tank was repositioned and lowered in the structure to help improve the handling.

On this occasion the car was driven all the way to Sicily and the driving team of Rauno Aaltonen and Clive Baker set about practice with enjoyment because, for some reason, this turned out to be a very attractive machine in which to tackle a 10-lap nearly 500-mile race.

On the event the car set a cracking pace until it was affected by the left front brake caliper, whose pistons developed a tendency to lock at all the wrong times. This resulted in one major pit stop where an attempt (by brute force) was made to make the caliper pistons work as they should. This proved not to be possible, so the car was patched up after spending 15 minutes on jacks and it could finish the event no higher than 15th.

TFR3 then spent much of the next few months and the winter of 1965/66 as Geoff Healey's own road car before being completely refreshed as a race car for the 1966 Targa Florio, becoming TFR4 in the process.

Competition Record		
1965 Targa Florio	Rauno Aaltonen/Clive Baker	15th Overall, 2nd Class

Le Mans 24 Hour 1965

REGISTRATION	DRIVER	ENGINE SIZE
ENX 415C	Rauno Aaltonen/Clive Baker	1293cc
ENX 416C	Paul Hawkins/John Rhodes.	1293cc

Because the Triumph Spitfires from the rival sports-car-making company just a few miles up the road had proved to be alarmingly rapid in the 1964 Le Mans 24 Hour race (though only one of their three cars had finished the race), Healey concluded that the works Sprites needed to be up-gunned for the 1965 French classic to keep them competitive with the domestic opposition. Much of the technical and aerodynamic work which went into producing the radically upgraded 1965 Le Mans cars had already been seen on the car which competed in the 1965 Sebring race, and on TFR3, which Rauno Aaltonen and Clive Baker had driven in the recent Targa Florio.

As noted in the 1965 Sebring report, much wind-tunnel work during the winter had been applied to TFR3, whose scrutineered dry weight, aided by the use of much light alloy in the bodywork, was a mere 1543lb, and it is worth noting that four-wheel disc brakes by Lockheed were part of the specification.

For these new Le Mans cars it was also decided to use the largest possible A-Series power unit, which effectively was a slightly over-bored 'S' unit of 1293cc. (It is not without significance that Triumph were not ready to enlarge their own race-car engines at this time, though such a modification was already being developed.) This BMC engine was now rated at 101bhp at 6700rpm and was fuelled by a single dual-choke Weber carburettor. It proved to be an update well worth all the effort, for the new 1.3-litre engined car recorded no less than 147mph on the straight and raised the overall race average to 96.5mph.

By comparison with what was to follow in the race itself, most of the dramas were centred around pre-race scrutineering. For reasons known only to the chauvinistic French, at pre-event scrutineering Healey were told that the colour of their cars, rather a fetching fluorescent green, was sporting-illegal, and that they had to run in British Racing Green instead! No amount of reasoned discourse could change this viewpoint so, with little time to spare, Healey found supplies of a dark green paint which was close to what the scrutineers might accept and made the cars 'sporting-legal' again.

In the race both cars, which were running No. 48 and No. 49, performed very well and consistently, and although one of them broke its engine with a bang right in front of the pits, the other, driven by Paul Hawkins and John Rhodes, came through in 12th place, averaged 96.5mph, and roundly defeated the 1.15-litre Triumph Spitfires. There was no 1.3-litre class in this race but no such car finished ahead of the gallant Sprite.

By the mid-1960s, the Warwick-inspired streamlined shape of the works Le Mans Sprites was thoroughly refined. This was the Hawkins/Rhodes car on its way to twelfth in the 1965 event.

Competition Record

1965 Le Mans 24 Hour Race	Rauno Aaltonen/Clive Baker	DNF
	Paul Hawkins/John Rhodes	12th Overall, 1st in Class

SEBRING 12-HOUR RACE 1966

REGISTRATION	DRIVER	ENGINE SIZE
HNX 455D	Paul Hawkins/Timo Makinen	1293cc
HNX 456D	Paddy Hopkirk/Andrew Hedges	1293cc

In the mid-1960s the Sebring race was still a great magnet for the Warwick team, especially as in previous years they had already proved that a good result would produce increased United States sales of road cars. For 1966, therefore, there was once again a full-blooded attempt to win their category class, not only by securing the services of the best quartet of drivers available to BMC, but also by commissioning two brand-new cars, HNX 455D and HNX 456D, whose engineering was effectively an upgrade of those streamlined coupés seen at Le Mans in 1965: peak power was now 110bhp at 7200rpm.

Once again Austin-Healey's sterling efforts were virtually ignored by the media of the day – not because they were insignificant but because they were competing in a World Sports Car Championship event which hosted a titanic battle between the latest Ford GT40s, Ferraris, Chaparrals and 2-litre Porsches. Even so, the team put in a copybook performance, for although a best finish of 18th does not sound outstanding, it was achieved behind 16 out-and-out racing sports cars (the Fords, by the way, had 7.0-litre engines!) and the sole works MGB.

If ever there had been a copybook demonstration of how to make a production sports car into a competition race car, this was it. Both cars, incidentally, were so healthy at the end of the 12 racing hours that they were brought back to Warwick, refreshed, and sent off to compete at Le Mans in June.

Competition Record

1965 Sebring 12-Hour Race	Paul Hawkins/Timo Makinen	18th
	Paddy Hopkirk/Andrew Hedges	29th

TARGA FLORIO 1966

HEALEY CODE	REGISTRATION	DRIVER	ENGINE SIZE
TFR4	EAC 90C	Rauno Aaltonen/Clive Baker	1293cc

For their traditional return to campaign in the Sicilian Targa Florio race in 1966, Healey decided not to build an all-new car but to evolve the TFR3 open-top race car (see above) into the TFR4 fixed-head coupé, whose style and construction were very close to those first used on the works 1965 Sebring 12-Hour and Le Mans 24 Hour race cars. To emphasise the carry-over from 1965 to 1966 yet further, the latest car was to be driven by the same duo of Rauno Aaltonen and Clive Baker.

Compared with TFR3, TFR4 had a fixed-head fastback style in aluminium alloy whose sweeping roof hid a more comprehensive roll cage than before. Under the skin, the running gear was much the same as in 1965 (with TFR3) and was of course equipped with Healey's by now familiar cast alloy wheels.

Unhappily this car's race was to be eventful and resulted in a finish only at 16th and third in class. There was rain before and on the day which made the open-road track slippery. At an early stage, with Aaltonen driving, the car left the road, hit a rock at the side of the track (no guard rails or anything like that!) and damaged the alignment of the rear axle. Hasty repairs were carried out back at the pits but on the very next lap, with Clive Baker at the wheel, a driveshaft broke and the car was immobilised for some time.

At this time the Healey race cars invariably started a long-distance race with a spare shaft on board, and with the help of British enthusiasts who were quite coincidentally on hand a change was made at the side of the road!

Competition Record

1966 Targa Florio	Rauno Aaltonen/Clive Baker	16th Overall, 3rd in Class

---

Le Mans 24 Hour race 1966

REGISTRATION	DRIVER	ENGINE SIZE
HNX 455D	Paddy Hopkirk/Andrew Hedges	1293cc
HNX 456D	John Rhodes/Clive Baker	1293cc

Two updated Le Mans-type/Sebring 1966-type Sprites (the same special coupé style, with twinned headlamps enclosed behind plastic covers, and with an adjustable flap controlling the amount of cold air which was channelled into the radiator) were entered for the 1966 event. Their engines were as before, with yet another transmission variation - a four-speed MGB gearbox with Laycock overdrive which effectively gave six forward speeds and meant that the engine would have a less hard time on the long Mulsanne straight. It had not been used on the cars at Sebring in March and this was the only time the MGB overdrive gearbox was used in the Le Mans Sprite cars; the final development, a five-speed gearbox, was to follow in 1967.

The driver line-up was changed shortly before the race (the original entry list mentioned Rauno Aaltonen as one of the drivers) but the team was otherwise well prepared. On this occasion they did not have to battle with the Triumph Spitfires, which had been withdrawn from motorsport because of a change in Standard-Triumph (which meant Leyland) policy – and their main opposition came from a fleet of works Alpine-Renaults.

It was not to be a good Le Mans year for the Maher-developed A-Series engine, as both power units let go after more than 19 of the 24 hours, suffering broken connecting rods. The only consolation was that the engineers at Longbridge then examined the wrecked engines, concluding that there were machining shortcomings and that they should make changes to all A-Series units to obviate this ever happening again. More robust rods were therefore designed.

In the meantime the cars had been found to reach 150mph on the straights and to hold that speed without any dramas, while they were holding a race average of 101.3mph just before the catastrophic engine failures occurred. This, it transpired, might not have been enough to beat the Alpine-Renaults (which were running with very special engines) but it was certainly enough to get their attention for most of the race!

HNX 456D was driven by John Rhodes and Clive Baker at Le Mans in 1966, where it regularly achieved 150mph on the Mulsanne Straight, but unhappily the engine blew in the latter stages of the event.

Competition Record

| 1966 Le Mans 24 Hour Race | John Rhodes/Clive Baker | DNF |
| | Paddy Hopkirk/Andrew Hedges | DNF |

SEBRING 12-HOUR RACE 1967

REGISTRATION	DRIVER	ENGINE SIZE
HNX 456D	Rauno Aaltonen/Clive Baker	1293cc
LNX 629E	Alec Poole/Carson Baird/Roger Enever	1293cc

Two very different looking works cars appeared in Florida in March 1967, one being HNX 456D, the other a standard-looking (but fully modified according to the homologation papers) machine which nonetheless carried many light alloy panels to help reduce its weight.

Following its unsuccessful outing at Le Mans in June 1966, HNX 456D enjoyed an autumn and winter lay off before being made ready to compete in the 1967 Sebring 12-Hour race. In some ways this was a déjà vu outing, for HNX 456D had been new for Sebring a year earlier and was driven by the same seasoned duo of Rauno Aaltonen and Clive Baker,

As usual, all the post-race headlines were made by the battle between Ford's monstrous new 7-litre machines, the Chaparrals and the Porsches, so the progress of Warwick's works Sprites was virtually ignored.

Throughout the 12 hours, however, the fleet little Aaltonen/Baker Sprite proved conclusively that it could keep up with the larger-engined works MGBs, which had been prepared at Abingdon, and would end up just one lap (in around 200!) behind them. In the end, too, the Sprite was credited with winning its capacity class.

Amazingly, this was not the end of HNX 456D's works career as once again it was shipped back to Warwick, there to be rebuilt in time to take part at Le Mans in June

The standard-bodied Sprite, which ran with its normal

soft-top erect, circulated well and reliably but could only achieve third in class against more specialised opposition.

It would be used again a year later, when for marketing reasons it was re-badged as an MG Midget.

Competition Record		
1967 Sebring 12 Hour race	Rauno Aaltonen/Clive Baker	1st in Class, 13th Overall
	Alec Poole/Carson Baird/Roger Enever	3rd in Class, 18th Overall

TARGA FLORIO 1967

HEALEY CODE	REGISTRATION	DRIVER	ENGINE SIZE
TFR5	LWD 959E	Rauno Aaltonen/Clive Baker	1293cc

Undaunted by the mechanical traumas Healey had encountered in previous years, a new car – coded TFR5 by Healey – was built for the 1967 event. The layout of this fastback fixed-head car was quite clearly based on a combination of the latest Healey Le Mans-car thinking and on TFR4.

Aerodynamically, clear and presumably effective differences included the provision of a more conventional front intake for the radiator and the use of headlamps which were not covered by streamlined cowls (TFR4 had used cowled lamps). The running gear, all hidden away under the smooth alloy bodywork, featured new-type Girling disc brakes with light alloy calipers, and double rear dampers at each axle extremity.

Even though this brightly-hued machine was driven in a very spirited manner, and was capable of lapping the circuit in around 44 minutes (yes, it was a very long lap), it could not figure among the class leaders and was eventually eliminated when Clive Baker (driving at the time) was obliged to swerve to miss an errant spectator who was dashing across the unguarded road ahead of him, the result being a crash which quite immobilised the car.

It was not used again.

Competition Record		
1967 Targa Florio	Rauno Aaltonen/Clive Baker	DNF

LE MANS 24 HOUR RACE 1967

REGISTRATION	DRIVER	ENGINE SIZE
HNX 456D	Andrew Hedges/Clive Baker	1293cc

For 1967 there was just one Sprite entered at Le Mans, driven by Andrew Hedges and Clive Baker. As ever, the 1293cc engine was built and prepared by BMC/Morris Engines in Coventry, producing 105bhp at 7000rpm with a compression ratio of 12.0:1 and a single dual-choke Weber carburettor. Yet another variation on the transmission theme saw the use of a sturdy five-speed derivative of the latest all-synchromesh MGB gearbox. The car was amazingly rapid, its top speed being recorded at nearly 150mph.

This was the phenomenal year in which a team of 600bhp 7-litre Fords were fighting for the outright win against 500bhp 4-litre Ferraris, and at one stage Clive Baker's Sprite suffered considerable rear body damage because one of the Fords was suspected of tripping over it. In spite of needing a lengthy pit-stop to stabilise the damage, the gallant Sprite finished the race, completing no less than 2421 miles and taking 15th at 100.91mph – the very first time a Sprite had ever achieved this mark.

Competition Record		
1967 Le Mans 24 Hour Race	Andrew Hedges/Clive Baker	15th Overall

Sebring 12-Hour race 1968

Registration	Driver	Engine size
LWD 959E	Clive Baker/Mike Garton	1293cc
LNX 629E	Jerry Truit/Randy Canfield	1293cc

For its annual appearance in Florida to contest the Sebring 12-Hour sports car race, Warwick once again entered two very different-looking Sprites. One was the already familiar special-bodied coupé (TFR5/LWD 959E), this time fitted with the newly-developed Lucas fuel injection (to replace the usual twin-choke Weber carburettor used on earlier works race engines), but the other was the standard-looking car that had raced at Sebring in 1967.

Compared with 1967, detail differences were that the special-bodied LWD 959E now sported cooling vents in the front wings (behind and above the front wheel-arch cut-outs), along with a bulge in the bonnet panel to provide the necessary space for the Lucas fuel injection system, while for publicity/marketing reasons in the USA market the standard Sprite (LNX 629E) had been slightly changed, with an MG Midget grille and chrome strips along the flanks, to run as an MG Midget, which fooled absolutely no-one.

The special-bodied car ran well at first but after only an hour Clive Baker brought the car back to the pits, complaining of an engine misfire. A change of sparking plugs and a petrol refill were made but soon afterwards the engine began to cut out completely. A lengthy pit stop and investigation finally discovered that there was water in the fuel, and it was only after two hours that the car could resume its race. Amazingly, it ended up winning its (prototype) capacity class, even though the overall result was 35th overall.

The standard-bodied car, on the other hand, circulated briskly and reliably throughout, and eventually won its own capacity class.

The newly-formed British Leyland entered no fewer than four very different cars to travel to Florida for the 1968 Sebring 12-Hour race. LWD 659 was one of the familiar special Warwick-built Sprites, while (on this occasion) LNX 629E was running with standard-looking but mostly aluminium body panels, and was badged as an MG Midget. Both cars won their capacity class.

Competition Record

1968 Sebring 12 Hour race	Clive Baker/Mike Garton	1st in Class
	Jerry Truit/Randy Canfield	1st in Class, 15th overall

Targa Florio 1968

Healey Code	Registration	Driver	Engine size
TFR6	LNX 629E	Rauno Aaltonen/Clive Baker	1293cc

By 1968 British Leyland had been formed (meaning that Healey had new political masters to satisfy) and BL's politics had suggested that Healey's race cars should look more like the road cars, which they had not done in the recent past. TFR6, therefore, may have been a successor to TFR5 but did not have the special coachwork of that car, instead looking like a production-bodied Sprite. It ran in the FIA Group 4 Sports Car class in the Targa Florio and was the car that had already raced in the Sebring 12-Hour races of 1967 and 1968.

While sticking to the FIA homologation rules, the bodyshell was lightened as much as possible by the liberal use of light alloy skin panels, though the Mk IV's under-platform, suspension and a much-modified dry-sump 1293cc A-Series engine were all retained. Not only that, but this car also had a 5-speed gearbox as used by other Sprites in the Le Mans 24 Hour race, and ran on magnesium alloy Minilite centre-lock wheels.

All looked promising: in practice Clive Baker lapped in

43min. 43 seconds, which was better even than had been achieved in 1967, while during the race the car led its class, beating several special lightweight Lancia Fulvia HFs along the way, but the engine blew its cylinder head gasket a long way from the pits, and by the time the car had been brought, steaming and limping, back to the mechanics the engine was ruined.

Before coming back to the UK the engine was rebuilt and the car refreshed to compete in he Mugello sports car race, where it won its class.

Competition Record		
1968 Targa Florio	Rauno Aaltonen/Clive Baker	DNF

NURBURGRING 1000KM RACE 1968

REGISTRATION	DRIVER	ENGINE SIZE
LWD 959E	**Clive Baker/John Handley**	**1293cc**

Two weeks after the Targa Florio of 1968, Healey sent their streamlined 'endurance' car to Germany, to contest the Nurburgring 1000km, with Clive Baker as lead driver and saloon-car specialist John Handley on board to partner him. John was more used to driving front-wheel-drive Mini-Coopers in sprint races, so a change to the rear-drive Sprite was a considerable upheaval for him.

While all the sound and the fury of this race was up front among the 5.0-litre Ford GT40s, the 3-litre Porsches and Alfa Romeos, the Sprite circulated regularly and without flamboyance, always lapped at well over 85mph, eventually winning the 1.6-litre prototype category in its last race as a works car.

Competition Record		
1968 Nurburgring 1000km	Clive Baker/John Handley	1st in Class

LE MANS 24 HOUR RACE 1968

REGISTRATION	DRIVER	ENGINE SIZE
HNX 456D	**Roger Enever/Alec Poole**	**1293cc**

Then came 1968, the last year in which Healey entered a Sprite for this classic endurance event. Healey consulted Lucas (and BMC/Morris Engines, of course), and was rewarded with a fuel-injected version of the 1293cc A-Series engine. Not only that, but an early example of the cast iron eight-port cylinder head was used, the result being that the engine produced no less than 110bhp at 7200rpm, with more torque all the way up the rev range.

Because the injector nozzles were mounted in inlet trumpets which pointed, semi-downdraught fashion, at the cylinder head itself, it was necessary to add a power bulge to the car's bonnet. The result was an extremely effective racing power plant (which for shorter distance races could have been super-tuned to 120bhp at around 7500rpm). As Geoff Healey later commented: "This was a wonderful system which we should have had years before... This injection equipment on the Sprite engines worked faultlessly throughout some very long races. As far as the Sprite was concerned, this 1968 series of engines represents the peak of development. If we had continued racing the power would have been increased to over 120bhp...'"

The proof of that pudding came in the 1968 race, when the injected car finished 15th, averaging 94.73mph on a much-changed circuit and reaching almost 150mph when flat out. No more proof about the worth of the amazing little A-Series engine was ever needed, and this was its last works appearance in a long-distance event..

Competition Record		
1968 Le Mans 24 Hour Race	Roger Enever/Alec Poole	15th Overall

CIRCUIT OF MUGELLO 1968

HEALEY CODE	REGISTRATION	DRIVER	ENGINE SIZE
TFR6	LNX 629E	Andrew Hedges/Clive Baker	1293cc

The last-ever official works appearance by a race-modified Austin-Healey Sprite came in July 1968 (after British Leyland's Sir Donald Stokes had decided to stop all financial support to the plucky little team at Warwick), when the standard-looking car which had already tackled three endurance races totalling 30 hours of motor racing was sent off to Mugello in Italy.

In many ways the Mugello circuit and its challenges were like those of the Targa Florio, for this was an open-road event, with a 66km/41-mile lap (the outright lap record time was almost 32 minutes) set in the rolling hills of Tuscany. The race was a non-championship event, sure to be dominated by Italian built and driven nationals, and was for cars limited to 2.0-litres. The standard-looking Sprite, while creditable and very well-equipped, would have to face up to a fleet of Fiat Abarth OTs.

As the 4hr 30min race unfolded it was soon clear that the Sprite had the measure of all the Abarths, and so it remained throughout, as Abarth after Abarth dropped out and the Sprite carried on, eventually to win its class. It was a sturdy and emphatic way to bring a works programme to a close.

Competition Record

1968 Circuit of Mugello	Andrew Hedges/Clive Baker	1st in Class, 17th Overall

---

TARGA FLORIO 1969

HEALEY CODE	REGISTRATION	ENGINE SIZE
TFR7	not registered	1293cc

Planned and mostly built before British Leyland imposed drastic budget cuts and prepared to drop the Austin-Healey brand name altogether, TFR7 was very much state-of-the-art as far as Healey was concerned. However, although it was specifically intended to be raced in the 1969 Targa Florio, it was not used in that or any other Healey-sponsored event, and was sold off to Ed Bussey, who was then the MG and Austin distributor in Florida.

In many ways, TFR7 was a further-developed but drastically lightened and uniquely-specified version of the 1968 Le Mans cars which have already been described. The major (and obvious visual) difference was that the Le Mans cars had been coupés, while TFR7 was an open-top two-seater. The familiar Sprite/Midget chassis/platform was retained but was topped by a Birmabright (aluminium alloy) bodyshell.

Forward of the driving compartment, the style and construction was like that of the shovel-nose 1968 Le Mans cars except that single as opposed to twinned headlamps were fitted and there were no bulges in the bonnet. There was a simple roll-over hoop behind the seats and the rather boxy tail featured a sharply cut-off Kamm style.

Under the skin, the engine was the very latest of the 1293cc Le Mans units, with the eight-port cross-flow cylinder heads which had been seen in works Mini-Cooper S race cars since 1967, allied to Lucas fuel injection, special racing camshafts, and a 12.5:1 compression ratio. It developed more than 110bhp and was the most powerful A-Series power unit ever used in a works Sprite. This was backed by a five-speed gearbox which had been evolved from the casing of the MGB and was akin to that used at Le Mans in 1967 and 1968. The rear suspension incorporated adjustable-length torque reaction rods/radius arms, and no fewer than four Armstrong dampers were used to keep the back axle in check

---

Competition Record

1969 Targa Florio	Never raced in works hands

APPENDIX
AFTER AUSTIN-HEALEY – THE SR37/XR37 LE MANS PROTOTYPE

By the later 1960s it was clear to the Healey family that BMC would not be offering them any major new project work to tackle, so DMH and his son Geoff set out to keep themselves busy with the design and operation of a specially-designed racing sports car which they intended to enter for the Le Mans 24 Hour race. Work began in the summer/autumn of 1967, and the incomplete car was shown off in an Autocar feature published on 22 February 1968.

Geoff Healey and Barrie Bilbie carried out the concept work on a car which they coded SR (Sub Rosa, a Latin phrase, bowdlerised and meant to be 'in confidence', or 'secret' – there was still time for a bit of humour in the Healey way of doing things). It rapidly took shape as a mid-engined two-seater with a simple but rugged sheet steel monocoque centre section

The original Coventry-Climax engined Healey SR race car looked magnificent before it went off to tackle the Le Mans 24 Hour race in 1968.

and a 32-valve 2-litre V8 engine from Coventry-Climax, actually the very unit which Jim Clark had used in 1965 F1 in a Type 33 Lotus-Climax and with which he had competed in the 1967 Tasman Series. The five-speed transmission came from Hewland.

Front and rear suspension were by Geoff and Barrie, the rack-and-pinion steering was a modified MGB assembly, and the rest of the running gear was gathered from the UK's prolific motor racing industry. John Thompson Motor Pressings made up the monocoque tub, and the 15in wheels

This was the artist's impression of the shape of the Coventry-Climax-engined Healey SR.

COVENTRY-CLIMAX FWMV ENGINE

Coventry-Climax, a Coventry-based maker of industrial power units and proprietary engines whose top people were all very friendly with the Healey family, built its first Formula One race-car engine, the 2½-litre V8 FPE, in 1953. It was bench tested but not installed in a race car, and for 1957 was followed by the 1½-litre four-cylinder FPF power unit, which became a great success in Formula Two. This eventually grew to 2.7-litres, did well in Formula One, and was an extremely versatile power unit. Walter Hassan (technical director) and Harry Mundy (chief designer) were mainly responsible for it.

When the F1 regulations changed in 1961 Coventry-Climax evolved an all new 90-degree V8 race engine of 1½-litres, coded FWMV (the design roots of which were in the twin-cam cylinder head of the company's tiny 0.75-litre FWMC sports/racing four-cylinder engine). Announced in 1961 and starting to win races in 1962 in F1 cars like the new Lotus 25, it was rated at 186bhp, and in the next three years peak output was gradually pushed up to 212bhp at 10,300rpm, that latter figure being achieved with Lucas fuel injection and four-valve cylinder heads.

F1 regulations changed again, effective 1966, with normally-aspirated engines of up to 3.0-litres authorised, which rendered the ageing FWMV engine obsolete. For one year, however, Coventry-Climax supplied Lotus with a strictly interim and final update of the FWMV, which combined the 72mm cylinder bore of the final cars with the original stroke of 60mm, resulting in a 2-litre capacity and providing 240bhp at 9000rpm.

Because these engines were only built to keep Lotus at the races until alternative (non-Coventry-Climax) supplies became available, just two of these engines were built, both of them eventually being returned to Coventry-Climax in 1967 as there was no obvious use for them in the future. It was one of them, together with suitable spares and support, that was supplied to Healey when the SR Le Mans project took shape in 1967/68.

The bodyshell of the Healey SR race car in constrction for the 1968 Le Mans 24 Hours.

As designed by Geoff Healey, the structure of the Healey SR was simple, rugged, and was engineered around the mid/rear-mounted Coventry-Climax engine.

carried Dunlop racing tyres. With a guaranteed 240bhp (see the panel on the previous page) in a sleek aluminium-panelled coupé body, it was thought that this car could be competitive with the other,more established 2-litre cars from Porsche and Alfa Romeo which would be in the Le Mans race.

Testing began in March 1968 – pictures exist showing that it carried the 1966 plate HNX 456D – and the SR competed at Le Mans with honour until the clutch operation failed. It appeared in the 1969 Le Mans race too, this time retiring because of an overheating engine in the low-speed queueing which followed an early-race accident to another car.

For 1970 the car (there was only one during Healey ownership) was rebodied, this time to have an open top, and after considering using a race-tuned Rover V8 power unit Healey decided to use a Type RB470 Repco-Brabham 3-litre V8 (as used by Brabham in his F1 cars in 1966 and 1967) which produced 322bhp at 8500rpm. Thus re-engined, it was also recoded as the XR37. The car performed extremely well at Le Mans until mere minutes from the end of the race, when an electrical wire severed and tragically killed the engine.

It never raced again. Soon afterwards it was sold off, along with all the parts, including the spare monocoque tub, the result being that in later years two Healey Le Mans came to exist, and to confuse historians for ever more.

Competition Record

1968 Le Mans 24 Hour Race	Andrew Hedges/Clive Baker	1st in Class, 17th Overall
1968 Le Mans 24 Hours	Clive Baker/Andrew Hedges	DNF
1969 Le Mans 24 Hours	Clive Baker/John Harris	DNF
1970 Le Mans 24 Hours	Roger Enever/Andrew Hedges	DNF